Nigel Cawthorne is the author of *Military Commanders* and *Vietnam – A War Lost and Won*. His writing has appeared in over a hundred and fifty newspapers, magazines and partworks – from the *Sun* to the *Financial Times*, and from *Flatbush Life* to the *New York Tribune*. He lives in London. His son, **Colin Cawthorne** helped to compile the first-hand accounts that make up this anthology. They have previously worked together on *The Mammoth Book of the Mafia*.

Football Hooligans

Edited by

Nigel and Colin Cawthorne

ROBINSON

Constable & Robinson Ltd
55–56 Russell Square
London WC1B 4HP
www.constablerobinson.com

First published in the UK by Robinson,
an imprint of Constable & Robinson Ltd, 2012

A copy of the British Library Cataloguing in
Publication Data is available from the British Library

ISBN: 978-1-84901-371-0 (paperback)
ISBN: 978-1-84901-767-1 (ebook)

Printed and bound in the UK

1 3 5 7 9 10 8 6 4 2

Contents

Acknowledgements

The editors would like to thank all those who made this book possible by letting us reprint the extracts listed below. Many thanks to Loreen Brown from Hodder Headline for use of "The Way In" from *Everywhere We Go: Behind the Matchday Madness* (Headline, London, 1996) © Dougie and Eddy Brimson 1996; "Why?" from *Barmy Army: The Changing Face of Football Violence* (Headline, London, 2000) © Dougie Brimson 2000; "No One Likes Us . . ." from *Capital Punishment: London's Violent Football Following* (Headline, London, 1997) © Dougie and Eddy Brimson 1997; "It's Grim Up North" from *Derby Days: Local Football Rivalries and Feuds* (Headline, London, 1997) © Dougie and Eddy Brimson 1997; "At Home" from *England, My England: The Trouble with the National Football Team* (Headline, London, 1996) © Dougie and Eddy Brimson 1996; "The Beginnings" from *Eurotrashed: The Rise of Europe's Football Hooligans* (Headline, London, 2003) © Dougie Brimson 2003; "Life's a Beach!" from *Tear Gas and Ticket Touts: With the England Fans at the World Cup* (Headline, London, 1999) © Eddy Brimson 1999; "The Police" from *Kicking Off: Why Hooliganism and Racism Are Killing Football* (Headline, London, 2007) © Dougie Brimson 2007; and for "Heysel Upon Us" from *Armed for the Match: The Trials and Tribulations of the Chelsea Headhunters* (Headline, London, 2000) © Colin Ward 2000. All reproduced by permission of Headline Publishing Group Limited. Thanks also to the following: Seonaid MacLeod at Mainstream Publishing for use of "National Pride" from *Who Wants It?* (Mainstream Publishing, Edinburgh, 2000) © Colin Ward and Chris Henderson 2000. Sarah Birdsey at Simon and Schuster for the use of "Robson's Boys" from *Steaming In: Journal of a Football Fan* (Pocket Book, London, 2004) © Colin Ward 2004 and Sarah McMahon at Random House for "Man U" from *Among the Thugs* (Secker & Warburg, London, 1991) © Bill Buford 1991.

Introduction

Football was first played in China as early as 206 BC. But it was a decorous game played after dinner at court with a ball filled with feathers. It became an altogether more boisterous game in ancient Greece – the Spartans were particularly fond of it when they weren't actually fighting.

In ancient Rome, football took to the streets. The Roman politician and orator Cicero (104–43 BC) recorded the first known incident of football hooliganism when an air-filled leather ball was kicked through a barber's window, killing a man having a shave. The Roman Empire and its legions spread the game throughout much of Europe. On holidays, neighbouring towns and villages would play "mob football" – called mellays or *mêlées* – with unlimited numbers on each sides, the goal being a geographical feature such as the opposing team's church. Medieval football matches involved hundreds of players, and were essentially pitched battles between the young men of rival settlements. Matches were often used as opportunities to settle old feuds, personal arguments and land disputes.

Such untamed free-for-alls inevitably led to violence. In Newcastle, County Down, in 1308, a spectator was charged with accidentally stabbing a player named William Bernard. Another man was wounded in Shouldham, Norfolk in 1321.

The game had got so out of hand that, in 1314, the Lord Mayor of the City of London tried to ban it. In 1363, King Edward III tried to prohibit "such idle games" as football. Richard II also tried to ban the game in 1389 because it took young men away from archery practice. There were other attempts to outlaw the game to preserve public order. They too were unsuccessful.

From the seventeenth century, the public schools began playing more orderly versions of the game. Eventually the self-styled gentlemen took over with the foundation of the Football Association in 1863. But while the FA laid down the rules for what happened on the pitch, what happened beyond the touchline remained a law unto itself.

In 1885, Preston North End beat Aston Villa 5–0 in a friendly. According to the newspapers of the time, this sent the crowd into a frenzy. "Howling roughs" pelted the players with stones, spat at them, punched and kicked them and attacked them with sticks. The following year, there was the first reported incidence of soccer violence away from the ground when Preston supporters took on Queens Park fans at a railway station. Preston supporters were in the headlines again in 1905 when they were tried for hooliganism following a match against Blackburn. One of the defendants was a seventy-year-old woman accused of being drunk and disorderly.

Later Millwall came into the picture. In 1920, 1934 and 1950, their ground, The Den, was closed due to crowd disturbances. Then in the sixties, when the game began to be televised, there was an upsurge in pitch invasions, riots and violence. This was seen in the anarchic spirit of the time as an attempt to reclaim the game for the working class.

By the mid-sixties ad hoc match-day alliances had formed between young men drawn largely from housing estates and working-class areas. These supporters staked out the goal-end terraces of football grounds as their territory, ousting older spectators and rival fans. The gangs formed on these terraces sought to intimidate or overcome rival "firms". Maintaining the firm's reputation became as important as the performance of the team they had come to watch. By the late eighties and early nineties, there were around five thousand arrests at League matches each season.

Firms began kitting themselves out in designer clothes, and organized confrontations away from the stadium. They were also seen as fertile recruiting grounds for Fascist organizations such as Combat 18, due to their endemic racism. However, black hooligans have now integrated themselves into some firms.

International matches stirred up old national rivalries. Hooliganism – especially in confrontations between England and Scotland – led to the cancellation of the British Home Championship in 1984. At least one tabloid newspaper portrayed the England–Germany match in Euro '96 as a resumption of World War II.

At the time, football hooliganism was dubbed the "English disease". However, it has spread right across Europe, and nowhere where the game is played is unaffected. There have even been incidents of violence in the US, where soccer is considered a family game. In 2008, some thirty West Ham fans took on over a hundred supporters of the Columbus Crew in Columbus, Ohio, marring an international friendly.

Many attempts have been made to stamp out hooliganism. In 1973, crowds were segregated to prevent fighting on the terraces, though this may have been counter-productive, strengthening the grip rival firms had on their team's supporters. Attempts were made to improve stadiums and, in 1989, the Football Spectators Act aimed to prevent known hooligans travelling abroad for international matches.

The Heysel Stadium disaster in 1985, where thirty-nine fans were killed at a match between Liverpool and Juventus in Brussels, and the Hillsborough disaster, where ninety-six Liverpool fans were crushed to death during a match against Sheffield Wednesday in 1989, led to the conversion to all-seater stadiums. In 1998, there were further limits on overseas travel for troublemakers, restrictions on ticket touting and bans on alcohol. Marketing men sought to alter the image of football, promoting it to a family audience, like sporting events in the US. There have been improvements, but these measures have not quelled the violence completely. In December 2010, after a local derby between Birmingham City and Aston Villa, there was a running battle on the pitch between fans and the police.

Over the years, football hooliganism has been portrayed in films, though many critics condemn them for glamorizing violence. A number of books have also been written on the subject of hooliganism, some by the hooligans themselves. A selection of extracts from these books has been reprinted here. Our aim is not to encourage hooliganism, nor to praise it. But it is a social phenomenon worthy of study, and its exponents, like everyone else, have a right to be heard, no matter how much we disapprove of what they do. These men, and they are largely men, tend to be tough guys from the streets. Some may find their language offensive. Be warned.

1

The Way In

Dougie and Eddy Brimson

Dougie Brimson is a fanatical football fan who has written extensively about soccer hooliganism and the social issues that surround it. He has written thirteen books on the subject over the last fourteen years and also penned the screenplay for the Hollywood film Green Street, starring Elijah Wood, which won numerous awards. Some people call him the "Yob Laureate". After spending almost twenty years in the Royal Air Force, including tours in the Falklands War and the first Gulf War, he co-wrote his first book *Everywhere We Go* in 1996 with his brother Eddy Brimson. This extract comes from that book.

Eddy Brimson, who has also written several books on football hooliganism, is a critically acclaimed stand-up comedian. The brothers are both lifelong Watford fans.

This chapter is an account, sent to us anonymously, which explains how a supporter became involved in violence. His life is, we believe, typical of many others. We reproduce it in full in order to show how one man's participation in hooliganism can evolve, and what it is that motivates him:

This is the story of how I became involved as a member of one of the most respected firms in the country and how, basically, I became addicted to football violence.

I come from a small Home Counties town, have a managerial job and live with my girlfriend and our two children. My father was a professional gentleman who ran his own business and I was brought up in a beautiful house with my younger sister and never really wanted for anything. I led a sheltered life away from the gang warfare of the local council estates, which was big news around our town at the time, so I was not a "face" and could, if I wanted to, travel to any part of the town without any hint of trouble.

Since I was eleven, my father and an uncle had taken me on occasions to watch Watford, our local team, and I loved it. But they only took me about five times a year and I began longing for more. One Saturday, when I was about fourteen, I did what most boys end up doing and went to Vicarage Road on my own without telling my mum where I was going. The thrill of that day is still with me – the thought that I might get seen and that my parents would find out made it all the more exciting, and when I got home afterwards, no one even asked where I had been. I had got away with it.

This started to become a regular thing as I attended almost every home game while my mum, happy that I was building a social life for myself, sometimes wondered why she never met any of my new friends. After about six or seven matches, I started to recognize some of the faces on the way to the game and one day one of the other lads of about my age came over and asked if I wanted to go with them as they all lived in my town and went up every week. That felt fantastic. I was no longer on my own but going to the game as part of a group of lads. Little did I know it, but these lads were to change my life.

When we got to the ground, we went to the opposite end from where I usually stood, and for the first time I found myself standing quite near to the visiting supporters. I will never forget that feeling in my stomach, looking across at about a hundred and fifty Newport County supporters who were doing their utmost to out-sing us. The lads I was with seemed to know everyone around us and introduced me to loads of people, and I really began to feel a part of something. It was quite an amazing feeling for a fourteen-year-old. The atmosphere was different from anything I had ever experienced – everyone was singing and shouting and when we scored, it wasn't the refined applause I was used to with my father and uncle, it was total chaos, absolutely brilliant!

At half-time, one of the lads told me they were going over to stand near the away fans and wind them up a bit for the older lads. He explained that this happened at every home game. Towards the end of the match, the older lads would drift over one by one, and once they had sufficient numbers in that part of the ground they would probably attack. I could not believe what I was hearing, there seemed to be no sense at all to it. I mean, "why?" was the obvious question. I had never been to a fight in my life.

I have looked back on the moment many times because it was a major turning point in my life. I have often wondered what would have happened to me had I not gone with them, but I was with a group of lads who had invited me into their little circle and there was no way I was going to look soft in front of them, so I followed. I remember thinking that, close up, Newport County fans were huge and quickly realized that any one of them could do me permanent damage, but the other lads were hurling abuse at them and they were getting very aggressive. I was getting very close to the point where I was about to run when the cry went up and I realized that all of the older lads had made their way over. Suddenly, all hell broke loose as people ran in every direction. Within seconds, the police appeared out of nowhere and I soon realized that we were standing in the spot the

Newport fans has occupied only minutes before and they were standing down in the corner by the tea bar. The police rounded us all up and moved us back to our original place while the rest of the crowd cheered as if we had won a great victory. As our group moved back, all the older lads patted us on the back for our part in their victory. We were part of it all. What a feeling!

The same thing happened over and over again at home games. We never got turned over and I never received anything more than the odd shove, but things took a very different turn in my first away game, which happened to be a midweek match at Brentford. There was always trouble at our place when we played them, and it was well known that this continued at their place, but the chance actually to go there and take them on was too good to miss. In those days, the silk scarf was the height of fashion and my friends and I had ours hanging round our necks to let everyone know who we were, something we quickly realized was not such a good idea as we were well and truly outnumbered and were on our own. We turned into a road and found a load of the older lads drinking outside a pub. Suddenly we felt more confident and a lot safer. This was more like it.

They were all on good form after a few beers and we began talking about Brentford supporters and past trouble with them when someone told us that they had heard that a mob from Chelsea were supposed to be coming up to fight with the Brentford mob, but they had bottled it. This was a standard rumour in those days, and even I didn't really believe it. But as we left the lads and made our way up the road we heard an almighty noise. When we turned, we saw the pub being attacked with bottles and bricks and our lot getting a bit of a hiding and being run up the road towards us. I could hear the odd shout of "Chelsea!" and ran for my life. This was a different game altogether. I could get hurt and I was scared.

Once we made it into the game, the atmosphere was very different from our place, much more intense, but our mob was much bigger than the usual one, which was probably something to do with us all being in the same part of the ground. All through the game we were attacking their fans and then they would run at us. I remember seeing one of our lads being taken out with blood streaming down his face after being hit – with a brick, I think – but as the St John's led him round the pitch, he turned and ran at the Brentford mob and dived in on his own. When he came back out, he just walked across the pitch and waved at us. What a hero!

When the game finished, all the Brentford supporters from the other end came streaming across the pitch towards us, but someone was shouting at us all to get up the back to the exits. As the first Brentford supporters came over the wall, a shout went up and all our lot turned and steamed down at them. Those they caught took a right hiding while the rest just ran – it was an amazing thing to see. As we left the ground we were so excited. We turned a corner to find a huge mob of Brentford coming up the road from the side stand. These were the people we had been fighting during the game. My scarf was off and down my trousers in a flash and I quickly ducked down behind a car. Once again the roar went up and the Brentford mob came running past; then we saw the familiar faces chasing up the road after them. We were now running after them. The scarves were out and off we went, running with the mob, not knowing where we were going or why, but what a buzz. The police finally caught up with us and after a while escorted us back to the tube station and away. We had been in another town and had been taking liberties: the feeling of power was incredible – we could have taken anyone that night. I was hooked.

Later that season we drew West Ham in the FA Cup down at Upton Park, and we knew that this would be the biggest test we had ever faced. This was the big time we had all wanted, but deep down we all knew that they would waste no time in trying to put us firmly in our place. Make no bones about it, that game was scary, mostly because we were travelling by tube and were well and truly sussed out long before we arrived in East London. The walk down the road to the ground was one of the most scary moments of my life. I saw a chip-shop window that had been put through and this bloke came up to me and told me that they had just thrown a Watford fan through it, and that he would be looking for me after the game as there were loads of other windows to aim at. At that point I would rather have slept on the terrace for the night than leave the ground and walk back down the road at full-time.

During the game it was going off all the time, and to be honest we did all right. At the end we felt that if anything our reputation had been boosted because we had gone to West Ham in good numbers and we had a go back.

Away games became the focus for us. Pitch invasions at Torquay, Scunthorpe and Bournemouth; taking the home end at Northampton and Crewe, where the wall collapsed and the match was held up for twenty minutes – all of these helped us to gain the reputation we were after. Promotion in that season meant that there were new challenges and we continued to travel and take people on whenever we could. Going to Old Trafford and beating them 2–1 in the League Cup and then getting mobbed up and taking the piss out of the "Mancs" all the way to the station was for me one of the highlights of the season. Taking a mob of four hundred up to Carlisle for a night game and setting fire to the programme stall was another, but we also came up against some bigger firms, such as Blackpool, who were more than up for it, and Plymouth.

The real turning point for us as a mob was the trip to Sheffield Wednesday. This was a big match – it was near the end of the season and we were both up for promotion, and it was estimated that we would be taking about six thousand supporters. We knew full well that Wednesday would give us a reception to remember. As we entered Sheffield, we saw loads of Watford supporters heading back to the motorway. We stopped at some lights and this guy opposite us got out of his car and came over to us. He told us that he was a Watford fan and that the Sheffield supporters had been turning cars over, the club coaches had been wrecked and more of their fans were running riot and throwing small steel bars at anyone they suspected of being a Watford fan. We had travelled in a small convoy of minibuses with some other people from our town, and as some of them had never been involved in any trouble, we pulled over to decide what to do. It was decided that one bus would turn straight round and anyone who wanted to could just leave while the rest of us would go to the game, but would wait where we were until the last possible moment. When we got to the ground, there couldn't have been more than seven hundred of our lot there. We felt gutted – our reputation had been completely shattered in just one game. I remember seeing the coaches as we left the ground and they had been well and truly hit. We had been turned over big-time.

That summer, I was to get my revenge on Wednesday. Myself and a friend who had been at that game went on holiday to Great Yarmouth and one night we were in this nightclub called Tiffany's. Also inside this club was a large group of West Ham supporters and a group of Wednesday fans. When we left the club, the West Ham lads had mobbed up outside. Once they realized that we were southern football fans they asked us if we wanted to help them out because they were about to turn over the Wednesday lot. Lovely. When the Wednesday supporters came out, they walked straight through the West Ham mob and we started to follow them. But when we got to the street corner, they turned and ran straight back at us. The West Ham lot were off like a rocket, leaving the two of us facing about twenty Yorkshire intent on beating the shit out of us. Now, there was no way I was going to take a hiding on the pretence of being a West Ham fan, so we also did the off, but the problem was that the Wednesday fans seemed more interested in the two of us than they did in the rest of them. I remember this big, fat northern bloke chasing up the road after me long after the others had given up. I was giving him loads of verbal while running just fast enough to be out of reach until he nearly had a heart attack and had to stop.

My friend and I were well and truly pissed off with this West Ham lot and decided that we would put on a show for the Watford. When we found the Wednesday mob, they had got back together and were on a roundabout making loads of noise. We quickly went through every garden we could find and collected about a dozen milk bottles and lined them up. We shouted down the road to them and started singing "The Watford". When they saw us, they came steaming up the road after us. When they got close enough, we let fly with the bottles and they went in every direction, although one got a direct hit and put this bloke flat on his arse. It was now time to leave, but we felt we had paid them back a little for the hiding they had dished out to us earlier that season.

By now, our club was doing all it could to drive us out. The ground had become much better segregated and then chances to get at the away fans were almost zero. After the Sheffield incident, many of the lads had dropped out of the group and although we were still having the odd big one, it wasn't at the same level as before. I wanted more action, and so I began to follow the England team.

Going to Wembley was a real eye-opener. The first match I attended was in 1979 against Bulgaria in the build-up to the European Championships to be held in Italy the following year. I remember walking around Wembley thinking that this was the biggest mob I had ever seen in my life (there weren't that many Bulgarians!), and the feeling of being proud to be English overwhelmed me. England qualified for the finals and some friends and I decided to take our first holiday abroad in Italy to follow the national side. Everybody was fully aware of the English reputation, but for me this only added to the excitement. We were going to Italy with the intention of giving them a good hiding in their own country.

When we arrived, we stayed on one of the campsites that the Italians had provided, which was right next to a bridge. Every night the locals threw bricks and bottles down on to us. As the police seemed determined to do nothing about it, the English fans were well and truly worked up by the time we went off to Turin for the first game. At the match the police gave us constant grief, along with the locals, who continually threw missiles at us. When the police moved in to take someone out, we had had enough and started to fight back, hitting out at anything that wasn't English. The police steamed back in and when they failed to gain control, they fired tear gas at us, which was really a bit over the top. But what struck me above all else was that the English supporters stood firm and fought it out as best they could. We were immediately branded as scum all over Europe, but of course no one was interested in the treatment we had been receiving, which was the main reason why it had gone off in the first place. All they were interested in was that we were animals. During the next few days, we started to knock about with some of the other groups of supporters on the site, mainly for safety reasons, and among those was a mob from one of the bigger London clubs, a group I was to meet up with again a few years later.

Later in the tournament we had to play the Italians, and you can imagine the hostility that had built up against us. Many of the English supporters decided to return home or move to another part of Italy and watch it on television. Along with some of the other lads, we decided to brave it, because this was an experience we would never forget and we didn't want to be seen to have bottled out. That game was frightening. Getting to the ground was a nightmare and rumours of stabbings were flying around, while the police were busy making it obvious that they were not there to help us out in any way at all. One of our lot was attacked on the way to the stadium because we were waving a huge Union Jack fixed to a wooden pole. This mob of Italians surrounded him and were trying to steal it, but he ripped it off the pole and stuffed it as best he could up his shirt and started to run. This mob grabbed the pole and went after him, one of them catching him across the back of the head. He went down but luckily managed to get up and away. The police didn't give a shit, despite the blood pouring down his face, and just pushed him, and us, into the ground as fast as they could.

During the game we were pissed on, spat on and had firecrackers thrown down on us, but the most frightening thing was when someone threw a small petrol-bomb into the area where we were standing. Thankfully, not many English fans had turned up and we had room to move away from the flames, because if the terrace had been full, a great many people could have got badly burned. Italy won the game, which seemed to calm things down a bit, and the police finally gave us protection but England were out of the competition and we decided to return home early. I still felt proud of myself for putting up a show, but the whole experience changed my way of thinking. If we were going to be treated like scum whenever we travelled abroad, we would behave like scum, and anyone who came to Wembley would be fair game, no matter where they came from. That view was shared by everyone who endured that trip.

Over the next couple of seasons, I continued to fight for Watford. We were on the up and support was growing, and those who had left the mob were being replaced by new blood. Promotion was firing people up again and it meant more derby games against London clubs. We had some great battles at QPR and Crystal Palace as well as at Norwich and Cardiff, but the one that sticks in my mind is Derby County on the last day of the season. We were already promoted and the First Division loomed for the first time in our history. Derby needed to win to stay up, and at a ground renowned for its atmosphere anyway, you can imagine what it was like. We had one of the biggest mobs I'd ever seen us take anywhere that day, and we were going for it big-time – opening the perimeter gates in an attempt to get on the pitch, the full works. The police were really pissed off with us and kicked the gravel from around the pitch into our faces and hit out with their truncheons whenever we got up on the fences. As it happened, Derby won the game and at the end invaded the pitch and came across to give us the biggie. We finally managed to get one of the gates open, about a hundred Watford managed to get on the pitch and Derby did a runner.

Outside we ran them everywhere. The police sent the horses in to sort us out and charged us down the alley that runs behind the end. Even though it was packed, the horses still came through and the police were hitting out at anyone.

One guy got trampled on and was badly hurt and, as you can imagine, we were starting to get really pissed off. Something made one of the horses rear up and a copper got pulled off. He had his foot or something caught in the stirrups and the horse started to drag him along as it tried to get out. He took probably the worst kicking I have ever seen anyone take in my life. The poor bastard had blood coming out of his eyes.

Since the battles in Italy, I had kept in touch with many of the lads I had met there. We had even been to an England game together, and they kept asking me to go to a League match with them to see a real firm in action. Club loyalties forced me to decline their offer, but promotion meant that we would indeed meet on the terraces – only this time we would be on opposing sides. We knew they would come to our place and put on a show. It was one of those fixtures you dream about at a small club but dread when it arrives, and my mates kept ringing me up and taking the piss, telling me what they were going to do to our place and everything else that went with it, including me. Come the big day, they took over the town and I remember thinking that it must be so fantastic a club with a following that big. They were in every pub and every street, and the Watford fans were nowhere to be seen – though in our case it was because we had decided to split up and get to the ground, where we would form up inside to repel the attack on our end that we knew would come.

When I got inside, it was clear that most people had been thinking along the same lines – we had gathered quite a decent mob together. We waited by the turnstiles to spot them as they came in and there were plenty of them to see, including some familiar faces. It was obvious that they were going for it in a big way. There was no way we could let them walk all over us like this, and when one of them spotted me, I decided to make a stand before they were all inside.

I went for this bloke while the rest of my group saw me go and followed. The police were over in a flash and got them away and into a corner, from where they were led out. I looked across at my mate and waved goodbye to him as he made his exit. He was not best pleased, but when I rang him the next day we were creasing up about it all; it was respect all round. During the game, the rest of their lot who had managed to make it in kicked everything off, but they were expecting to have bigger numbers and were surprised at the size of the mob we had ready for them, so things ended up pretty even on the day.

I continued to hook up with these lads at England games and eventually took them up on their offer of an away League trip. I had always wondered what it would be like [running with a top firm] and there was only one way to find out. It was an eye-opener. We travelled up by train and stopped at the first pub we came to. By 11.30 we were beginning a serious session; by one o'clock, the place was packed with blokes who had formed into a serious mob. The time had come for them to introduce themselves to the locals and let them know we had arrived. The feeling was fantastic – this was more like it. It had been a long time since Watford had gone on the offensive at an away game (other than at derbies and the Derby match), and it was interesting to see things from a different perspective – there but not involved, if you understand what I mean. The police were on us immediately, but it didn't really matter to anyone. We just went where we wanted and they just shadowed. As we made our way through the town, we could see the local firm up ahead. They started to give us loads of verbal and threw the odd milk bottle while the police just blocked our way and stopped us moving.

It was just like the old days, only better, and I could appreciate what was happening much more now than I had before. The police thought they had it sussed, but some of our lot had slipped round them and let out the signal for us to run at them. Before they realized what was happening most of the group had got past them and were up the road after their firm. After a minor ruck, the police managed to get everyone else rounded up and herded us to the ground and inside. Although the match went off without trouble, the day wasn't over for this lot. There had been talk all day of stopping off at a mainline station on the way back and ambushing the Leeds fans – Leeds had been playing in London that day. Everyone seemed up for it. It was all new to me and really got me buzzing.

When we arrived at the station, we all got off and made our way to the buffet and waiting rooms. If the Leeds fans had a special coming out of London at the usual time, it would stop here in about thirty minutes' time. We sat and waited while some of the others went to get themselves tooled up. In all there must have been about a hundred and fifty of us waiting for them. When it came, the noise was deafening: we just let fly with everything we had. We could see that some of the Leeds supporters were getting off and coming for us, but most of them didn't have a clue what was going on and were shitting it. We steamed up the stairs to meet them on the bridge but they turned and ran because we had them well outnumbered. We followed them across the bridge, picking the odd one off, but not down on to the platform because there we would have been outnumbered ourselves. The train pulled out quite quickly after that and, luckily for them, they all managed to get on board before it went. After about ten minutes the police turned up in force, gathered us together and got us on the first train back to London without arresting anyone. What a great day and a great introduction to running with a top firm.

Over the next few seasons I ran with that firm more and more, particularly at the games where we knew the opposition had a serious reputation. I still went to Watford, but the buzz of going on the offensive had got hold of me and it wasn't really the same any more. By the start of 1989–90 season, I was more committed to this firm than any other, including the Hornets. They soon introduced me to members of one of the top Scottish firms and we went north of the border several times for big derby and grudge matches.

Much of the connection with the Scottish clubs is political, and our firm do have a number of members with right-wing beliefs. But for me the politics don't come into it: I go for the "offs", pure and simple. Many of the lads from our firm go to England games and get accused of being racist and all that stuff, but to me that's not correct. Personally, I consider myself to be nationalistic and will fight to defend our flag – that stems from the Italian experience – but I won't boo black players or refuse to cheer when a black player scores, the "black goals don't count" mentality. There are still a few racists about, although there are fewer and fewer these days, thankfully.

In the last couple of seasons, we have continued to be active and have fought all over the country on our travels. We've also planned some great hits – one in particular on a pub in Oxford where one of our lot had a pitchfork stuck up his arse – but it has not always gone to plan. We had planned to do a return visit to Leeds to turn one of their pubs over, but we were followed, and when we turned up, they were ready and waiting for us. Fair play to them, though, they had us well and truly sussed, but I'm sure we'll meet again.

During this last season [1991–92], it has become clear to me, and the rest of us, that the violence is beginning to creep back into the game on a wider scale, but, as a member of one of the worst firms around, I can't really say I'm sorry, can I? The English clubs abroad and events in Dublin are testament to this, while the treat of CCTV has worn off and all-seater stadiums never had any effect anyway. Over the years our club (I still feel uncomfortable saying that) has tried everything to get rid of the hooligan element, but it just will not work because there are thousands of people like me who just live for that buzz. The feeling you get when you're out with a load of blokes and actively looking for trouble is what keeps it all going. And it's not just at football: go down the tube on any Saturday and you'll see it. I've even been to a rock concert for a pre-arranged "meeting" with two other firms. The game won't stop us, it has to accept that; it may make things difficult for a while, but we'll change our tactics, which will make it easier to hit other mobs until they catch up with what we are doing. Trust me, we're here to stay until we decide to give it up on our own – and, personally, I can't see that happening for a good while yet.

2

Man U

Bill Buford

Among the Thugs is probably the most famous book about football violence. It was written by an American journalist, Bill Buford, who became obsessed with football violence and British hooligans. He spent eight years going to football matches, befriending supporters and witnessing riots in order to document football hooliganism.

Here we get an account of a match he attended between Manchester United and West Ham, and all the violence that ensued. He sets the scene with a quote from *The Observer*.

"The Stretford End . . . is a kind of academy of violence, where promising young fans can study the arts of intimidation. This season the club installed a metal barrier between the fans and the ground. It resembles the sort of cage, formidable and expensive, that is put up by a zoo to contain the animals it needs but slightly fears. Its effect has been to make the Stretford terraces even more exclusive and to turn the occupants into an elite."

The Observer, 1 December 1974

The weekend after my visit to Turin, I took the train to Manchester. Manchester United was at home to West Ham, the East London team, and I had been told to come up for the match. I had been accepted. I had been accepted for the simple reason that I had travelled with the supporters to Italy and had been with them when it had "gone off". I had witnessed an experience of great intensity and – like the other supporter returning to tell stories to the friends who had remained behind – I was among the privileged who could say that he had been there.

I was told to show up around mid-morning at the Brunswick, a pub near Manchester's Piccadilly station, but if I was late then I was to go on to Yates's Wine Lodge on the High Street. By one, everyone would be at Yates's.

I arrived just before noon and got to the Brunswick in time to meet some of the people I had heard about. There was Teapot and Berlin Red and One-Eyed Billy and Daft Donald. Daft Donald was the one who had tried to reach Turin but never got past Nice. Daft Donald showed me a canister of CS gas. He said that he always travelled with a canister of CS gas. It stuns them, he said, so that you can then take out their teeth without any resistance.

I spotted a lad named Richard, whom I recognized from Turin. He was flicking through an envelope of photographs that he had picked up that morning from Boots, surrounded by four or five of his friends. They had stayed home; Richard had gone, although he told me later that, because he had gone without first getting permission from his boss, he had probably lost his job – assembly-line work at a machine factory. The reason he could say only that he had "probably" lost his job was because, three days later, he still hadn't showed up for it. But for the moment it didn't matter; he was a celebrity: he had been in Italy when it had "gone off".

For Richard, being one of the lads was the best thing a person could be. He became serious and a little sentimental when he spoke about it. The shape of his face changed; it seemed to soften and round out, and his eyebrows knitted up with feeling. "We look forward to Saturdays," he said, "all week long. It's the most meaningful thing in our lives. It's a religion, really. That's how important it is to us. Saturday is our day of worship."

Richard wanted to explain to me what it meant to be a supporter of Manchester United. I didn't know why at first – whether it was because I was an American and was thus ignorant about these things, or because I was a journalist who might put the record straight, or because I was the most recent member to be admitted into the group – but Richard wasn't the only one. Other people went out of their way to do the same; they wanted me to understand. All day long people stopped me to illustrate, to define, to comment upon the condition of being one of the lads. I cannot remember meeting people so self-conscious about their status and so interested in how it was seen by others. They were members of something exclusive – a club, cult, firm, cultural phenomenon, whatever it might be called – and they valued its exclusivity. They were used to the fact that the world was interested in them and were accustomed to dealing with television and newspaper journalists in a way that few people, however educated in media matters, could hope to be. It was a perverse notion, but they believed that they were involved in an historical moment, that they were making history. And now that they didn't have to hide from me that their thing was violence – now that the pretence of being a good supporter could be abandoned – they all wanted to talk about it.

This put me in an awkward position. What was I meant to do with what people were telling me? I was uncomfortable with the idea of writing in my notebook in front of everybody. I knew that I couldn't pull out a tape-recorder, that something so blatant would destroy the trust. So what did that make me? Was I the reporter or had

I been genuinely admitted to the group? And if I had been admitted should I be explicit about the fact I would be writing about the very people who were befriending me? In retrospect, my confusion, that I was suddenly unsure of my role, was a symptom of the way this sort of group works – the way it takes you in, proffers support and expects loyalty – and I resolved the matter in a simple way: I avoided it. I ended up excusing myself constantly to get into one of the stalls in the lavatory, where I sat down and, secure in my privacy, scrawled down everything I had been told. I was being told so much that day that I was having to disappear with considerable regularity – there is only so much you can hold in your head – and I finally had to own up to having stomach problems.

I re-emerged from one lavatory visit to discover a lad who looked exactly like Keith Richards. The likeness was uncanny. What's more, it wasn't Keith Richards at just any time of his life; it was Keith Richards during the worst time. The lad had the same long, leathery, lined face; the druggy offhand manner; the endless cigarettes; the dazed and exhausted appearance of sustained personal abuse. He, too, had been in Italy, but I didn't remember seeing him there. That, he said, was because, through the whole match, he had sat at the bottom of the stairs with his head between his legs vomiting upon his feet. He showed me his boots, still caked with the dry splatterings of the horrors that, at one time, had been contained in his stomach.

It would be, I offered, such a waste to clean them.

The Keith Richards lookalike was disconcertingly self-aware. He knew what a journalist was hoping to find in him and that he provided it. He worked in a factory, making soap powder. "The perfect profile of a hooligan, isn't it?" he said. "He works all week at a boring job and can't wait to get out on a Saturday afternoon."

I nodded and grinned rather stupidly. He was right: the disenfranchised and all that.

He sneered. It was a wonderful sneer – arrogant, composed, and full of venom. "So what do you think makes us tick?" he asked. "If *we*," he said, not waiting for my answer, "did not do it here at football matches then we'd simply end up doing it somewhere else. We'd end up doing it on Saturday night at the pub. It's what's in us, innit?" He had an intense, but rather practised, look of contempt.

"What's that?" I asked. "What is it that's in us?"

"The violence," he said. "We've all got it in us. It just needs a cause. It needs an acceptable way of coming out. And it doesn't matter what it is. But something. It's almost an excuse. But it's got to come out. Everyone's got it in them."

Keith Richards was interrupted by Robert. Robert was the one who arrived in Turin by an expensive taxi from Nice. He was also the one who had been telling people in Italy that I worked for the CIA – such was the threat to international stability that the supporters of Manchester United represented. Robert had concluded, even if only tentatively, that I probably wasn't CIA – he was not entirely certain – and that, regardless, I was a good geezer.

Robert was tall and Irish and good-looking and could not take too many things too seriously for too long. He had been listening to Keith Richards's account of the violence and thought it sounded a little too earnest. "All that's true," he said, "but you've got to see the humour. You can't have violence without a sense of humour."

The time was called out – it was one o'clock – and it was agreed that we should all be moving on to Yates's. Once the move was announced, the pub, although packed, emptied in seconds.

I fell in with Mark, the British Telecom engineer whom I had also met in Italy. Mark was of a philosophic disposition.

"I've been going to matches for years," he said , "and I still can't put a finger on it." Mark was trying to describe the essence of the thing.

"For most lads," Mark was saying, "this is all they've got." He nodded, as we were walking out the door, towards a cluster of supporters whose common feature was, I must admit, a look of incredible and possibly even unique stupidity.

"During the week," Mark continued, "they're nobody, aren't they? But then, when they come to the match, that all changes. They feel like Mr Big." The implication was that Mark – skilled job, career prospects, pension-fund, wife, future family – was different, that he was somebody. Somebody or nobody, the experience wasn't any less intense for Mark. "Every now and then," he said, "even for me this is something spectacular, something that makes you feel different afterwards. The Juventus match was like that. That was a once-in-a-lifetime experience.

He described Italy. "You remember the moment we entered the ground? Everybody started throwing things at us – bottles, cans, stones, everything. I've got a scar on my forehead from where some Italian jabbed me with a flag-pole. There were only 200 of us. It was us against them, and we had no idea what was going to happen. There was so many different feelings. Fear, anger, excitement. I've never felt anything like it. We all felt it and every one of us now knows what we have been through something important – something solid. After an experience like that, we're not going to split up. We'll never split up. We'll be mates for life.

"I will never forget these blokes. I will never forget Sammy. For as long as I live, I will be grateful that I could say I knew him. He is amazing. He's got this sixth sense that keeps him from getting caught, and he knows, somehow, when something really big is about to go off, and that's when you find him there at the front. If there was a war, Sammy would be the bloke who'd return with all the medals. He'd be the hero. It's funny isn't it? Sammy could be put away for years if they knew even half of what's he's done, but if he did the same things in a war you'd see his picture in the papers."

Yates's Wine Bar was a pub and café. As we entered it, a supporter was standing on the table, singing, "Manchester, la-la-la, Manchester, la-la-la." Nobody was joining him; despite his antics, the mood was subdued.

Mark was still explaining. "You see, what it does is this: it gives violence a purpose. It makes you somebody. Because we're not doing for ourselves. We're doing it for something greater – for us. The violence is for the lads."

Mark brought me a pint, but we didn't end up staying at Yates's for long and I hadn't finished my beer before I noticed that people were starting to drift out of the door.

I was greeted by Steve. Mark may have been right, that football provided meaning for supporters whose lives were otherwise empty, but many supporters had their lives remarkably well sorted out – at least financially: they had money and prospects of getting more. Steve was one. At the age of twenty-two he had a colour television, an expensive camera, a video player, a car, a van, CD and stereo equipment. He was married – his wife was a hairdresser – and was about to secure a mortgage for the purchase of his first home. He lived in one of the southern commuter-belt garden cities not far from London. Like Mick, Steve was an electrician, but, unlike him, Steve was self-employed and running his own business, was already fully informed about the rhythms of cash flow, tax fiddles and the tactics needed to deal with the VAT man. He had opinions about most things and a gentle way of expressing them.

Steve had been on that early-morning coach that took me

up to Manchester airport. I had spent quite a bit of time
with him already. I would spend more. In fact, for a while, I
went out of my way to spend time with Steve, if only
because, being articulate and intelligent, he was good
company and because I always believed that he would be
able to reveal something about why he, of all people, was
attracted to violence of this kind. If the *Daily Mail* had been
asked to create a twenty-two-year-old with his life sorted
out, it could have presented Steve.

There was the language that he used. I mentioned
Sammy, and Steve would say, "Ah, yes, Sammy. Me and
Sammy go way back." I mentioned Roy, and Steve would
say, "Ah, Roy. I've know Roy for years." Steve was only
twenty-two. These phrases were an old man's; they sounded
like his father's. And when he talked about the violence, he
could have been assessing a small business's marketing
problems. "We've got one of the best firms in the country
– as you carry on with your research you'll find that very
few clubs get the support that Manchester United gets
every Saturday – and the last time we played West Ham in
London our boys filled three tube trains. There must have
been two thousand people. Two thousand people had come
to London from all over the country with the sole purpose
of routing West Ham. Those are very big numbers. But then
nothing happened."

Extensive preparations had gone into Manchester
United's last meeting with West Ham – coaches had been
hired, with complex routes into the city to evade the police,
the arrival times staggered so that everyone did not appear
en masse. "Our trouble," he said, "is one of leadership. We
have too many leaders, with the result that we have no leaders at all. We're always getting dispersed or split up. West
Ham has Bill Gardiner – I've known Bill since I can remember – and you will see him later today. He is always the first

man out, flanked on either side by his lieutenants, with everyone else behind. And what he says goes. He is the general. He doesn't fight much himself any more – when it goes off, he tends to step back and disappear into the crowd – because he can't afford to get arrested."

Problems of leadership, organization, "big numbers", a hierarchical command structure: the technocrat phrasing did not obscure that what Steve was describing was a civil disturbance involving several thousand people. Every now and then, I would butt in with a "*why*?" or a "*how*?", but Steve would simply say something like "It's human nature, I guess," or "I don't know, I never really thought about it," and then he would be off describing one of the current tactical problems. And in this, he had very developed views.

His essential complaint was that football violence emerged out of such a coherently structured organization that the authorities should just leave it alone. The members of each firm knew those from all the other firms – without a moment's hesitation, Steve could also run through the leaders of Chelsea, Tottenham, Arsenal, Millwall and Nottingham Forest – and, in their ideal world, they should be allowed to get on with fighting each other without unnecessary impediments: "We know who they are; they know who we are. We know they want it and so do we." It was a matter of freedom and responsibility: the freedom for them to inflict as much injury on each other as they were prepared to withstand and the responsibility to ensure others were not involved; with some pride Steve mentioned watching a fight on the terraces that was interrupted to allow a woman and child to pass, then promptly resumed.

Steve blamed most of the current troubles on the police. "The police have now got so good," he said, "that we're more constrained than before. We just don't have the time that we used to have. The moment a fight starts we're immediately surrounded by dogs and horses. That's why everyone has started using knives. I suppose it might sound stupid but because the policing has got so good we've got to the point where we have to inflict the greatest possible damage in the least amount of time, and the knife is the most efficient instrument for a quick injury. In fact these knifings – because there is so little time – have become quite symbolic. When someone gets knifed, it amounts to an important victory to the side that has done the knifing. If the policing was not so good, I'm sure the knifing would stop."

People were leaving Yates's. Steve said it was time to get moving, and I followed him outside. Talking to Steve was a curious experience. Everything was exactly the way it was not meant to be. The police were bad because they were so good. Knifings were good because they had the potential to be so bad. The violence was good because it was so well organized. Crowd violence can be blamed not on the people causing it but on ones stopping it. In themselves, these would be curious statements to consider. What made them particularly unusual was the way Steve presented them. He was rational and fluent, and had given much thought about the implications of the thing – that this was socially deviant conduct of the highest order, involving injuries and maiming and the destruction of property. I don't think he understood the implications; I don't think he would have acknowledged them as valid.

Everyone left Yates's and made his way on to the High Steet. There were about a thousand people, milling around "casually", hands in their pockets, looking at the ground. The idea was to look like you were *not* a member of a crowd, that you just happened to find yourself on the High Street – at the time that a thousand other people happened to have done the same.

The next London train was due at 1.42, a matter of

minutes, and it was known that the West Ham firm would be on it. The Manchester United firm intended to meet it and had a plan. From Yates's, the High Street led straight to the ramp of Piccadilly station, and, at the agreed time, everyone would charge up the ramp, burst through the station entrance and attack the West Ham supporters as they were coming off the platform. I thought that the plan was preposterous, but, if it could be pulled off, it would be spectacular – in the sense of a spectacle that was extraordinary to behold. I tried to remember the station. The police had been there this morning when I arrived but not in numbers great enough to have stopped a thousand supporters crashing through the station's entrance with the momentum that would have built up and been sustained over the length of the High Street. And that was what had been described to me: that everyone would charge up the ramp at full speed. I remember the shiny floors – I had noticed someone was washing them – and imagined the fight that would break out. For some reason, a very vivid image of blood arose in my mind. The blood was deep red and had formed into a thick puddle and sat, swelling, jelly-like, on the shiny white floor. The image would not go away.

I found it breathtaking to think about – genuinely breathtaking in that I detected my own anxiety in the way I was now breathing – but also exciting. I didn't want to miss it and intended to be as close to the front as I could get. I wanted to experience this thing fully.

A police car pulled up, stopped and drove away. I was sure that the policeman knew what was going on, but was surprised he didn't stay. There were no other police.

Another minute passed. Nothing happened. The street was busy with Saturday shoppers – families, older women all carrying Sainsbury's carrier bags – but no one knew the nature of the thing that was forming around them.

Another minute, and the supporters drifted into the middle of the street. There was still the studied casual look, but it couldn't be maintained. As the clusters of people came together, a crowd was being formed, and, as it was in the middle of the High Street, it was conspicuous and intrusive. The crowd had blocked the path of a bus, and the traffic behind it started to build up. Someone tooted his horn.

I found myself in the middle of the group, which was not where I wanted to be, and I tried to work my way to the front, but I was too late. The crowd was starting to move; it had started off in the direction of the station. It proceeded in a measured way, nothing frantic, at the pace of a steady walk. I could see the confidence felt then by everyone, believing now that they were actually going to pull this thing off. The pace accelerated – gradually. It increased a little more. Someone started to chant, "Kill, kill, kill". The chant was whispered at first, as though it were being said reluctantly. Then it was picked up by the others. The pace quickened to a jog, and then a faster jog, and then a run.

An old woman was knocked over, and two carrier bags of food spilled on to the pavement. There were still no police.

Halfway up the ramp, the group was at a full sprint: a thousand people, running hard, chanting loudly, "KILL, KILL, KILL". I was trying to calculate what was in store. The train from London would have arrived by now if it was on time, although it was possible that it was late and that we would burst through the station doors and find no one inside. But *if* it was on time, the West Ham supporters would be clearing the ticket barrier and heading for the main waiting area – that shiny floor where I kept seeing a thick, coagulating puddle of blood.

I couldn't see who was leading the group or what was up ahead. I had people on all sides and couldn't get past them, but we must have been within yards of the entrance. They were going to get away with it, I thought. It was about to happen. It would only be a few seconds more.

And then suddenly something had gone wrong. I crashed into the person in front of me: hard, bumping my nose. He had stopped and turned with cartoon-like speed, his legs whipping round, while the momentum of the run carried the rest of his body forward. He had a look of intense panic on his face, his hand flapping in the air, grabbing at anything, everything, me, the person next to me, the railing. His eyes were wild with fright. He was desperately trying to run back down the ramp. So were the others. I was turned round by the force of the people in front and then had to concentrate on not falling. I don't know what had happened; I could hardly think about it because we were running so hard. Someone was squealing, "Dog! Dog! Dog!" I didn't understand this. The moment before they had been chanting, "Kill, kill, kill". Now they were screaming, "Dog! Dog! Dog!" It was only when I reached the bottom of the ramp that I understood what had occurred.

The police had known all along what was taking place and simply waited for it to unfold. They had judged the moment with precision and had placed two dog-handlers on the other side of the entrance to the station. As the first supporters pushed open the doors, they would have been greeted by two husky German shepherds going for their throats. Two dog-handlers – there were no other police – had turned back a chanting mob of a thousand people intent on violence.

The dog-handlers then came hurtling down the ramp. One supporter fell and the handler let the dog run over him. The dog went for the arm, biting into the flesh. I recognized the handler, a big man, with an Old Testament beard, whom I had seen on previous trips to Manchester. This was his

beat, and he was very practised at it. He then jerked the dog
up off the supporter and went after the next one, who had
also tripped him up, and the dog was allowed to run up over
him, tearing noisily at his sleeve. And then he was off again.

The supporters had split up and were scattered in all
directions. Other police arrived, but not in big numbers.
This was the dog-handlers' show. I ran fast and hard – I was
determined not to be part of it – and so I missed the appearance of the West Ham supporters. I did not notice them
until they reached the bottom of the ramp.

There were about five hundred. They had walked down
in three columns. Once they reached the High Street, they
stopped, still in formation. At the front was a big, broad-
shouldered man, about thirty-five. This was Bill Gardiner.
He stood there, feet planted apart, crossed his arms and
waited. Next to him were his lieutenants, who had crossed
their arms, their feet already apart, and waited. They were
all dressed in the same manner: jeans, open leather jackets,
T-shirts. Many had the same scar on their faces: the serrated
hook across the cheeks, a knifing scar.

There were no shoppers or traffic, and the West Ham
supporters remained in the middle of the High Street, waiting. People started throwing stones and bottles – arching
high in the air, hurled from the different, scattered positions
where the United supporters had found themselves – and
the glass broke around the feet of the people in front. No
one flinched. They stood there until the police had cleared
away all the United supporters.

And then it was over. The police appeared with their
horses and escorted the West Ham supporters to the
ground, and that was that. But, according to the rules of
engagement, West Ham had humiliated the supporters of
Manchester United. The language – rich, as usual, in military metaphors – is important: the firm from East London

had entered the city of Manchester and had taken it. They had made a point of showing that they could take whatever liberties they wanted to. They had walked into the city as if it had been their own.

I walked with the United supporters to Old Trafford. There were recriminations.

"We've been humiliated," someone said. "They're going to laugh at us now when they get back to London."

"Fucking yobs," someone else said. "They had to start chanting when they went up the ramp."

"We should have had them."

"We should have had them."

"But didn't you see them waiting for us?" someone said, referring to that rather majestic moment in which Bill Gardiner stood his ground, flanked by his troops. "They were waiting for us to charge. But no one would chance it. There was no one around."

"This doesn't happen abroad. That's where we show what we're made of."

"It didn't happen in Italy."

"It didn't happen in Luxembourg."

"In Spain, forty of us would have taken on fifteen hundred of those bastards."

"Why can't we fuckin' do it? What's the matter with us?"

There were skirmishes throughout the day – outside the ground just before the match; outside the ground just after it. A tram ran from Old Trafford to Piccadilly station, and the West Ham supporters were put on it by the police. Sammy, knowing the routine, had taken a hundred of his "troops" to one of the stops. He came charging down the stairs of the station, his lads just behind him, filling up the staircase, their chant – "Manchester, la-la-la, Manchester, la-la-la" – echoing loudly. When the tram approached,

Sammy ran up to it and pulled apart the doors with his hands. And then he stood back. The station was ringing with the noise. There were not many police, only two or three buried deep within the carriage and unable to get out.

"Come on," Sammy was shouting, standing in front of the door, waiting for the supporters behind him to follow on down the staircase.

"Come on. We've got them."

Only they didn't come. Sammy turned round angrily, incredulous that he was standing alone on the platform: "What are you waiting for?" The doors closed and the tram left.

The moment had come and gone. It was not meaningful, except for me and only in one respect. Just before the tram pulled up, Sammy turned round and surveyed the supporters he had brought with him. He did a head count, one by one, looking everyone straight in the face. I was included in the head count. Sammy shook his head and cursed, realizing he had made a mistake. And then he looked at me again, started, and counted me in. I was pleased.

What did I think I was doing?

3

The Beginnings

Dougie Brimson

During the eighties and nineties, the so-called "English Disease" of football violence spread right across Europe. Writing in the lead-up to Euro 2004, hosted by Portugal, Dougie Brimson takes a look at the spread of hooliganism across Europe. Taken from his book *Eurotrashed*, the following extract looks at the varying degrees of severity of football violence across the continent. He discusses how, with the intense media coverage English hooligans were receiving, there was a general ignorance of the troubles in other footballing nations such as Italy and the Netherlands. The levels of violence in other countries often exceeded that in England, although this was not as well reported.

It may come as a surprise to discover that although the English game has been blighted with incidents of crowd disorder since as far back as the fourteenth century, hooliganism is a relatively recent phenomenon on mainland Europe. Indeed, in some countries, it is all but impossible to find anything significant that occurred prior to 1980.

That is not to say that there were none. In Italy, for example, one of the first recorded examples took place in 1920 at the end of a game between Viareggio and Lincques.

Following a fight between the two teams at the end of the game, the police went pouring on to restore order but during the subsequent skirmish, the referee was shot dead. The ensuing rioting spilled out of the stadium and resulted in widespread civil disorder and vandalism. And in what was the former Yugoslavia, the fifties saw a wave of trouble sweep through the game. Labelled Zuism – a Serbo-Croat acronym for killing – the worst incidents involved large numbers of fans storming pitches to fight with knives, metal bars and chains.

Yet such incidents were extremely rare, and the fact remains that the stranglehold the hooligans began to exert on the English game from the early sixties onwards was not replicated on the mainland until the mid- to late seventies if not even later. However, rather than examine why there was a delay, we should instead look at why it happened at all. After all, hooliganism isn't an obligatory consequence of football, it is a product of the mood and atmosphere created around it. And, as was proved only too well during the 2002 World Cup, football without hooliganism can be a positively breathtaking experience. So why did the European game, having watched the hooligans drag football to its knees in England, sit back and do nothing as it too became infected? The answers to that question can be found, inevitably, within the history of English hooliganism.

Much of this history was documented in my previous book *Barmy Army*. However, what that book did not examine was the European dimension and, given its relevance here, it is vital that people understand not just why, but how, the problem first left these shores. Because no one should be in any doubt that the English game was – as was the growth of television – instrumental in the eruption of violence within European football.

In the mid-sixties, when England's football terraces were no place for the faint-hearted and certain town centres would regularly become no-go areas on match days, television provided the ideal alternative for the law-abiding football fan. Watching games on the small screen was not only easier and cheaper, it was also a great deal safer. As a result, people began staying away from grounds in their thousands. While this in itself was bad enough for the game, the knock-on effect was that in purely percentage terms, as the crowds fell, the number of hooligans rose. Not surprisingly, so did the amount of violence.

The situation was not helped when, alongside the actual games, television began showing graphic footage of fighting in the crowds. Not only did this provide both entertainment and encouragement to the hooligans but, more worryingly, it also provided a new avenue of publicity. The tabloids had for years sensationalized football violence to the extent that being seen in the papers had become almost a national pastime. Indeed, for many, the keeping of scrapbooks was almost an obsession. That now changed to being seen on the telly. And, increasingly, the cameras acted as a catalyst. Wherever they appeared, the fans would play up, sure in the knowledge that if they escaped arrest on the day, nothing would or could be done to try and bring them to justice.

Across the Channel, the European game was watching what was happening with unease. The terraces battles being seen with monotonous regularity on our shores were now being broadcast to a bewildered continental audience and, with English clubs enjoying success on the bigger stage and significant numbers of fans travelling to watch them, the big fear was that sooner or later something bad was going to happen. Inevitably, it did. And in 1974 Tottenham Hotspur supporters gained the dubious honour of being the first

English hooligans to become involved in large-scale violence outside the UK.

The occasion was the UEFA Cup Final, a two-legged affair against Dutch side Feyenoord. Following a 2–2 draw at White Hart Lane, the Spurs fans crossed the Channel in their thousands determined to drive the team on in the hope of securing an unexpected victory. For many, it was to be their first trip aboard, and the alcohol, coupled with the arrogance that had already become an inherent part of the English hooligan scene, made for an intimidating atmosphere on the streets of Rotterdam. The police, totally unprepared for what was going on, simply adopted a high-profile stance, but it was not enough. As the drinking continued, trouble erupted in numerous bars and, by the time the Spurs fans arrived in the ground, their mood was decidedly hostile. When the referee disallowed what looked to them to be a perfectly legitimate goal, they erupted, tearing down fences and attacking the home supporters. The team were shell-shocked and Bill Nicholson, the then Spurs manager, was forced to make a loudspeaker appeal at half-time, but to no avail. Only when a squad of riot police arrived and began baton-charging the visiting support did things inside the ground calm down, but afterwards it started again and continued for most of the night. The resulting tally of 200 injured and seventy arrested heaped shame on the club and the country.

UEFA were furious and ordered Tottenham to play their next two home games 250 kilometres from White Hart Lane.

Despite UEFA's anger, English hooligans started to wreak havoc on their travels. Only a year later, Leeds United supporters left a trail of wounded locals and empty shops as they made their way to Paris for the European Cup Finals against Bayern Munich. Sadly, their conduct inside the ground was also less than exemplary and, following a riot that was beamed live into homes across the continent, UEFA banned the club from European competition for four years.

Yet if they were hoping it would act as a deterrent they were wrong. And as the hooligan scene in England grew, seemingly by the week, it was becoming increasingly obvious that their actions were not only being closely watched by supporters across the continent, they were also starting to be copied.

The Dutch fans, having witnessed at first hand an entirely new method of supporting, began to look at how they could replicate the behaviour of the English fans and, within months, Dutch clubs such as Ajax, Feyenoord and Utrecht discovered that hooliganism had found them.

The football authorities in England realized that unless something was done to stop it, and quickly, the problem was going to spread. The trouble was, no one knew what to do and so nothing was done. This resulted in things suddenly getting dramatically worse. And then some.

The murder of a Millwall supporter at New Cross station in December 1976 was taken so seriously that police in England even called for the game to be suspended. Yet even as football was still reeling from this disaster, it was dealt a further blow when television stepped back into the equation with the broadcast of the now infamous *Panorama* documentary about Millwall and its hooligan following.

It is impossible to overstate the impact this programme had on the hooligan scene not just in England, but also across Europe. Suddenly, Millwall were *the* hooligan club and The Den went from simply a nightmare place to visit, to being home to a collection of identifiable individuals who belonged to gangs – gangs who, for the first time, had names: The Treatment, F-Troop and The Halfway Liners.

Within days, this phenomenon was repeated at clubs the

length and breadth of Britain and, as both Liverpool and Manchester United carried the yobs' torch across Europe, fledgling hooligans on the continent lapped up reports of what was going on in what had already come to be regarded as the spiritual home of football violence: England.

Yet still it got worse. When England supporters caused mayhem in Luxembourg in October 1977, both the media and supporters across Europe suddenly realized that this was a new and potentially frightening dimension to the problem. For not only were the hooligans putting aside their club loyalties to travel with the national side but, with the right wing already making inroads into the game in England, the potential for a political dimension developing was immense.

More importantly, the envious eyes that had been cast in our direction from the mainland suddenly recognized that hooliganism went way beyond simple violence. It was about excitement, adventure, but above all, it was about power. That realization signalled a sharp rise in incidents involving both Italian and German supporters. Many of which, according to a number of commentators, aped what was going on in England, albeit on a much smaller scale.

By 1980, local hooligans on the continent were even looking to have a go back at their less welcome visitors. The most famous example of this involved fifty Manchester United fans who had to be rescued by German riot police when they came under attack from FC Nuremberg supporters. Yet such incidents were few and far between, and with English football in the grip of the burgeoning casual movement – a movement which ironically was fuelled by Liverpool supporters' exploits in Europe – things were only ever going to get worse before they got better.

It has been said many times before but, in the early eighties, the casual movement *was* football violence in England.

Revolving as it did – and to a certain extent still does – around designer clothing and arrogance, it was tailor-made for the hooligans who suddenly found themselves with not just an identity, but a uniform. However, while the Europeans continued to regard the English scene as the ultimate manifestation of the hooligan culture, they never embraced the casual scene to the same degree as supporters did in this country. Instead, hooliganism developed along different lines. In many instances, this involved far more overt displays of passion and support than were seen in England as well as, increasingly, the involvement of politics. This was particularly so in Italy where the Ultra groups, who had been around since the sixties, now took on a new and added significance.

Unlike the English hooligan gangs who were largely disorganized and existed purely for their own devices, the Ultras were extremely well organized and motivated. They provided their predominantly youthful following with a focus which often went way beyond football, and so successful were they that they quickly spawned similar movements in other countries such as Spain, France and Greece.

However, at the core of the Ultra movement was pride and it was inevitable that as incidents of trouble continued to increase around the European game, a clash of cultures was coming. The first signs of that came, somewhat predictably, in Italy during the 1980 European Championships.

Instrumental in what happened were the Italian media who, having covered the activities of the Ultra groups for a number of years previously, now whipped them into a frenzy about the forthcoming invasion of the English hooligans. As a result, the English support was baited and abused at every turn and by the time the travelling fans arrived in Turin for the Belgium game the mood was already ugly. When the Belgians scored a first half equalizer, the Italian fans in the stadium began taunting the English support who responded in time-honoured fashion. Immediately, the Italian riot police baton-charged the English and then fired tear gas at them – a tactic that resulted in the game being held up for five minutes as the gas drifted across the pitch. When an apparently perfectly legitimate England goal was disallowed later on in the second half, things erupted again and continued afterwards. In all, a total of seventy people were hospitalized and UEFA hit England with a huge fine. But, for the Italian fans, it had been a huge result, and the claim that they "ran" the English is one still being made to this day. More importantly, it set the scene for two things: a sudden explosion of hooliganism across Europe and a period of violence involving English football fans the like of which the game had never experienced.

With UEFA's threats still ringing in their ears, both the British authorities and the English Football Association went on the offensive. They were determined to clean up the game no matter what it took. But to the mobs, this merely added to the challenge. By the time the new season kicked off, they had already started to become more organized and when, in September, a seventeen-year-old Middlesbrough fan was stabbed to death outside Ayresome Park, it was clear that English domestic football was in for a rough time.

Abroad, the pattern continued. English clubs caused mayhem whenever they crossed the Channel and the followers of England did likewise. But increasingly, problems were being seen in the domestic leagues of our near neighbours and, with the local police usually ill prepared, incidents often became incredibly violent.

Worryingly, at least for the English, the locals were also starting to go on the offensive. When Spurs travelled to Amsterdam in 1981, they were expecting some degree of trouble, but what they got was something else. For almost the first time, an English club ran up against serious local opposition, as gangs of Ajax fans, in some cases 200 strong, went for them in the biggest possible way. At least three Spurs fans were stabbed and over twenty were arrested but, significantly, the Dutch police laid the blame squarely at the feet of the Ajax fans.

Just a year later, England, having seen its supporters cause trouble in Switzerland and Norway during the qualifying rounds, travelled to Spain for the 1982 World Cup. With the Falklands War still taking place even as the tournament got under way, tensions and xenophobia were running at an all-time high. Inevitably, it all went badly wrong but, for once, the followers of the England side were on the receiving end as Spanish fans, fired up by anti-British rhetoric, attacked anything that moved. Even the British media were aghast and went to town on the Spanish authorities, accusing them of doing nothing to protect their English guests. Both UEFA and FIFA seemed strangely quiet. The inference was obvious.

Later that same year, English fans were again the victims when they came under attack from local gangs before a World Cup qualifier in Denmark. However, this time, convinced that the local police were happy to see assaults on English fans go unpunished, the hooligans decided to exact their own brand of justice. As the final whistle blew, trouble erupted which, according to some sources, was among the worst violence English football fans had ever been involved in.

Inevitably, neither UEFA nor the FA made any comment on the fact that the England fans hadn't started the trouble, but what UEFA did point out was that if things didn't improve soon, they would have no alternative but to ban England and English clubs from overseas competition.

However, while all eyes had been fixed on the English, of

growing concern to UEFA was the burgeoning hooligan scene in the rest of Europe. Incidents were becoming increasingly frequent, particularly in Germany where violence between rival gangs was becoming extremely vicious. In one example, a sixteen-year-old boy was killed when the train he was travelling on was set alight.

For the English hooligans, however, trouble and travel continued to go hand in hand and, in 1983, Tottenham Hotspur fans were involved in more violent scenes during a trip to Rotterdam. Significantly, the first leg in London had seen the appearance of a hooligan group from Feyenoord. Although their activities were well policed and nothing of note happened, the fact that they came at all sent a clear message to the Spurs fans who travelled for the second leg ready, and more than willing, for the inevitable violence. With a large group having purchased tickets in the home end of the Feyenoord Stadium, fighting broke out early on and continued after the game, resulting in over thirty serious injuries. As a result, Spurs were hauled up in front of UEFA again and fined nearly £8,000. However, if that was meant to send a warning to other English clubs or to English fans, it failed dismally. Just a few months later, England travelled to Luxembourg and, despite a 4–0 victory, the team failed to qualify for the 1984 European Championships. The fans ran riot and once again UEFA stepped in with a warning that if anything happened again all English clubs would be banned from European competition.

Despite this, in February 1984, English hooligans were involved in more trouble – this time in Paris when local skinheads mobbed-up and attacked the visiting fans in the Porte de Saint-Cloud area of the city prior to an international against France. After the game, there were more incidents that resulted in some eighty wounded, forty arrests and a reported £700,000 worth of damage. Even more worryingly, later that year, a Tottenham supporter was shot dead in a Brussels bar prior to the first leg of the UEFA Cup Final against Anderlecht, a game that also saw some two hundred Spurs fans detained by the Belgian police.

Yet despite having issued numerous warnings, UEFA once again failed to act. Just a year later, that failure was to result in a tragedy of previously unimagined proportions.

There can be no doubt that 29 May 1985 saw one of the darkest but most significant events in the history of European football. The condemnation which poured on the English game in the aftermath of the death of thirty-eight Juventus fans and one Belgian at Heysel was immense, well deserved and, to be fair, long overdue. What many people do not realize, however, is that it was the final link in a complex chain of events that had begun the previous season.

In the early eighties, Liverpool, then possibly the greatest club side in world football, was one of the few major English clubs without a significant hooligan following. They had been involved in trouble for sure, but nothing compared to the big London clubs, Leeds or Manchester United. Instead, their reputation was for humour, noise, passion and, on occasions – particularly during their many European excursions – the "liberation" of property.

In 1984, having made it to their fourth European Cup Final, the team travelled to Italy looking to build on what was already a formidable reputation. However, unlike previous occasions, this time they went as underdogs. For the game was to be played in Rome and on the home pitch of their opponents, AS Roma.

Inevitably, with so much at stake for the local side and a support that outnumbered them by many, many thousands, the reception given to the Liverpool fans was less than welcoming. As they entered that stadium, stewards and policemen confiscated coins, bunches of keys, watches and even cameras, which, if anything, fuelled a degree of hostility among the Liverpool support especially when they soon came under attack from a hail of missiles.

Despite the obvious tension inside the ground, the English side went on to win the game in a penalty shoot-out, but even as the players celebrated on the pitch, things on the terraces began to take a very nasty turn.

Almost immediately, the police became openly hostile towards the Liverpool fans and it quickly became clear, especially to the seasoned travellers, that there would be trouble outside the ground. What no one expected was that it would be quite as bad as it was.

While some of the Liverpool support managed to make their way to the centre of the city to be pictured dancing in the famous Trevi Fountain, others headed for their hotels and supposed safety. However, they soon found themselves the target of local youths who seemed totally indifferent to the fact that many English supporters were family groups some of whom included quite young children. Worryingly, the police seemed unsympathetic to their plight and in many cases actually became a part of the problem, lashing out at the English fans as they pleaded for protection. Inevitably, the situation deteriorated. Scooter gangs began chasing the Liverpool fans along narrow streets and slashing out at them with knives as they rode past. In one horrific incident, a thirteen-year-old was almost hacked to death and required over two hundred stitches to his wounds.

To make matters worse, coach drivers who had been due to take some of the Liverpool fans to Rome airport after the game simply went home leaving them stranded and at the mercy of the roving gangs. Equally, some hoteliers, whether in fear for their premises or resentment at the result, refused entry to their English guests, some of whom were forced to seek sanctuary in the British Embassy. It was a shameful episode, and the fact that it received so little media attention in both Italy and England caused outrage among the Liverpool support as well as among the English hooligan community. Revenge was sworn and, only a year later, the opportunity to take it arrived when the team, having made it to the European Cup Final yet again, discovered that they were heading for Belgium to face another Italian side, Juventus.

Even leaving aside the simmering tensions, quite how or why the Heysel stadium was chosen to host this fixture is something of a mystery. The ground failed to meet any of the basic safety standards, and a lack of investment meant that large sections of the terracing were crumbling and covered in knee-high weeds while security for even domestic games was regarded by the locals as something of a joke. For a fixture of this stature, it was simply laughable.

Ironically, the Liverpool fans arrived in Brussels in a subdued mood. Just eighteen days previously, the game in England had suffered a horrific double tragedy when fifty-six fans had died in a fire during a game at Bradford and a young supporter had been crushed to death at Birmingham City when Leeds fans went on the rampage. Sadly, their mood didn't last.

Trouble erupted in Brussels early on as Liverpool fans, many of them veterans of the game in Rome, once again found themselves the target of an Italian Ultra group. This time, however, they were ready and fought back. More importantly, elements among the Liverpool support took the Italians' aggression as a sign that they had called it on. As a result, as far as they were concerned, the opportunity to avenge the events of the previous year had now been handed to them on a plate.

Despite this, the Liverpool fans did not immediately go on the offensive. Instead, they merely sat back and responded where necessary until the Belgian police, who seemed totally unprepared for what was happening, eventually decided that rather than arrest or detain people, the best tactic was to get the fans into the ground as quickly as possible. It was to prove to be a huge mistake for one simple reason: poor segregation.

The ticketing situation had been a shambles from the start. Many of those who had bothered to buy theirs from official sources found themselves separated from the Italians by a flimsy fence and a few uninterested stewards. Others, who had bought their tickets from touts or simply worked out that they could get into the ground by climbing under, over or even through the perimeter fencing, ended up spread around the terraces. As a result, segregation was almost non-existent and with over two hours to go, in a stadium full of some of the most embittered supporters the game has ever seen, small pockets of Liverpool fans soon began to gather together. It was payback time.

Ironically, it was the Italian fans who kick-started the trouble inside the ground when the bulk of the Liverpool fans, who were gathered together on one half of the large Western terrace, came under attack from a barrage of bottles, coins and flares. This quickly escalated into direct violence as Juventus supporters began attacking groups of Liverpool fans located in other areas of the ground. As the Scousers fought back, and with the police seemingly unable or unwilling to take control of the situation, these small skirmishes rapidly escalated into large terrace-battles.

At approximately 8.45 p.m. local time, a section of the Liverpool support on the Western terrace decided enough was enough and forced their way through a fence and charged at the mass of Juventus fans who had been hurling a steady stream of missiles at them. Immediately, panic set in among the Italians, who turned and fled. However, with the other three sides of the terraces surrounded by a concrete wall, they simply had nowhere to go.

The Liverpool fans, unaware of what was happening continued to attack the Juventus supporters, who by now were desperately climbing over each other in an effort to escape. As the police were still trying to work out what to do, the inevitable happened and the crumbling wall at the eastern end of the terrace collapsed. The release of pressure sent the helpless Italians who had been crushed against it tumbling to the floor. Yet even as they lay there, the remainder of the Juventus support poured through the gap, crushing their fellow supporters underfoot.

As the rest of the ground witnessed the tragedy unfolding, all hell broke loose. Italian fans in other parts of the ground invaded the pitch in an effort to get at the Liverpool support and at one stage it even appeared that a Juventus supporter was firing a gun into the English section (it later turned out to be a starting pistol). With the situation now seemingly out of control, the Belgian police were finally spurred into action and when reinforcements arrived, supplemented by units from the Belgian army, order was quickly restored.

Incredibly, despite the deaths of thirty-eight Italian fans and one Belgian, and with neither set of players wanting to take part, the decision was taken that the game had to go ahead. The reasoning being that if it didn't the fans would cause even more mayhem in the streets of Brussels. So, in one of the most controversial games in the history of football, Juventus won the 1985 European Cup Final 1–0. But the result was meaningless.

With the game being broadcast live, pictures of the disaster were seen around the world and, inevitably, every ounce of blame fell on the Liverpool fans. The Belgian authorities, in a desperate but ultimately flawed damage-limitation exercise, accused the Englishmen of being "fighting mad" and told of one who had to be injected with enough tranquillizer to knock out six horses before he would calm down. There was even talk that those held in custody would be charged with mass murder.

But, almost immediately, stories began circulating that among the Liverpool fans had been known hooligans from a variety of clubs including Chelsea, Newcastle, West Ham, Millwall and Leeds. Desperate for a new angle on the hooligan issue, the tabloid press jumped on these rumours and informed the world that Heysel had actually been a planned show of strength by the English hooligan elite as revenge for the events in Rome the previous year. It was also claimed that it had been a group of Chelsea fans that had kicked everything off.

However, in all the research I have ever done on this incident, no one has ever provided a shred of evidence that supports that claim. Where the rumours came from is still unclear, but given that Liverpool have always enjoyed a wealth of support across the whole of England, it is possible that regional accents heard at the time have more to do with these theories than any ounce of reality. Indeed, many Liverpool fans I have spoken to who were at Heysel, angrily refute the suggestion and make it plain that this was very much their fight and it was one they wanted.

Whatever the truth of the matter, what is clear is that National Front literature was found on the terraces afterwards but, at a time when the right wing were still heavily involved with English football, that was nothing unusual, especially considering what had gone on the previous year. Official condemnation was instant. A stunned UEFA finally acted against the hooligans and all English teams were banned from European competition for five years with Liverpool having to serve a further two-year ban on top of that. Equally, the authorities in England went on the offensive like never before. A number of high-profile police operations took place that saw various hooligan groups torn apart. Others who had been actively involved in terrace violence simply gave up, too shocked at what they had seen on their television screens to take any further part.

Surprisingly, the ban didn't include the England side but, thankfully, largely due to the cost and distance involved in getting to Mexico, the 1986 World Cup was remarkably trouble-free. However, just a matter of weeks later, English football was once again dragged on to the front pages by its travelling fans – although this time they never actually made it on to foreign soil.

Unbeknown to many, in the wake of the World Cup and a 50 per cent reduction in trouble at domestic league games, UEFA had relaxed the ban on English clubs travelling abroad to play pre-season friendlies. Two of the first to take advantage of this were Manchester United – who had arranged a fixture with Ajax – and West Ham, who had accepted an invitation to take part in a tournament in Groningen. To avoid any repeat of previous problems, both clubs took the decision to keep news of the trips secret from their fans. However, it wasn't long before it leaked out and travel plans were soon being made.

On 7 August 1986, the ferry *Koningin Beatrix* sailed out of Harwich with a couple of hundred football supporters on board. A good proportion of those were simply fans of both teams intent on enjoying a trip to Holland to watch their respective sides play, but drinking heavily in the bars were a group of a hundred and fifty Manchester United lads. More importantly, sitting in first class were fourteen of the main faces from West Ham United's ICF – the notorious Inter City Firm who had hit the headlines in 1985 when the now infamous documentary *Hooligan* had been shown on British television.

With a trip of several hours ahead of them and an intense rivalry between the two sets of fans that dated back to 1967, a confrontation of some kind was inevitable and it took just over two hours before it exploded.

After the usual exchange of verbal abuse and a small but violent skirmish, the outnumbered ICF retreated to the sanctuary of first class and prepared for the inevitable attack. Using a variety of weapons including bottles, fire extinguishers and even a fire hose spraying at full blast, they stood firm at the top of the various stairs leading up from the lower decks and repeatedly drove back the United fans who tried desperately to get up at them.

As the fighting continued seemingly out of control, and with the stairs and decks awash with blood, the captain decided that the journey was simply too risky to continue and, having sent out a distress signal, turned the boat around and headed back to Harwich where it was met by hordes of policemen and a huge media circus.

Over twenty Manchester United fans were taken off the boat and rushed to hospital while eleven were arrested for their part in the fighting, which had been so fierce that a group of *Hell's Angels* who happened to be on the boat heading for a rally in Holland had refused to become involved, telling the West Ham lads that they were simply too violent.

In hooligans' terms, it was a result that cemented the ICF's reputation as a legendary firm but, for the English game, it was nothing less than a disaster. Not only did it end any lingering hopes of an early end to the ban but UEFA actually increased it by an additional year as a punishment.

Clearly relieved that they had been handed a reason to postpone the return of English clubs to European competition, UEFA sat back and got on with the business of running football. What they failed to notice was that across Europe hooliganism wasn't just developing, it was actually catching up with the English game.

Proof of this came in 1987 when Feyenoord fans en route to Aberdeen for a UEFA Cup tie caused havoc on the ferries taking them to Scotland. Not only was this the first example of any club bringing trouble *to* the UK, it also sent a message to the English hooligans that the fast-approaching Euro '88 was going to provide a severe test of their reputation.

The British media immediately jumped on this and began whipping up both the fans and the public. The *Sun* newspaper even compiled a league table of the participating nations based on the performance of their hooligans and, much to the annoyance of the English, placed the Dutch firmly at the top.

In the event, despite the best efforts of the media to say otherwise, the warnings proved to be false. Trouble involving England fans in Germany was fairly limited with the only major incident taking place at the main railway station in Dusseldorf where England fans came under attack from German hooligans but ended up giving them a good hiding. Of more significance was the riot in Hamburg that resulted in a number of Irish and Dutch supporters being given serious beatings by German hooligans.

Despite the fact that out of 1,200 fans arrested, only 381 were English (over 800 were German) and the majority of them had simply been rounded up and deported, the English FA withdrew a planned application to have the European ban lifted on the grounds that the fans were not to be trusted. As a result, the then Prime Minister Margaret Thatcher warned that the very future of the game in England was in serious doubt as a result of the continuing problems associated with the hooligans.

However, as the end of the decade approached, what no one realized was that hooliganism was already on the decline in England. Not because of the police or the media, but because of music and, more importantly, drugs.

The rave scene that exploded across the UK in the late eighties took lads away from football at a quite amazing rate. To a certain extent, it was also successful in making hooliganism unfashionable. Yet the impact that the new dance culture had on the hooligans was nothing compared to the effect that the events of 15 April 1989 had upon the English game.

The death of ninety-six Liverpool fans at Hillsborough changed football in England for ever. The subsequent report on the tragedy by Lord Justice Taylor saw the fences surrounding pitches torn down and the terracing of the top-flight clubs replaced with seats. More importantly, it forced the police to go on the offensive and the hooligans to go undercover or, in many cases, simply give up altogether. It also attracted an offer from UEFA who told the fans that if they behaved at the fast-approaching Italia '90, English clubs would be readmitted to European competition.

What happened in Italy had been well documented elsewhere, but what is important is that not for the first time England supporters came under sustained attack from both local fans and the police, the majority of whom seemed intent on exacting revenge for past misdemeanours. In one incident, for example, twenty-five England fans were attacked by a group of approximately five hundred Italians but, when they fought back, they were beaten by the police and arrested.

Incredibly, the English media saw what was happening and reported the provocation accurately and sensibly, with the result that when the fans came home they were perceived not as scum but as victims. Even UEFA recognized what had happened and rewarded the fans by readmitting Cup-winners

Manchester United and League runners-up Aston Villa back into European competition. Champions Liverpool were still barred. Astonishingly, they also invited England to bid for the 1998 World Cup.

To all intents and purposes, the bad times surrounding English football on its European travels were apparently over.

4

Heysel Upon Us

Colin Ward

On 29 May 1985 the European Cup Final between Liverpool and Juventus was played at Heysel Stadium in Brussels. The stadium was fifty-five years old and in a state of severe disrepair. It may have been Belgium's national stadium but it was not a suitable venue for a match like the European Cup Final where 60,000 supporters would be packed into its crumbling stands. There were already tensions between the two sets of fans and the terraces were segregated. An hour before kick-off a group of Liverpool fans breached the fence separating them from the Juventus fans. As the Juventus fans retreated towards the concrete retaining wall many were crushed. Then the wall itself collapsed. Thirty-nine people died, and 600 were injured.

From the book *Armed for the Match*, Colin Ward looks back at this terrible disaster, later described as "the darkest hour in the history of UEFA competitions".

In 1984, Liverpool played AS Roma in the final of the European Cup. The match was played in the Olympic Stadium in Rome, which also happens to be the home of AS Roma. Those Liverpool supporters who declined to be bussed in and out of the city by a force of 5,000 police were subjected to a terrifying ordeal of systematic brutal attacks by the Roman Ultra thugs. One Liverpool fan foolish enough to walk the streets alone, thinking he was a gentle tourist, was viciously and repeatedly stabbed and lay close to death for many weeks, eventually returning home to England never to be the same person again. The Roma fans had done the same thing to a Gothenburg fan earlier in the tournament. A group of Swedes were ambushed and ran, but one fell, and the last thing his friends saw was the repeated slashing and stabbing movements of frenzied fans. He died on the operating table.

Twelve months later, Liverpool again reached the final of the European Cup, where they faced another Italian club, Juventus. The same system that had seen an Italian club awarded a European Cup Final on their home ground now deemed Brussels' Heysel Stadium fit to host this match. Heysel, when it was built, was probably a modern safe stadium. Now, in 1985, it had become a crumbling relic with rotten, rust-eaten fences, open cracked concrete terraces eaten away by years of frost, and rickety perimeter walls ready to fall down which anybody without a ticket could scale to gain entry. It had been that way for many years, yet nobody had bothered to check on its worthiness to host a match expected to attract a sell-out crowd, with more outside clamouring for tickets. Liverpool fans would be coming there with anger in their hearts, caused by stories of Italians attacking their mates the previous year; Stanley met Roma salami and Stanley got sliced. Aye wack, those Eyeties are all blade merchants.

Heysel was going to have 50,000 people crammed inside on a warm May evening. Tales of Stanley in the cooked meat counter spread like wildfire on the terrace bush telegraph and the ferries leaving Dover, until every fan from Liverpool knew at least one story of their mates getting bushwhacked. As the Scouse invasion converged on the centre of Brussels, the salami stories sparked into life again. Liverpool fans being attacked by groups of young Italians with knives. At Brussels North Station, the paranoia was hanging in the air.

"There's bleeding mobs of Italians going round slicing anybody with a red shirt on."

"That's rubbish, that is."

"Yeah? Well if it ain't true, then why are people telling the stories? Those Italians really worked it to us last time with their dirty great knives. We're gonna be ready this time."

Paranoia is paranoia, no matter how you bottle it. Hope and pray that the bottle doesn't smash.

UEFA had imposed segregation with a neutral zone but before kick-off it was obvious that this was only wishful thinking. With that neutral zone next to the Liverpool sections was a large group of Juventus Ultras. The Liverpool fans within had moved towards the comfort zone of the dividing fence looking for a transfer into their own section but that didn't stop a small group being attacked by a larger group of Italians just before kick-off. One lad ran over the fence pleading for the help from the huge contingent of Liverpool fans.

"Come on, lads, they're doin' us!"

Fear was in his voice. The dread that they'd be left at the mercy of the vicious Italians. His pleading went up an octave as terror and adrenalin combined.

"Help us!"

Young Stanley and the rest of those on the Liverpool side of the fence reacted with fury. Full of anger and Belgian lager after a serious seven-hour session, they were never going to walk away or call for the police to sort it out. The boys will sort this one in a drunken charge. Sort this out the way disputes should be sorted out – the English way.

"Come on! Are we gonna let them humiliate us? Are we

gonna let them Eyeties do us again? Let them do fellow Liverpool fans while we stand and watch?"

Arms were waved. The harder lads, ace faces, front-line terrace punchers, surged over or were beckoned over. People looked around for faces who would be prepared to go over the fences and go in first. It took a few minutes but, once the Scousers got their act together, they led a charge to help their mates. Hands against the mesh, pushing, shouting, rocking. Police whacking their hands, making them let go with pain. Soon hundreds were rocking the fence. Only six police officers stood between them and the Italians. The police were frightened.

"Take the fence down! Do the Italian shits! They're doing us again!"

The roar of the charge came up from the throats. A roar of anger, one of grinding teeth and pent-up aggression. The Italians beckoned them forward, cockily holding their hands out and gesturing with their fingers because there was a fence and a line of riot police.

"It's their main firm. Come on, let's have it! Are we gonna have it or what?"

"You bastards! You're gonna cop it, you shitbags."

First one, then another, up close to the fence, close enough for the Italians the other side of the thin police line to smell the anger and hatred. The rusty metal groaned and bent over the concrete as it rocked to and fro. Then a surge from behind.

"Go, go, go! Come on, come on! Do the shirtlifters!"

People pushed from the back into the others simply finding themselves on the front line. There is a stage when part of the crowd is reluctant, but there comes a point when it becomes one and the charge is inevitable. The Italians stood looking tough and resolute, still hitting prostrate Liverpool fans, as the fence and the line of police guarding them seemed to be holding firm. Desperately the fans surged forward over the fence and between its concrete pillars. The dam had burst and, like sea washing away sand, the charging fans went through the police line, which melted away in terror, to punch the Italians in a mad frenzy and exact revenge.

Reasoning had departed. Over the mesh they trampled with clenched fists, punchers wanting action. Fear and loathing in equal amounts, this was their moment: "Avenge Rome." Here comes Stanley and wack. Across went one Scouser and nutted a young Ultra right between the bridge of his nose and his eye socket. Those close enough heard the crunch of nasal bone being compressed and an eye-socket shattering. Blood squirted out over his friends' designer label. Now cool was fast being replaced by panic among the Italians. Where were their front-line boys? Those that hit the floor were kicked with real venom and then stamped on. Now it was Stanley's turn to slice salami. The Italian Ultras on the front line weren't so tough now it was unarmed combat, eyeball to eyeball, fist on face – so they ran.

"RUN! RUN! RUN!" Panic in the Italian voices. Italian, an emotive language where the panicky words come out faster than Anglo-Saxon. Now the hunters were the hunted. In their fear they pushed those in front of them out of the way as they desperately tried to escape. Huge gaps appeared on a previously packed terrace. Some Italians were caught by the Scousers, but the surge to get away created a wave of panic.

When a terrace crowd runs, it creates a rumble sound as those fleeing utter a noise that comes from within. Guttural and instinctive, an avalanche of sound, the rumble of hell on the move. Fearful air rapidly exits the lungs trying to shout for help while 30,000 feet stamp at the same time, trying to keep upright against the uneven surface beneath their feet. Arms in front pushing, shoving – move, move, move, faster, faster, head half-turned to see how close behind the pursuers are, the eyes giving a manic full-moon madman look, the mouth twisted. Who or what is in front of them becomes unimportant, everything must just be pushed out of the way as fast as possible. Behind them is the terror, the unknown. When it's a few on the move it's easy to stop. When the terrace is packed with thousands then collective kinetic energy propelling that crowd forward is immense. Cattle stampeding towards a barbed-wire fence spring to mind. In the case of a football terrace, the edge is a brick or concrete wall. The crowd propels itself forward until the mass of bodies squashes into a smaller space at the edge of the stadium, preventing the crowd progressing any further. An unstoppable force meets an immovable object but when thousands go forward in a human wave, something has to give. Usually among the squash of flesh the crunch of bone is heard, then the panic relents and calm is restored.

In Heysel's case, frightened Italian flesh and bones met crumbling concrete, brick and mortar. Those near the edge of the terrace ran away from an unseen foe and were crushed up against a wall, which collapsed. Over and down they went, with the momentum of those behind still coming forward on top of them. In the chaos that ensued, thirty-eight Italians and a Belgian were crushed to death while hundreds more were injured. The whole world watched as the event unfolded on prime-time television, myself included. Back in England the watching masses recoiled in shock. Like the Vietnam war when it was broadcast into American living rooms, this was drama of a different kind.

And something or somebody had to be blamed.

Plenty of people saw it clearly. It was the English hooligans. Parliament the next day demanded retribution.

An empire had been built on the need to have someone

be seen to walk down the road for a crime. At the helm of this English principle this clear May morning was Margaret Thatcher. In the *Guardian*, Eric Heffer, an MP representing Liverpool constituents, tried to shout above the parapet that the deaths had been caused by a wall collapsing and that there should not be a lynch mob as there might be reasons other than pure hooligan bloodlust for the outbreak of trouble. But his voice was drowned out. This was England in full vengeful mode. From the Tolpuddle Martyrs onwards, England has never liked those who upset the established order.

Mrs Thatcher immediately set up a Cabinet committee. In England's wars the first casualty is rational thinking and, with Thatcher, propaganda was truth. Authority good, hooligans bad. The TV scenes had made her blood boil, so she would speak for everybody and nobody else had a view that counted. "Everything has to be done that needs to be done to bring football hooligans to justice." We'd heard it all before. In the dark recesses of power, people nodded because someone would be seen to pay for this. Authority good, hooligans bad. Bad football fan equals hooligan. Get hooligan, any bloody hooligan.

In the reports that followed blame was immediately apportioned.

One British supporter said that the ground was littered with British National Front leaflets, some overprinted by the British National Party with their address. One witness spoke of passengers on the boat crossing the Channel with National Front insignia singing songs of hatred and exhibiting violence.

Mr John Smith of Liverpool Football Club spoke of how six members of the Chelsea National Front – skinheads with Cockney accents – had boasted to him of their part in provoking the violence and said that they seemed proud of their handiwork. Ex-Liverpool manager Bob Paisley said that a man claiming to be a Chelsea fan had forced his way into the directors' box. People stated that they saw a party they observed as Londoners leaving Brussels North station carrying Union flags and having National Front and swastika tattoos. A contingent of men displaying National Front insignia on flags were supposedly seen moving around the terrace just before the main fighting erupted.

In Britain, there had to be an Official Enquiry, chaired by a learned judge, in this instance Lord Justice Popplewell. Britain's great system of justice and order meant that the pronouncement of and apportionment of blame were seen to be fair and equitable. Now, at long last, the buck-passing would stop because the Prime Minister had decided that football hooligan gangs had gone too far. And those given the task of removing football hooliganism would be granted proper resources to get to the heart of this depravity. Priorities established, no more the operational inspector who regularly lost his men on a Saturday to some other task. No, this was right from number one, so nobody would touch this budget or cut men from this duty for something more vital. These hooligans had been cutting a swathe across the continent for years now, destroying the country's reputation, but England was powerless because the police had no authority to stop them. Now the order had been megaphoned through from Number 10, the Prime Minister who had used the law and the police to break the power of the unions. Maggie had defeated the miners when everybody said it was impossible; Maggie had shown the world that she alone would make a stand against everything that was wrong and corrupt in England and the world. Trade unions, Argie dictators. So a few football hooligans held no problems for her. Off-the-record lobby briefings to the newspapers told us what the establishment was thinking:

"The tragedy at Heysel has hurt our standing in Europe. Never again do we want to see this on the TV. These people are not above the law because they are in a foreign country. These actions must be terminated. People want some action from this moment on – bodies brought before the courts."

Very soon the initial clarion call to arms by Mrs Thatcher was translated into action. Some saw it as an intelligence matter, but the Chelsea boys were part of the Metropolitan Police jurisdiction so the Met would get first bite at the cherry. The Met Police had achieved results before, but the culture of football hooligans was new so there was no precedent.

Perhaps the briefing for the Fulham police was a formal one, or it may have had other ways of going down the chain of command. Whatever, they had picked goods lads, the sort that England has always relied upon to help her through a crisis. These were good old British bobbies, the kind that Americans loved to be pictured next to as they patrolled the King's Road. Somewhere in this highly charged rhetoric and Thatcher-driven results culture, Operation Own Goal was born. Exactly what went on during this period is unclear, but the pressure was on to gain a result. The orders were coming from the highest level and they demanded it. Results will be achieved.

Young police constables would be in the terrace front line, grimy station backstreets or wherever the protagonists did their worst. They would be gathering evidence against people they saw flouting the law every Saturday right in front of their eyes. They didn't mind football fans having a good time, but these people were taking the piss. There was a determination to eliminate the vermin that had planned and executed the violent acts which had culminated in Heysel.

History would be the judge of who was really to blame for Heysel, but many a legend started out as an apocryphal story that gained a special life of its own as fact met fiction and intermingled in the course of time. Someone always knew of someone who'd told someone else the truth. And every football fan knows how much Scousers love a story. At the opening match of the 1985–86 season, following Heysel, the Liverpool programme featured numerous pictures of people whom the police wanted to trace, with an anonymous contact number. There was a rumour floating around that when one group of Liverpool lads were questioned by the police, they had stated firmly: "Aye, it were Chelsea. They were the Chelsea NF boys – they caused it. I saw them getting the boys fired up in and around Brussels North station. Them Chelsea boys that are always around when it goes ballistic with England. Right tasty cases, they are, carry shooters sometimes. Plus they know all the main racist geezers on the Continent, you know, Combat number crew."

"Combat 18."

"Yeah, that's them. Really well organized. They were there waiting to have it with the Eyeties. Some of 'em don't drink, just organize, point here and there. They rallied the boys inside near the fence then led the charge, they did it. It was that Hickey [Stephen 'Hickey' Hickmott] and his mob. Everybody saw them."

5

It's Grim Up North

Dougie and Eddy Brimson

In the North of England football means everything. There are so many big clubs in cities and towns across the North with intersecting and complex rivalries. Manchester United have their obvious cross-city rivals Manchester City, but Man U fans also harbour a deep hatred for Leeds United that is more than reciprocated. Supporters of the three big Northeast clubs – Newcastle, Middlesbrough on the A66 and Sunderland (the Mackems with their Stadium of Light and Seaburn Casuals) – all intensely dislike each other and all live within spitting distance of each other.

In this extract from *Derby Days*, Dougie and Eddy Brimson explain some of these rivalries. They describe the intense passion that football generates in the North of England and how this passion often boils over into violent encounters.

Those of us fortunate enough to live in the South of our glorious country know only too well that the North is good for only one thing: it provides a buffer zone between us and Scotland.

In the case of football fandom, the North provides ample excuse to travel with our clubs and experience the joy of returning south after our team has, hopefully, done the job it was supposed to. We also get to experience such culinary delights (?) as meat and potato pies and mushy peas, although, to be fair, the best chips are always found up north. But we are not here to sing the praises of North or South, just to talk about the local rivalries that exist within the game. In the case of the North of England, they are many and are all too often ferocious affairs.

For this book, we expected a great deal of material from both Manchester and Sheffield but, despite our best efforts, received little. The reason for that escapes us, because the Sheffield clubs are certainly among the most passionate rivals in Britain.

Clearly, every soccer thug relishes the prospect of a local derby game, both on and off the field. The fact that the fans at the other end of the ground live in the next town, the next street, or even the next bedroom, gives the whole day added significance. In the North-east, when the "big three" meet, the possibilities for violence are very real. Indeed, as J. H., a Newcastle fan from North Tyneside, relates, the clubs don't even have to meet on the pitch for the fans to indulge:

The Geordies

One weekend, we thought we'd treat ourselves to a good day out and have a pop at the scum (Sunderland), who we hate with a passion. On the Saturday in question, we were due to play Middlesbrough away and although many think that this is a local derby, they're over forty minutes down the A19 and as far we're concerned, it's just another game. The Boro had been getting a good name for themselves over the years, although they've never created much when they're on our patch. Lately, though, they'd resorted to giving our lads grief in and around the local nightclub circuit, so it was about time they were taught a lesson by the top boys in the north-east.

All the old faces were contacted – including a few who had settled down and had been well out of it for a good while – and on the day, we had an evil mob of around 100 milling around "the Shrine" of Newcastle Central station by about nine o'clock. However, this wasn't all down to the attraction of a day out at Boro. We were also going to pay the scum a surprise visit, as the Mackems were playing at home.

Everything was organized to escape the police clampdown, because we knew that once they got hold of us, that would be it. So we brought the train tickets and went past Boro to Darlington. Once there, one of the lads had organized a pub owner to open his bar for us at about ten. So there we were, having a few sherbets and getting into the mood.

One o'clock came and we all set off to the station. The two carriages we took over were rammed full of lads 'up for it', and not one runner among us. Anyhow, talk about coppers being thick as pigshit, for when we pulled into Boro's station, the platform and entrance was full of plods looking menacing . . . but we were coming from the other direction, so our platform was empty! We seized the chance and the carriage emptied within seconds. It was five to two and we knew Boro would be in or around the two pubs situated within yards of the station. Everyone was at the pace of a quick walk on the unmanned platform, and we made it out of the station just as the police finally realized what was happening and they were screaming at us to stop. Some chance!

All our eyes were focused on the first pub as our relatively quiet mob steamed across the road. Outside the pub there were a couple of their smart lads, who looked at us in sheer terror. They lobbed their pints at us, but it was too late. We were on top of them, fighting to get through the pub entrance.

Tunnel vision took over as the Boro were getting whacked left, right and centre, but all the surroundings were a blur. The sound of windows breaking, shouting and screaming, not to mention approaching police sirens, only heightened the buzz. Someone had let off some CS gas, which must have been one of them as we weren't tooled up at all. At that point, we pulled out and as the police were stuck in the pub, we steamed down to the next pub, which was about a hundred yards away.

We must have looked like a swarm of wasps going down the road. By this time, some of their lads, about twenty, had come out of the pub and were giving us the come-on, but we were all on a roll and just ran into them, fists and boots flying. There were a number of lads sparked out completely and a couple huddled up in a ball just trying to get out of it, but once again the police were soon in the middle of it and we pulled out. Due to our numbers, we were now in control of our own movements and we gathered at the corner of a crossroads to regroup. Still no one was around to have a pop at us, probably because they didn't have a clue what the fuck was going on and they were shitting it. By the time we decided to move, the coppers were all over the place with horses and dogs, so we moved off into a housing estate and began moving through the back lanes.

With everyone still on a giant high, we saw a massive mob of their lot, about a hundred and fifty lads, and they were angry as fuck. Before they could see us, we just went at them as fast as we could. Before we could get there, though, three riot vans appeared and drove straight in front of us. They almost ran down some of our faster runners, but they stopped us going forward and then another couple of vans pulled in behind us. The bastards had us trapped in a little back lane, while the Boro lads were lobbing stuff at us over the top of them before the coppers moved them on.

Realizing that the police meant business, myself and four others (including two members of Shrewsbury's English Border Firm who had been invited along for the day, a friendship that had been formed during Italia '90 after we'd been locked up for the night together) decided to leg it between the vans, the main reason being that one of the lads couldn't risk another court appearance.

Walking around an area you don't know well is bad enough, but when the locals are hellbent on killing you, you could say the five of us were well on edge! It was too risky going to the game and far too dangerous to risk going back to the station for a while, so we had a few pints in a shitty little pub until after kick-off.

When we arrived back in Newcastle, we were astonished to find all our lot on the other fucking platform. The Boro coppers had decided that the only way to deal with such a big mob was to get it out of town, and fast. So they had just searched them all, took a few videos and then put them on an express train back to the "Toon"! The five of us would have been better off 'supposedly' getting lifted! Once the dozy coppers had escorted them back to Newcastle and fucked off, our lads had just crossed the platform and were waiting for the next train to Sunderland.

Apparently, the scum weren't expecting us until after the home game, about six o'clock, the chosen venue being the Windmill pub. Fuck Queensberry rules, we decided to use the element of surprise again and turned up at about 4.30. But as we walked out of the station, it was clear that their pub was still full of lads, and a couple of scouts soon sussed us. As we took off towards them, they came pouring out of the pub and we met head-on on some waste ground. As usual, they were flapping around like headless chickens, totally unorganized and shitting themselves, and we stood our ground for a good few minutes. We certainly had the upper hand, anyway

– not just because of the fact that we had already been at it and were full of confidence, but because we're full of hatred for them. The coppers then came screaming in and unfortunately, some of our lads were arrested as our soft, sad rivals did a runner.

The ones who made it home certainly had a good drink that night in the Bigg Market, and the whole day's events are talked about on a regular basis. In the space of a few hours, we humiliated our two closest "opponents" and proved that they're nowhere near being in the same league as the Geordies.

With both Sunderland and Middlesbrough being relegated from the Premier League at the end of the 1996–97 season the re-emergence of the clubs' traditional rivalry was inevitable, given their disappointment. However, the 1997–98 season saw the activities of the supporters plunge to new depths and there is simply no excuse for some of the things that have gone on between these two sets of fans. The fact that both sets of supporters attempt to justify their actions in any way makes it all the more astonishing. An example of this was sent to us by Mike, who describes himself as "a Boro boy through and through". He sent us his account of what was a particularly nasty and dangerous incident that could have had fatal consequences.

The A66

Now there's never been any love lost between the Boro and Sunderland. Just like any derby game there's always a little trouble but this season had seen more than most and has ensured that, from now on, there's going to be more and more. Here's how it all started.

We – the Boro – travelled to the Stadium of Shite early in the season fully expecting a bit of bother because we had kicked the shit out of their lot down at our place the year before. But the scenes we were faced with were very unexpected. We won the game 2–1, but a good ten minutes before the end we could see their lads leaving the ground. We were bracing ourselves for a bit of a ruck, but what followed was a full-scale riot.

The police were shite and seemed virtually non-existent as their "lads" were kicking the shit out of our shirts, which is fucking out of order. I personally saw an OAP get smashed in the face and loads of our lasses being spat on! We went for it with any of their lot that had the bottle to fight real men, but it didn't last long as eventually the bobbies got their act together. However, they smashed our coaches up, full of families, and even had the cheek to throw bottles and pint glasses at our disabled supporters' bus as it passed a pub. Even Chelsea or Millwall at their worst wouldn't have resorted to that. Anyway, because of this incident, they were sure to receive a warm welcome next time they came down here. So imagine our delight when we drew them in the Coca-Cola Cup, at home!

We didn't even bother to organize our lads because we were sure that revenge was on everyone's minds due to the fact that their attack on our disabled bus had been widely reported in the local press. Come the night of the match, we were looking for anyone and anything wearing stripes: women, children, old fogies, it didn't matter. We wanted to send a message out loud and clear that no cunt fucks the Boro about, let alone the fucking Mackems! All the old boys were out, the original frontline, and, boy, were they up for it. I even saw one of my old teachers and my ex-driving instructor!

We heard of a few confrontations before the game but didn't witness anything ourselves. We were concentrating on after the match and didn't fancy getting locked up for slapping some shirt when the chance to do the poxy Seaburn

Casuals was out there. We all agreed to congregate outside the away end ten minutes before the final whistle, but the pigs beat us to it and, when we got there, they had a line of horses between us and the back of the stand. This allowed us to hunt around for missiles (not very difficult given that the Riverside is sited on a huge wasteland) and we were tooled up with all sorts: bricks, broken bottles, planks of wood, the lot. We were just waiting for them to show, shouting their mouths off behind a line of police just like they always do. Anyway, they came out and just as planned gave it the biggie. "Come on Boro" and "Soft as shite" rang out from the daft cunts before we shut them up with a shower of gifts. This didn't impress the police, but they couldn't hang on to any of our lot long enough to get the cuffs in as we just barged them out of the way.

By now, our mob was about four hundred strong but because we were all together and the exit from the Riverside is only one long road, the bobbies soon got hold of us and it was easy for them to move us along even if it was like a death march. It took them thirty minutes to move our lot ten yards but eventually, when a load of extra police and dogs arrived, they managed to get us away from their coaches and off up the road.

Around fifty of us eventually decided to split up and meet again at the A66 roundabout to try and meet up with their coaches. We managed to brick a few minibuses, but no cunt dared stop and get out, and one bastard even had the cheek to drive his P-reg XR3i past with four passengers all wearing those fucking stripes we all hate. Poor bastard, he took some punishment! It was paradise: no police, because they were in town searching for us, and an endless supply of ammunition as we were running into the road to retrieve the bricks we were using!

We'd been there a good fifteen minutes when we realized

that God himself is a Boro fan. What did we see approaching us with no escort? Only the fucking Sunderland team coach! We showered it with every-fucking-thing in sight and when the windscreen went in, the driver's face was a picture. There's nothing you can do when your vehicle's getting smashed up by the opposition fans; if you get out you get done and if you drive through, the coach gets fucked up. So all you can do is put your foot down and hope. Thinking back, it's a wonder he didn't crash because he was watching us not the road!

Most of us saw this as the funniest thing we had ever seen in our lives, but it was also revenge for the attack on the disabled lads (and lasses). If nothing else, it makes it certain that this is one rivalry that is going to get more and more serious.

Yorkshire can be a dangerous place to visit for any football fan. It goes without saying that the Leeds hooligans are in a different league to anything else the area has to offer, mainly due to their greater numbers, but there is plenty of additional activity taking place, as certain elements of support from Bradford, Barnsley and Huddersfield battle it out. It is a part of the country that, like London, could fill a book of its own.

One of the most dangerous aspects of life among the football fans of Yorkshire is the apparently increasing use of weapons, a subject of great concern to us personally. From things we have heard over the years, we would go so far as to say that in parts of that region, we believe it is almost out of control. The following story shall remain anonymous and tells of the revenge one Bradford fan craves, following the loss of a friend:

Trouble in the People's Republic

There was a time when I would go to all the matches, week after week, but not now. The derby games with Leeds, the two Sheffield clubs and Barnsley were never to be missed but Huddersfield were the team I really hated. As I said, I don't go any more. I don't trust myself, because the passion with which I hate them hurts so much that I could really go over the top. The reason for this? One day, one of my best friends was stabbed to death by two Town fans who jumped him. He was just eighteen. Can you imagine how much I hate them for that? All he was doing was walking around the shithole in his shirt.

The matches between these two have always produced their fair share of problems. One of the most talked-about occasions took place in 1994, when fans involved with Bradford's firm the Ointment attacked a known Huddersfield pub. The whole attack was filmed by an undercover police unit and the evidence was used to sentence fifteen fans to a total of over twenty years in jail. All the Huddersfield fans involved claimed they were the victims of an unprovoked attack and were acting in self-defence; all escaped punishment. The question as to the excellent timing of the undercover police unit that "just happened to be passing" has never been answered. What should be remembered is that some innocent fans could have avoided injury if the police had acted to prevent such an outbreak of violence, rather than sit safely back and film it!

Following this incident, trouble between the two showed no signs of calming down as, despite the prison sentences dealt out by the courts, both firms continued to turn out in numbers. G. gives an account that proves that the police, with a little pre-planning, can actually get it right:

We Don't Need No Ointment

The police and the clubs had been appealing for calm for weeks in the build-up to this match. They knew that both sets of fans were out to prove just who were top lads, and all the appeals in the world would never stop that from happening. Some lads from the Huddersfield Young Casuals (HYC) had been in contact with their opposite numbers in the Ointment, so we knew they were coming in numbers and they knew we were ready and waiting. The police swamped the area. They must have some good intelligence up here, as they were all over their lads when they arrived and got them straight to the ground without anything going off. Fair play to Bradford, they had brought a tidy firm and on seeing that we knew that at some stage it would go off.

As the game started, Town were getting slaughtered. The team were 3–0 down before you knew what was happening and the City fans was really winding us up and taking the piss. Word went out for our mob to leave, even though it was still only the first half. A fair few had already made their way up the steps when Town pulled one back. The police were all over the place – they realized that something was about to happen, but didn't have a clue what. Some of the lads still wanted to make a move, and were having a go at the others to leave, when Town scored again. Now it was 3–2, there was no way anyone would leave now. Just after the start of the second half, we equalized. Their shit fans shut right up. Midway through the half, some Town fans outside fired two rockets over the stand and on to the pitch. We could see the red tracers coming over, but the players didn't and the rockets just missed them.

One of the City players started to act up that he had been hit. What a cunt. That could have cost the club thousands, as well as starting a riot in the crowd. The Town fans gave him shit and amazingly, he made a sudden recovery and came charging over, giving us the big one and shouting at us to fuck off. Players think they are so fucking hard, they make me die. I would just love to see one of them front any lad from a firm and see what would happen. They wouldn't last five seconds.

The game finally ended 3–3 and now the fun was about to start. I swear I have never seen so many police at Huddersfield. We mobbed up outside, but the police had to keep us moving and get us away so they could let the City fans out. It was getting really heavy and the police were filming everyone, so we moved off and broke up into small groups, making it difficult for the police to keep an eye on all of us. The Bradford fans were let out and their lads tried to force their way free of the police escort, but they were all over them.

The only people to get turned over were those that travelled by car. Our lads wouldn't usually target these fans, but for a derby match any scum are fair game. Make no mistake, the two firms will have their meeting another day. The police can't keep us apart for ever.

While the police got it right in the above account, they can also get it wrong – and this they did on a monumental scale in 1996, in the full glare of the television cameras. The game concerned was between Bradford City and Hull City, both clubs with a very volatile following. What follows is an examination of the Hull City fans as well as a look at the events of that fateful day. It is based on information supplied anonymously.

To Hull and Back

For many supporters viewing from a distance, the obvious derby fixture for Hull City would be Grimsby Town.

However, if you look at a map, it shows that the clubs are actually sitting out on their own and have various derby fixtures to choose from. Indeed, the recent fortunes of the club have seen the games against Grimsby drifting off into the distant past, leaving matches with clubs such as Scunthorpe, Doncaster and Scarborough as the main focus for local rivalry.

As the club fell down the League table, the average home attendance inevitably fell with it. Unfortunately, in a pattern repeated at numerous other clubs over the years, the hooligan element that follows the club has not fallen away in such great numbers and, as a result, now forms a greater proportion of the club's support. Here, the old chestnut that those who cause trouble are not "real" supporters is clearly shown to be untrue. Like them or loathe them, these are the very people who form the hard core of the club's support, and they continue to follow their side through what are obviously hard times. Those who do not bother to go – or, worse, go somewhere else – would do well to remember that, because it is a fact that is all too often overlooked.

During the relegation season of 1995–96, even the police admitted that the hard core of hooligans at Hull City could reach up to 200 once trouble flared up. Trouble started early that season, as the Hull firm known as the Hull City Psychos (HCP) caused problems. In the first leg at Highfield Road, the HCP tried to steam the home end following the final whistle. The police managed to keep them at bay before the firm rampaged through the adjoining streets, damaging cars and smashing windows. For the return leg at Boothferry Park, hooligans from both clubs turned out in great numbers. To keep the two groups apart, the police were forced into mounting a large-scale operation that cost thousands of pounds.

Once again, the HCP went on the rampage through the

street prior to the derby fixture at York City on 16 December. The trouble continued during the match, as police dogs were used in order to halt a pitch invasion by the Hull hooligan contingent. Fighting also broke out in the seated areas as rival fans clashed. However, not all the trouble associated with the club at that time was the result of hooligan behaviour. A number of demonstrations took place as anger grew among the fans towards those that were running the club.

The next serious incident didn't occur until the final away game, at Peterborough United's London Road stadium. The team had struggled all season and relegation beckoned. The hooligans, looking to go out with a bang, caused problems before, during and after the match and it was here that plans were laid for the final fixture, at home to promotion candidates and serious hooligan rivals Bradford City. Indeed, it is the HCP rivalry with the Bradford firm the Ointment which leads many Hull fans to look upon Bradford as one of Hull City's biggest "local" rivals.

The Hull city police had decided to hand over the home end of the stadium to the Bradford City supporters, much to the annoyance of the home fans. The logic behind such a decision was based on the fact that Bradford, who were playing for promotion, would bring more fans with them than there would be Hull fans attending on the day. Although this did in fact prove to be the case, such a decision was always likely to lead to only one thing on the day: serious crowd trouble.

Intelligence gathered by police spotters at the Peterborough match gave them prior warning as to the intention of the Hull hooligans to "take back" their traditional home end and confront the Ointment on the pitch, so perhaps they might have reconsidered their original decision.

On the day, the build-up of Hull hooligans began at around 11.30 a.m. and by 12.30 the police estimated that a hard core of approximately a hundred hooligans had gathered together in order to "welcome" the Bradford fans arriving on the 12.37 train. But the first incident of the day took place on Anlaby Road nearly an hour later. As the two groups fought, police with horses were called and forced the fans apart. The Hull fans moved off towards the ground, calling in all the pubs en route to gain greater numbers. By the time the mob had reached the Griffin pub, their number had grown to 150 and fighting broke out once more as they tried to gain entry to the bar. Once again the police moved in, but by this time the mob had become highly charged and vocal. The police escorted the mob towards the stadium, as they clearly announced their intention that the place to be, for all those looking for trouble, was the South Stand. Once the group had reached the car park, they split in all directions with the intention of getting on to North Road, where the majority were, but small fights broke out as the atmosphere grew more hostile by the minute.

A large group had now decided that the best avenue to the Bradford fans would be to enter the ground and charge across the pitch! As the police continued to contain the situation outside, it was left to the club stewards to keep the peace inside the stadium. Police expected that club stewards would be responsible for all safety matters within the ground, as well as the control of the turnstiles and searching of selected supporters. This decision turned out to be an error of judgement and placed members of the public in a highly dangerous situation. The police had also gathered intelligence that the Hull hooligans had intended to continue making trouble in the ground. If they hoped that they had defused the situation outside, they were proved wrong, as the stewards were unable to cope.

Ten minutes before kick-off, the Hull hooligans who had gathered in the north-east corner invaded the pitch. The stewards offered little resistance, which is hardly surprising considering that many of them had taken on the job expecting to help people enjoy their day, rather than face a volatile mob intent on causing trouble. The Bradford fans retaliated by invading the pitch themselves and fighting broke out. Police on horseback were called in from outside and quickly cleared the pitch. Due to this action, the match was able to kick off on time. But the mood for the afternoon had been set.

The match got underway and Hull City soon took the lead, but as the home fans were still celebrating, Bradford equalized. On seeing their team score, some Bradford fans ran on to the pitch, an action that prompted the Hull hooligans to do the same, sparking off one of the worst incidents of the day. The game was held up for eleven minutes as the police tried to keep the fighting groups apart. At the same time, the police set a ring of officers around both sets of goalposts, so that they could not be damaged. If they had been broken, then the game would have to have been abandoned. This was a particularly good move by the police, as they would certainly have faced increased problems for any rescheduled match. The match finally got restarted once the police had cleared the pitch and placed a large presence around the perimeter of the playing area, an action that, had they taken it originally, might have helped avoid the situation occurring in the first place.

Fighting continued throughout the game as the Hull hooligans on the North Terrace tried in vain to gain the upper hand. With fifteen minutes remaining, a police support unit were ordered to kit themselves out in full riot gear, as it was feared that a Hull defeat would spark a further invasion of the pitch. The match finished with Bradford winning, much to the delight of the travelling fans, who left the stadium without causing further problems for the police. The Hull hooligans were clearly not happy and looking for more confrontation with their rivals. The mob regrouped and, on seeing such a large police presence inside the stadium, they left to attack the Bradford fans outside.

The two groups clashed at the crossroads of Boothferry and North Road. Bricks were thrown as the Hull fans led the charge in some of the most frightening scenes ever witnessed at a Hull City match. The Bradford hooligans certainly played their part in the violence, but many families and children were caught up in the battle. The police officers in charge had made a mistake in allowing both sets of supporters out at about the same time, and the subsequent fighting lasted for some twenty minutes before police on horseback forced the groups apart. Indeed, it was made known to those in charge by the officers in the front line that if it had not been for the excellence and bravery of the police on horseback, then the situation would have been lost.

The details for the match are as follows: the home fans totalled just under 3,700 whereas there were almost 5,300 Bradford supporters present; despite the level of violence seen at the match, only six arrests were made inside the ground, with a further eleven arrested outside. The officers in charge of the policing of this match would appear to have got it badly wrong in this instance, with innocent supporters and stewards suffering as well as their own officers. Fortunately video footage of the trouble was extensive and helped identify many of those involved.

However, of more importance is the fact that there are a number of lessons to be gained from this game, and we can only hope that those in charge actually bother to learn them. The key one is that prevention is better than cure. It is also better than containment, reaction or evidence-gathering for expensive court cases, many of which will never even happen. The police had already made the game a Category C (almost guaranteed trouble) fixture as a result of the intelligence gathered at previous games, but if they knew so much, why could they not gauge the feeling among the home supporters and give them back their traditional end, and keep the Bradford fans in for a while? It may be simple with hindsight, but isn't the purpose of intelligence gathering to give you foresight?

The one saving grace for the police was that the video footage that came out of the violence caught many "known" faces in the act and led to numerous arrests and convictions.

Barnsley are another Yorkshire club who have built a reputation for trouble, and derby games involving them can be very dodgy affairs. G. also told us how problems between the HYC and Barnsley's Five-O have escalated:

The Five-O

The Barnsley lads had been busy trying to build their reputation, and to be fair, they were doing the business and getting a good firm of around forty lads together. They had been spouting off to some of our lads about Huddersfield and coming down to give us a lesson, so we were expecting to wait until we next played them. They had a different plan and paid a visit to town following an FA Cup game at Oldham. They walked through the town singing, "Barns-ley, Barns-ley", and stopped off at various pubs, fighting with the locals. Word soon got around town and the Huddersfield lads started to mob up. We had a couple of lads following their movements who came back and told us that they had finally pulled up and stayed in one pub.

We mobbed up and steamed down the road and straight in

at them. There was no fucking about because if the police had arrived, we wouldn't have been able to have it away and they would have claimed a complete victory. We couldn't allow them to say that they had come to town and taken the piss. The pub got blitzed. Tables, glasses, everything went through the air. The fighting moved out into the street, where two Barnsley lads had their faces slashed.

When we played them in the League Cup a few years later, they came down in greater numbers. They were mad for a result, following the pub fight, and their firm had certainly grown in reputation. This time, they had come armed with CS gas and were attacking Town fans as they made their way to the ground. During the game, the police had things under control and the fans were behaving themselves. Then, with twenty minutes to go, all the Barnsley lads got to their feet as if they were about to leave. They obviously had pre-planned something and someone was calling the shots. The Town fans stood up as well. Then came another gas attack from the Barnsley end. The place went mental, as it mostly affected kids and families. Following the game, we were desperate for revenge. The Barnsley lads were not ready to leave town themselves and shook off the police before taking over a pub down the river. The Town mob that night was fucking massive – the gas attack had really wound people up. Again the pub was steamed. It was one hell of a ruck, as over £2,000 of damage was caused to the pub. That's twice they have come down now, so fair play. Maybe it's time we took it to them.

Leeds United find themselves surrounded by much closer and more obvious rivals than those from over the Pennines, yet they regard these teams as we would a spot on our backside. It's irritating and you wish it wasn't present, but you know it's nothing serious and in a few days you will have forgotten it ever existed. Steve A. gives a brief insight into the spots that plague the top side in Yorkshire:

So You Hate Leeds? Big Deal

There are a few teams that claim to despise Leeds with the same passion and gut-wrenching hatred that we reserve for the scum from the poor county lying across the hills. For them, we are the enemy, yet contrary to what these sad, sad souls believe, we at Leeds don't give them a second thought, as they are worthless nothings. This only frustrates them more, and as they realize their feelings go totally ignored, the resentment grows and festers inside. Still, never mind. The likes of Bradford and Huddersfield would love Leeds to hate them, as they feel it would somehow give them some kind of meaning, a useless kind of importance. It's heartbreaking, really. Let me give you a brief outline of how we view these lesser people.

Bradford City: geographically our local rivals, these poor nobodies hate Leeds most of all. This hatred is born mainly out of seeing 90 per cent of the population of their city catching buses and trains to Elland Road on Saturdays rather than going down to their own little toilet of a ground. As a side, they measure success at not being relegated rather than by League Championships, Cup Final wins, European glory . . . shall I go on?

Huddersfield Town: sadness itself. Give a team a new ground and promotion from one shit division to the next (wow!) and they get all excited. We visited their new show-house for a pre-season friendly and what can I say, it's . . . well, new really. During the game, these saddos showed how low some will go by treating us to fine renditions of "Glory, glory, Man United" and "Ooh aah, Cantona". Bizarre, to say the least, as this was not only an obvious admission of their own lack of importance, but for any Yorkshireman to side with anything Lancashire is degrading. I would like all Yorkshiremen to bear this in mind if ever they come across such scum as those Huddersfield supporters that joined in that singing. They are not the kind of men we need in the Democratic Republic that is Yorkshire.

The two Sheffield clubs: Wednesday and United are way too busy hating each other really to bother about us. The mentality of wanting to be the top club in Yorkshire's second city seems enough to keep them occupied. Obviously, Wednesday have to come to terms with the fact that there is only one team in Yorkshire capable of winning silverware. As for United, well, being second to Wednesday says it all, really. They can both be good to laugh at, though, because they actually think we care.

Barnsley: now this is a bit of a strange one, because most Leeds fans have a soft spot for Barnsley, just like the Man U scummers do for Stockport or Cockneys do for Orient. This, I feel, is about to change somewhat, as Barnsley have now got above themselves. They can no longer be patted on the head or visited for a night out when all the pubs, clubs, cinemas, corner shops, etc. are closed. One consolation here is that Barnsley seem to hate everyone else in the area more than us, especially Wednesday. At last, another Yorkshire club with a bit of sense.

York, Rotherham, Doncaster Rovers and Hull City: what an exciting bunch, eh? In the words of Mavis Wilton, 'I don't really know.' They say they don't like us, but surely they should hate each other, or any other shit team. All these sides suffer from having such a giant casting a shadow over their futile lives, and that must be as difficult for them as they are meaningless to us. Listen, lads, Scarborough must need some excuse for existing. Go on, hate Scarborough.

On a final note, all these teams, and others from further

afield, love to sing, "We all hate Leeds and Leeds . . ." as if they invented the song. Well, sorry, people, you may hate us but as far as we are concerned, you lot just happen to fill up the fixture list between the matches with the real scum. Leeds hate one team and one team only, and as for the rest, you are merely pimples waiting to be squeezed. Altogether, now: "Who the fuck are Man United . . . ?"

Yes, for Leeds, the rivals they hate with a passion are Manchester United. This may not be a truly "local" derby, but both teams also look upon themselves as being the true representatives of Yorkshire and Lancashire, and you can't get more local than that. Ian S. sent us his thoughts on this intense rivalry:

On the Sixth Day . . .

On the morning of the sixth day, God created football. Come 2.50, he pulled on his white shirt for he was cold, yet pure. At three o'clock, he was done and ready for a cup of Bovril and a pie. At thirty seconds past the hour, the Devil arrived wearing red and tripped the Lord's little footballers up from behind, only to start whingeing that he never touched them. Much flying of fists was to follow and therefore, by thirty-five seconds past the hour Leeds United, God's own work, hated Man United, the bile of Beelzebub.

As was to prove itself through the ages, it was the Devil's children that were the cause of all trouble, so the Lord dressed Leeds in righteous white, in order that they should be pure and a shining example to all that were to follow. The Devil's spawn were dressed in red, the colour of danger yet a little bit girlie. The Lord truly did great work that day. The Devil's boys were to change their colour in order to confuse the meek, but the righteous were not fooled, for they knew tossers when they saw them. Referees, though, were fooled, as were those working in television, for they were tossers also. The fatherless one in black would award penalties and free-kicks at will to the Devils in red, while the pundits, unlike the blind man (John 9:7), would fail to see.

The Lord, in his wisdom, has moved in a mysterious way. Somehow, within our hearts, it is our mission to find forgiveness and pity those that follow the dark ones. The hymn "Who the fuck are Man United?" is to be sung, in order that they may somehow find themselves before attending one of their spiritual meetings at the church they call Old Trafford. Fortunately, many of the Devil's followers never find their way to this pit of shame – 98 per cent, apparently. No, the Naughty One tries to reach them through the power of the airwaves and television (and Lord knows, he has that one sewn up all right).

The Devil would like his brainwashed soldiers to take on the rest of the world, for here they have been sussed. When the Reds continually fail playing among their own in the Greed League of Europe, many lost souls will return. For defeat brings darkness to the shirt of evil, as it remains locked in the same cupboard with the old Liverpool and Arsenal shirts, from the time when they were giving false testament. For these people are fickle and easily led.

When the day comes for these sad individuals to finally meet their Maker, they will have one final chance to gain salvation. On that day, all the Devil's men will be given the chance to pull on the white shirt of Justice and therefore save themselves from endless re-runs of defeats at the hands of the mighty Galatasaray (!). It brings great comfort to me that there will be such a time of suffering. What brings greater comfort is the fact that all those that had previously led a pure existence will be there to see you doing it. Praise the Lord."

* * *

For the Manchester clubs, there is, of course, only one derby, and whatever your opinions of Manchester United fans living in Suffolk or beyond, it is a truly local affair. Sadly, the misfortunes of City have robbed football of this tremendous fixture for far too long now. Hopefully City will soon be up there with the big boys again, if only because we have always believed City supporters to be among the most loyal bands of sufferers in the country.

We received two United fans' rants about City which rather sum up the whole thing. The first is from Andy of Cheshire and the second was sent to us by Phillip from Manchester:

Come On, City, We're Waiting

I'm getting rather bored of hearing Man City fans singing, "Who the fuck are Man United?" I mean, they may well ask, because we're not on their fixture list. Why not try looking at the top of the Premiership and not the middle of Dickvision One? The song might be of some relevance if the roles were reversed and we were utter shite, but we're not and you are, so shut the fuck up!

Anyway, don't rattle your brains singing such a complicated song, you should be concentrating on finding out who your new manager is this week.

The amount of City fans who don't go to games yet live within throwing distance of the ground is pathetic, and is proof in itself that Man City is a dwarf club pretending to be a giant. Stop singing crap songs about United and sing songs in support of City. The thing is, you don't even need to be a member to get in at Maine Road, so you've no excuse, you sad bastards.

God created Manchester City so that people could exercise their laughter glands and also give "shit" an accurate definition.

I mean, any group of supporters who go twenty-one years without winning fuck all, claim to be a massive club and talk of themselves in the "same league" (you fucking wish) as a team who've just completed four League titles in five years must have either taken a stupid amount of hallucinogenic drugs or be on the same thinking plateau as Francis Lee.

The Government should make a law that every Manchester City fan has to have immediate surgery to remove their blue-tinted spectacles, and then they should be sent to laboratories for extensive research to find out which planet they come from. Why are NASA spending hundreds of millions of dollars trying to find alien life on Mars, when all they need to do is spend £12 on the gate at Maine Road and see thousands of little Liams and Noels with blue faces and hooves, torturing themselves? Please, please get promotion, City, so that we can take humiliation to new heights.

The Sad Manc

There's a bloke who lives down my road who guarantees me a good laugh every weekend. Every Saturday, without fail, I see him leave his house in his City shirt and go to watch that shit they serve up at Maine Road. The poor fuckwit, he hasn't got the intelligence to work out that his club are crap and have as much chance of making it to the big time as I have of winning the Lottery.

I have tried to convert him, of course. As I walk out to go to Old Trafford (on whatever day it is these days), I always ask him if he wants to come along and see some real football, but he always tells me to fuck off. Still, some people enjoy a bit of pain, don't they, and I know full well that he'll be going in to watch it on Sky anyway. Hopefully, the poor cunt will realize what he's missing one day.

I mean, it can't have been much fun watching your local rivals rule the roost over the last few seasons, can it? Especially while your bunch of has-beens go from joke to joke. At times, I've almost felt sorry for them, if for no other reason than they're so fucking depressing. The only time you ever see a City fan smile is when United lose, and thankfully, that's been rare the last few seasons. The highlight of last season for them was hearing that Cantona had retired. Fuck me – if that was what football was like for me, I'd have slit my wrists years ago!

All this bollocks about "only City fans come from Manchester" is a joke as well, but they trot it out as if it's some badge of honour: "I support Manchester City, so I come from Manchester." Fuck off! All it says to me is that "I support Manchester City, so I'm a stupid, sad bastard who hasn't got the sense I was born with."

I mean, look at them, they're a joke and yet they go on about United as if we're the ones who have consistently let our supporters and the city down for season after season after season . . . Correct me if I'm wrong, but isn't the trophy room at Old Trafford bulging at the seams after the last few seasons? I did hear that when Denis Law retired, he took the key to the trophy cupboard at Maine Road home with him by mistake. He found it last week and sent it back, but no one had realized it was missing.

The latest trick they're trying, in their quest to gain some decent support, is to convince people that it's trendy to support Manchester City. What the fuck is that about? I mean, if I meet a City fan, the last thing I think is, "Wow! What a trendy bloke!" I just think, "You sad wanker!" I suppose it all started with the two Gallagher brothers trying to be hard. All that "We'll save City" shite they came out with might have impressed a few teenage girlies, but anyone with an ounce of brain knew exactly what they were up to. Still, that might explain why most City fans fell for it. Still, anyone whose eyebrows meet in the middle of their foreheads should be kept off the streets anyway, too fucking scary!

If City ever make it back to the top flight, we'll welcome them with open arms at Old Trafford and then we'll take them for the jokes they are, on the pitch and off it. Still, I'm not holding me breath.

6

Why?

Dougie Brimson

Most of the chapters in this book are accounts of football violence. They give us the who, what, where and when of soccer hooliganism. But in his year 2000 book *Barmy Army*, Dougie Brimson asks: why does football hooliganism occur at all?

That is, of course, the wrong question. People should not ask *why* people indulge in hooliganism at games, they should ask why *can* they? When well over a century has passed since an incident of football violence at a game in England was first recorded and over thirty years have elapsed since it exploded on to the front pages of the popular press, why has so little been done to stop it? That is the big question, and one we will return to later on.

However, the question of why people go to football and cause trouble is one I have been asked more than any other over the last four years. While it is not impossible to answer, it is bloody difficult, primarily because most of the people who ask it believe it is nothing more complicated than a few lads running around getting mouthy or slapping each other. It is, of course, far more complex than that but if you are to supply an answer, it is important to understand that whatever you eventually come up with has to be a generalization. I mean, if you get 20,000 people in a ground, you're always going to get two of them who don't agree, but what makes an individual suddenly decide that jumping on to the pitch and attacking a linesman is a good idea? And why do people get off on travelling to places under the banner of their club and actually go looking for trouble? How can you understand, let alone explain, that kind of mentality?

Before we get into that, we really have to ask another more specific question: what actually constitutes football hooliganism? Or to put it another way, what is a football hooligan?

To some, a hooligan will be something as simple and innocent as a teenage kid in a replica shirt walking along singing. But to others, it will be a lad who starts off a hit by hurling a CS gas canister through a plate glass window. An individual's perception of what constitutes a hooligan can only be decided in one of two ways: either by his or her own experiences or through the media. And it is fair to say that for many people who have no interest in football, let alone any experience of football violence, the stereotypical shaven-headed, racist thug so beloved of the tabloid press has become so ingrained in their perception of football fans that the two are almost inseparable. That is tragic, not only for the game but for every decent, law-abiding football fan in this country.

But for those who have actually tasted the rough end of football hooliganism, whether they are fans of the game themselves or not, their perception will be all too real. Anyone who has ever been confronted with a baying mob knows how frightening it can be, but if you are unprepared for it, it must be absolutely terrifying. Only recently, I met a man who told me of an incident he had found himself caught up in a few years ago. He asked to remain anonymous for obvious reasons, but even as we spoke it was clear that this had had a profound effect on him. What made it worse was that he has no interest in football at all.

I had been at a meeting in London all day and having been taken out to dinner by the client, had drunk too much wine to drive home so took the train. It was late, about 10.30, and I was sitting alone in a carriage at Euston waiting for the train to pull out when this group of men got on. There were about fifteen of them, I suppose, all about 20-21, and although they were smartly dressed, even I could tell that they were football fans. A few other people got on as well and one of them was this lad of about fourteen wearing a football shirt. Anyway, once the train pulled out, they started singing songs – nothing really abusive, just a bit colourful. But after a minute or so, a couple of them moved over towards this lad and started giving him a bit of grief. He supported a rival club, I suppose. He stood up to move away from them, but one of them shoved him back down and started being even more abusive. Eventually, one of them hit him and he started crying and so this other man got up to tell them to leave him alone. Well that was it, they started on him and he was punched in the face for his trouble, while all these other lads were just laughing. They then became even more abusive and some of the things they were saying to the women were outrageous. Yet despite the fact that I watched all this, I did nothing to stop it and, when they got off, I felt not just embarrassed but totally humiliated. The looks the women on the train gave me were of outright disgust and I couldn't get off there fast enough.

Now I hate bullying, and that's what this was. And even after all this time, I am ashamed that I didn't do anything to stop what was happening and it made me take a long, hard look at myself, that's for sure. I know I could never sit by and watch something like that again. But if that's what football is about for these people, then they can keep it. I can't even watch the game now without thinking of that night.

This incident illustrates perfectly the consequences of hooliganism in terms of public perception. The lads involved would probably have forgotten all about it by the time they were off the platform, yet for the people on the train that must have been a terrifying experience, and one which will have tainted their view of football fans for ever.

But it is fairly accurate to say that incidents such as this involving active football hooligans are becoming rarer. One of the reasons for that is that hooliganism has developed into a "game" with specific rules and a certain code of honour. The people involved tend to shy away from such encounters with the general public and are interested only in confronting each other, because there is nothing to be gained in terms of status or reputation from being aggressive towards innocent members of the public or even other, non-violent football fans.

It wasn't always thus. In the sixties, seventies and even the early eighties, one of the main objectives of the travelling mobs was to terrify the locals. Steaming down high streets and smashing windows was the norm for many groups of fans on match days and I well remember banner headlines in the *News of the World* sometime in the early seventies registering outrage at the fact that a gang of Chelsea fans had taken a pram containing a baby from outside a shop and steamed off up the road with it. These days, the focus has shifted from the local population as a whole to the opposing mobs, and hooliganism has become a far more insular and underground beast. Consequently, the individual lads' perception of their own role in it has changed. For example, as I have already mentioned, I may have been involved in trouble at games but I never regarded myself as a hooligan. To me, hooligans were the boys who travelled around looking for it, hunting around back streets for opposing fans or hurling missiles at us from pub doorways. But to the locals, watching me from behind net curtains as I ran around, that was exactly what I was.

The simple answer to this question of defining football hooliganism is that it is a blanket term that can be applied to any kind of anti-social behaviour which damages the image of football, be it foul and abusive chanting or fifty lads ambushing a pub using baseball bats. As a descriptive word it is valuable only to the media and ranting MPs, but as a culture it is of interest to us all. Because if you ever end up in court for a football-related offence, be it drunk and disorderly or affray, the fact that the culture exists, and you are a part of it, will have major repercussions for you in terms of the sentence you receive. For many people, of course, the allure of the hooligan culture is what drew them into it in the first place. In the "caring, sharing" nineties, it is almost unique in that it lets the average male behave in a manner that is totally at odds with what is normally expected of them.

We will look at why and how individuals become involved in hooliganism in the next chapter, but first we should look at what it is about football that invokes such emotions in people that they will willingly indulge in intimidation, violence and even murder in its name. Just as importantly, why football and not any other sport? After all, if what we are led to believe is correct, hooliganism is unique to football, and other sports are watched in an atmosphere of tranquil serenity devoid of any aggression at all. The truth is that almost every other mainstream sport has crowd problems of sorts. Admittedly, such problems are usually minor and in most cases of an entirely different nature to football, but they are problems nevertheless. Cricket has had some major problems with crowd trouble in recent years, primarily at internationals but also at county level, as has boxing. The fact that it happens but is rarely reported is simply because, in general, it is not newsworthy. Football has a long, dark history of crowd trouble and also, let's be honest, more of it. But we should not hide the fact that it takes place elsewhere, although the governing bodies of many of these sports are quite happy that we do so.

So what is it about football that makes it the focus of all this? Why can twenty-two men running around chasing a ball cause so many problems? To explain that, we need to examine what being a supporter is all about because, in part, that will supply the answer.

Football is the most popular sport on the planet. As kids we play it, at home we are force-fed it via TV, newspapers or obsessed parents, and eventually a good number of us go to watch it. As fans, our links with our chosen club, be it Bath City or Manchester City, rapidly become a part of our personality to such an extent that many football fans, me included, regard themselves as an integral and essential element of their club and the club as an essential part of them. We use expressions such as "I'm a Gooner" in the same manner as we say "I'm an engineer" and expect people to know just what that means (which, of course, they usually do!). Our clubs are followed through thick and thin and we accept the bad times in the hope that one day, the good ones will come along. In short, we support their efforts on our behalf. Yes, we hand over our money at the turnstiles but we also bring with us something that money cannot buy: passion.

The passion generated by supporters is what breathes life into a football club. Many supporters believe, with some justification, that they are its heart and soul. The players and the staff are simply passing through and will be gone

one day, but they, as fans, will carry the aspirations of their club with them until their dying day. That may sound dramatic if you're not a football fan, but it is uncannily accurate. We want our clubs to be the best of the best and the dream is that one day they will be. More importantly, when it happens, we want to claim our part of it and say we did our bit. That's why football fans resent those who jump on bandwagons. Anyone can suddenly come out and say they support Arsenal or Manchester United, but they are not true supporters. They are simply hijacking the loyalty shown by others and riding along on the back of current success. Don't get me wrong, I've often whiled away a boring 0-0 draw against clubs like Bury or Rotherham wondering why I support Watford and not Arsenal. But I know that you can't just change clubs because times are bad. Do that and you have no right to enjoy the good times or, for that matter, to call yourself a true fan. Being a football supporter isn't about watching great football, it's about putting time in and belonging to something, the entity that is a football club. And that club isn't just a grass field and eleven men, it's much, much more than that. It's about history and tradition. That's why people go to watch clubs like Barnet and Torquay United, and that's why football fans throughout the country unite when a club is about to go under. We may not understand why they support a different club from us, but they are our soulmates and we need to protect each other, because no one else will.

But inevitably, where you have passion and pride, you have rivalry. If you want your club to be the best, then at some point they will have to defeat others. Football is, after all, a competitive sport. And so supporters will sing, chant and shout to spur their team on in the hope that they will react and do the business on their behalf. Not only that, but on occasions the actions of the supporters can have a major influence on events on the pitch. The fans can, literally, earn the club a result, as Mick from Birmingham explains:

> We were playing Tranmere at St Andrews a couple of seasons ago and as anyone knows, they have always been a dirty bunch of cunts. Anyway, one of their players took a dive right in front of the Kop and got one of our lads booked. What was worse was that when he got up, he had this fucking great grin on his face. Well, we all saw that and we went mental at this twat from then on. Every time he touched the ball we gave him shit and in the end, he bottled it. His crosses were going all over the fucking place and he had a bloody nightmare. In the end, he was subbed and I tell you what, as that cunt walked off, we gave ourselves the biggest fucking cheer of the day. The team won in the end and Trevor Francis went in the paper and said the crowd had made a massive difference. It made us feel fucking great, I can tell you.

At the other end of the ground are a group of rival fans, who also aspire to victory. They will also be singing and shouting, and so you get atmosphere. Generally that atmosphere is good-natured but on occasions, as we have just seen, it can spill over into hostility or worse. Something happens on the pitch, a bad foul or a crap decision, and the mood will go from jovial to aggressive. Usually that aggression will quickly evaporate as soon as the final whistle goes, or if it doesn't, it will only show in bad moods or moaning. As you walk away from the ground, the smiles will return and by the time you're in the pub or the car, it will almost be forgotten. After all, you cannot change what's happened. But on occasions that aggression will not be forgotten, it will leave the ground with you and be carried along, a point best illustrated by JL from Ipswich:

I've never been one for trouble at football. It just isn't my thing and to be honest, I don't really understand it at all. But at the end of last season, after ten years following Ipswich Town, I just snapped.

I was walking away from the ground after watching us lose out in the play-offs for the third season running and I was totally devastated. I still am. I mean, what else do we have to do? Anyway, I just wanted to get home, so I'd left my mates and headed for the car when this Bolton scarfer comes up to me and holds out his hand, all friendly like. I stopped and just told him to fuck off, which isn't like me at all, and he said something like "There's no need to be like that, it's only a game." Well, it might only have been a game to him, but it was a fucking sight more than that to me and for some reason I just snapped. I don't know why, frustration, anger, who knows? But I turned round and really lumped him one. I was ashamed of myself straight away but I was bollocksed if I was going to apologize. I don't know what made me do it and I hope I never do it again. But I have to say, it sure as shit made me feel better.

While this illustrates how an individual can just snap at football and do things totally at odds with their normal behaviour, it also illustrates the essential difference between "normal" fans and the hooligans. Because for the latter, taking those rivalries and passions out of the ground and beyond what most people would regard as acceptable is not only routine, it is an essential part of their match-day experience. For them, what happens off the pitch is as important as what happens on it, because they regard the reputation of the team and the fans as one and the same. If someone does something to affect that, be it a player or a rival mob, then they will try and redress the balance by exacting revenge in the only way they can. It is the fact that they overstep that boundary that marks them out as hooligans and what they do as hooliganism.

It is essential to recognize one point here: football hooligans are football fans. The media and the game may think otherwise, but that simply betrays how little they understand the nature of the problem. At the root of the hooligan issue is the game itself, and there is nothing to suggest that if any of these lads stopped going to matches they would cause similar trouble elsewhere. Indeed, most rivalries between particular hooligan groups or even individuals rarely, if ever, extend beyond match days. On the very few occasions that they do, it will inevitably involve something ridiculous like a group of lads on holiday, Sunday morning football or even another sport where there are links with specific football clubs. The prime example of that is boxing. Certain clubs, such as Birmingham, Cardiff, Millwall and L*t*n [Dougie Brimson is such a fanatical Watford fan that he affects not to be able to mention rivals Luton at all], have very close associations with individual fighters. When those fighters meet each other, it is often an opportunity for the rival football mobs to kick things off.

So what are the root causes of hooliganism? Why does football attract a sizeable minority of normally rational people who do not simply shake hands after a good game and have a beer and a laugh together but instead step over that line and adopt a movement which is, in effect, a sinister sub-culture akin to gang warfare? The academics have their theories about social deprivation, rebellion, etc., but to me, even if I gave them any credence (which I don't), these are excuses, not causes. No, as far as I am concerned, the vast majority of hooliganism as we know it today is caused by one of two things, which are interlinked: history and reputation. The history of a certain fixture or the reputation of a certain firm.

Mention any football club to anyone who either is or has been involved in hooliganism and they will instantly equate it to the reputation of their mob or a specific incident of trouble. A certain club in south-east London illustrates the point perfectly. If ever a club evoked instant thoughts of crowd violence, it is Millwall. Even today, fourteen years on, I can readily conjure up images of their fans rampaging across the pitch at Kenilworth Road, hurling plastic seats before them. Those images formed, or rather enhanced, a reputation that has stuck with the club ever since, despite their best efforts to remove it. That has two key knock-on effects. The first is that many people outside the game, and a few within it, continue to think that hooliganism and Millwall are inseparable, which means that all Millwall fans, old or new, are immediately tainted. The second is that when Millwall – and the same applies to any club with a history of trouble – travel around the country, the police will be on the offensive and the locals will be either hiding or looking to have a pop to build up their own reputation. The losers are the decent, law-abiding members of the Millwall support who only want to watch a game of football and not be herded around like sheep or abused by rival fans whenever they travel away.

Conversely, if you take my own club Watford, which has become known as "the family club", the idea of it being associated with any degree of football violence astonishes some people. When they come to Vicarage Road, visiting supporters do not expect to experience trouble. Nor do they when the Watford fans visit their ground and, in the main, they do not. Yet despite this image, the club has always had a small element of troublemakers among its support and in recent years that element has become increasingly violent. Eventually, through travelling around and fronting up more active firms at places such as Bristol City, the Watford firm's reputation will grow to the extent that when other clubs play Watford, their own firms will expect trouble and so will bring trouble when they come. And again, there will be a knock-on effect for everyone else at the club.

Of course, the ultimate example of a team with a bad history is England. A reputation formed on the streets of Luxembourg and Rimini continues to haunt England fans wherever they go, to such an extent that it actually becomes the cause of more problems. English supporters, as an entity, are still perceived as trouble abroad and are, more often than not, treated accordingly. But if you expect trouble and prepare for it in the manner that many countries do, you will inevitably get it. And while that is especially true of the authorities in other countries, as we saw during the 1998 World Cup, it is no less relevant to the plight of clubs such as Millwall in this country.

We should not forget, however, that if a group of fans have become saddled with a reputation, it will only be because it is richly deserved. Furthermore, there will be people who play up to that reputation and so, in effect, keep it going. And while certain groups may go through periods of inactivity, every so often they will explode back on to the scene and let everyone know they are still active. One of the most obvious examples of that came at Lansdowne Road, Dublin, in February 1995 when rioting England fans, fired up by the involvement of a few political extremists and exploiting some of the most inept organization ever seen at a professional fixture, forced the abandonment of the Republic of Ireland versus England match. It reaffirmed the impression that England fans and trouble go hand in hand.

Another example of a club suddenly bursting back on to the scene with a vengeance came in February 1999 when Millwall, who had been reasonably quiet on their travels for most of the season, took a massive mob to Maine Road for their Second Division clash with Manchester City, who had been relegated the previous season. There was always going to be trouble at this fixture. Both clubs are well known for having active and violent hooligan followings and it was fairly obvious that each would want to establish themselves as better than the other. Yet very few people could have guessed quite how bad it was to become.

The build-up to the game had not gone well. In the encounter at the New Den the previous September, there had been numerous incidents involving the fans, including a massive pitch invasion during the match. The City manager Joe Royle even claimed his team had been victimized. Not only had a player been sent off, but Royle claimed that his striker Shaun Goater had been subjected to horrific racial abuse from the home fans. As the game in Manchester approached, Royle told the City faithful that his team would "settle one or two old scores" at Maine Road, a statement that did not go down well with either the police or the Millwall board. Despite this, or maybe because of it, the Greater Manchester police turned down a request for increased capacity and security for the Millwall fans. It was clear that the mood on match day would be ugly, and so it proved.

Things started badly when Millwall supporters clashed with groups of both City and Manchester United fans at Stockport railway station. Running battles broke out which soon spilled over into adjoining streets before the police took hold of the situation. By lunchtime, Millwall had an estimated 1,500 lads in the centre of Manchester and more trouble erupted as the game approached. By kick-off time, the atmosphere in the ground was manic and when Paul Dickov scored for City in the second half, the Millwall fans charged at the North End, ripping out seats and hurling them at the home fans. Police in riot gear came in and baton-charged the Millwall fans, quickly restoring order, but the pattern had been set. Shortly before the final whistle, with City 3–0 up, the police announced that the Millwall fans would be kept in until the home crowd had dispersed. Twenty-five minutes later, the Millwall fans left Maine Road to find three of their coaches without windows and one of the drivers badly hurt after a gas canister had been thrown through a window. As police escorted a large group of them to Piccadilly train station there was more trouble. Shop windows were put through and missiles thrown both from and at the group. Yet Millwall hadn't finished yet. Later that night, a group steamed down the so-called "curry mile" in Rusholme and put through a number of restaurant windows before heading back to London. In all, eleven people were arrested, eight from Millwall, and nine police officers were hurt, one with a broken wrist. For a time, every cell in south Manchester contained supporters who had been detained as a result of trouble surrounding the game. It had been, according to an inspector from Greater Manchester police, "a return to the dismal days of the past" and Millwall were once again dragged under the scornful gaze of both the media and the FA.

The reason this fixture generated these problems is, as I have already said, because of the history of both hooligan groups. Now, of course, as a result of what happened at this game, when the two teams next meet the rivalry between the fans will be rekindled, and so on ad infinitum. Each encounter simply adds a new chapter to the history.

Yet while hooligan firms having digs at each other is one of the more usual methods of firing up these rivalries, they can be started in any number of ways. Local derbies or even inter-county affairs such as Leeds–Manchester are some of the more traditional causes, but others are less obvious. What follows is one such example. It was sent to me by Martin, a Stoke City fan from Oldham:

In October 1995, we drew Newcastle in the Coca-Cola Cup at our place. We were really up for it and had lads out all over looking for their mob. Eventually we found out that they were drinking in a pub in Fenton but we couldn't really get near them as the police were all over us. In the end we gave up and went to the ground, but once we got there we heard that the sick Geordie bastards had beat the shit out of this young Stoke girl for no reason. As if that wasn't bad enough, they sliced her up as well.

Well, this spread through the lads like wildfire and after the game it was like World War Three. Stoke lads were attacking them from everywhere, from the ground right up to the train station. It was mental and I even heard that one of their buses got turned over on to its side. But I tell you this, if we ever play them again it'll be even worse. It's one thing having it away with lads, but picking on kids, well, that just ain't on.

Another way a feud can start is if a club or even a city experiences some kind of tragedy. If such a thing happens, it is, sadly, inevitable that at some point a group of rival fans will use it to upset or taunt their opposite numbers. Manchester United have suffered more than most from this as songs about the Munich air crash have been heard at many grounds over the years, while back in the late seventies and early eighties, Leeds United supporters were taunted with songs claiming that the Yorkshire Ripper, a notorious serial killer of the time, was beating the local prostitutes 12–0. Furthermore, Spurs fans were for many years subjected to groups of rival fans hissing at them (and if you don't know, I'm not going to explain it). Such taunting has never been one of the more attractive sides of fan behaviour yet it seems to be on the increase. In November 1998, Chelsea visited Leicester City, a club with whom they already had a long history of trouble, and their fans were subjected to a barrage of songs about their former and much loved director Matthew Harding, who had been killed in a helicopter crash. The Chelsea lads went mental and major trouble erupted outside the ground. Undoubtedly, certain elements among the supporters of both clubs will carry this on whenever the fixture list throws them together.

Another example involved, shamefully, my own club. In August 1998, Bradford City came to Vicarage Road. What follows was sent to me by one of their supporters, Simon H:

I do wonder sometimes about the mentality of some people. I mean, what kind of bloke thinks holding up a lighter and then dancing around pretending he's on fire is funny? I tell you what kind of person, shall I? A cunt. And as for the songs, well, let's just say I hope the lads with me managed to catch up with the twats who were singing.

I've been about a bit and at Bradford we've certainly had a fair share of problems, but there are some things you just don't do and one of them is take the piss out of things like that. I mean, fifty-six people died in that fire and some of them were friends and family. That isn't something you forget. We'd only ever heard it from three other clubs before and the last place we ever expected it was at Watford. I mean, aren't they the so-called family club? Some fucking family.

I know that some of the Bradford fans complained but from where I was, I couldn't see anything being done. All I can say is that your lads better keep a low profile when they come up here. If they don't, they'll pay for that.

Another way to wind up an opposing mob and spark off trouble is to taunt them about specific hooligan incidents. One of the best examples of this involves two clubs who are party to one of the most long-standing and violent rivalries in English football. Ironically, neither of them are English at all. They are, of course, Cardiff City and Swansea City. As most supporters will be aware, the history of confrontation involving these two sets of fans is long and bloody. Yet despite the many hundreds of incidents between them over the years, there is one in particular that has stuck in their collective memory: the swim-away story.

If you talk to followers of the two clubs, you will hear hundreds of different versions of this incident. Indeed, it now seems that there were actually two episodes. The first took place on a May Bank Holiday in the early seventies when some Swansea fans were attacked by a group of Cardiff supporters at Barry Island. But the second, and more important, took place in Swansea towards the end of the eighties.

The basic facts as I have uncovered them are these. Cardiff had travelled to Swansea and, as usual, were busy causing mayhem in the city centre. The Cardiff group the PVM (Pure Violence Mob) from Port Talbot were playing an active part in this but, for some reason, about ten of them had travelled independently of the main party and, rather than go into the city centre, had made their way down to the seafront. Unfortunately, they ran into a large Swansea mob and came under attack. Despite standing for a time, the PVM lads were forced to run into the sea to escape the Swansea fans and finished up standing chest-deep in the water. Rather than follow them in, the locals began bombarding them with rocks until the police came and rescued them.

Despite the Cardiff fans' assertion that this was only a minor defeat and had more to do with the numbers involved than the quality of their firm, the incident quickly settled into local folklore and even now, over a decade later,

Swansea fans will taunt their Cardiff opponents by mimicking the front crawl. It usually has the desired effect.

It is stating the obvious but the one constant in all of the above is history, and the same can be said of almost every other incident of football violence that occurs. Football fans have long memories and hooligans even longer ones, and if something has happened in the past to fire up anger or rivalry between two sets of fans, inevitably one day someone will do something to exact revenge or exploit it. It could be as simple as walking round a corner and getting a slap from an irate Norwich fan or as frightening as walking on to a tube station teeming with West Ham. But if you are part of a mob and someone turns you over, you are duty bound to respond and gain recompense. This is why I firmly believe that history is the most important factor behind trouble at football and the tragedy is, it is all but impossible to deal with. You simply cannot change what has already happened.

Occasionally, however, past events, at least sporting ones, play no part in this issue at all. Sometimes the hooligans will not be guided by history, they will try and make it. What follows was sent to me by a good mate of mine who, although a Watford fan, has a sad affection for Hull City. It illustrates perfectly how crowds can, on occasions, have a massive effect on the future of their particular club:

It was the last game of the 98–99 season and Swansea needed a win to guarantee a play-off place, although given that they had beaten Cambridge a few nights earlier, it would have taken a mathematical disaster for them to miss out.

Anyway, I had been told that because of a massive storm, there would be a pitch inspection before the game as the surface was swimming. But given the situation, it seemed almost impossible that it would be called off and so I confidently took my place outside the turnstile of the Hull City end.

Just about 3 p.m. the game was called "on" and the gates opened, which meant the kick-off would be delayed for a time. Panic then set in as I was told it was all-ticket and having travelled over from Bristol that morning on the off-chance I would see the game, I didn't have one. Fortunately, they had relaxed the ticketing arrangements at the final minute, as Hull could not go down and the expectation of a large away following had diminished. In fact, there were still several hundred Tigers milling around, but outside the Swansea entrances the roads were packed. In the end, I had a child's ticket shoved into my hand by someone with a spare, and after a moment of holding my breath as I walked through the turnstile, I ended up on the piss-poor excuse of a terrace.

Within a few minutes of opening the gates, the Swansea end was packed and immediately it was clear that the locals weren't taking anything for granted. The "lads" congregate in the corner nearest to the away fans, and although there are a few advertising boards preventing fans from getting on to the pitch, at about 3.30 a roar went up and about three groups came on and ran towards the Hull contingent. Virtually every advertising hoarding was ripped up straight away and the triangle supports at the back of them were being thrown into the visitors' enclosure. A few Hull boys who were more than prepared to show their colours ran down to the front of the stand, but the barrage was forceful and swift and no one stood a chance. A couple of umbrellas were hurled like javelins into the Hull fans but, after about ten minutes, the police and stewards managed to clear the pitch of both people and debris and the game was near to starting.

So, as half-time happened everywhere else, the game in

Swansea was just kicking off. That meant that, as every other game was finishing, the second half was about to start! Swansea had a distinct advantage of knowing exactly what they had to achieve, although the pressure was lifted when, after about half an hour, Swansea scored and the second big invasion occurred.

The whole thing seemed so contrived and to be honest, without wanting to credit the Swansea fans with any merit, they knew exactly what they were doing. The boys created a diversion, while other groups ran on from other directions. One guy spent the whole game baring his backside at the Hull City fans and as a result took the attention of both police and stewards. The invasions came from nowhere near this guy, even though the main congregation of yellow jackets were in the area of the "lads".

With about twenty minutes to go it was obvious this game was over. Hull had lost, Swansea were there and at 2–0 up the game was over. All that remained was the inevitable third pitch invasion at the end of the game, this time with no foreseeable end to it, and many, many more people involved. Most of the Hull City fans wanted to leave, but were held in "for your own safety"!

As the final whistle approached, I asked a steward if I could leave and showed her my Watford shirt, but she just accused me of stirring up all the trouble. After all, what was a Watford fan doing in the Hull enclosure? In the end, I was taken out across the front of the main stand in full view of the Swansea fans, who sussed that people were leaving rather too early.

I made it to my car and got the hell out moments before the final whistle and yet another pitch invasion. The thing that struck me most was that if the other results had gone against Swansea, meaning that they would have missed out on the play-offs, there was no way that game would have finished. Such was the atmosphere, the ref would have abandoned it without hesitation, leaving the final say in the hands of the FA. He seemed to be giving everything Swansea's way to such an extent that Hull fans thought he might as well have had a number 12 on his back. Thank Christ Hull didn't need a result, that's all I can say, because the whole thing was a bloody disgrace.

Although incidents of crowds genuinely affecting results are rare in this country, they do happen. In October 1997, Watford travelled to the home of the old enemy L*t*n and by half-time were 4–0 up. Such was our dominance it could actually have been many more, and would have been were it not for one important factor: the Watford goals were scored in front of the home fans. As each ball hit the back of the net, they became more and more agitated to the extent that after the game, the referee all but admitted that he had not given an obvious penalty to Watford because he feared that the locals would riot had he done so. As it was, by the time the players came out for the second half, mounted policemen had been forced to come on to the pitch in an attempt to calm things down. Thankfully, things settled down a little after that but, for a while, many Watford fans at the game feared the home support would cause enough trouble to force it to be abandoned.

One reason trouble of this nature is on the increase in this country is because the clubs are now telling the fans to create it. Be it a cup tie, a play-off game or even an important League game, managers are now coming out and firing up the crowd in the local press. They call for an intimidating atmosphere and, as such, are asking for the crowd to be aggressive. But they know that generally speaking, the bulk of that aggression will come from the hooligan element and "the lads", and it will manifest itself in abuse and hatred. To me, such requests border on incitement because while we all like a good, passionate atmosphere inside a ground, it inevitably has a knock-on effect off it. If a firm gets wound up, there is no way it will leave that mood behind as it walks out of the gate. Such appeals go unpunished, but the fact that they are made confirms that clubs know just how influential supporters can be.

The fear is that one day, a group of supporters in this country will pre-empt the request or even turn it on its head and, in return for the creation of atmosphere, make demands of the club they follow. To take that a few steps further, how would any club react if the leader of their main firm walked into the chairman's office and demanded free tickets or subsidized travel in return for not causing mayhem at a specific game?

In Italy, such things are the norm. The Ultras who follow the clubs there know they have power and frequently wield it, to such an extent that no one puts up a banner inside a ground without the permission of the leaders, or *capi*. In the past, the Ultras have used various tactics to register their displeasure at something, including turning their backs on the pitch at specific times or even watching games in complete silence. And on occasions, things get more sinister. Despite the fact that it is against the law to have any dealings with the Ultras, there have been many occasions when a club's refusal to supply tickets has resulted in crowd violence or serious vandalism. There have even been a number of cases of the Ultras influencing player selection and even dictating who the club should, or rather should not, buy. One famous example came three seasons ago when word spread among the fans at Verona that they were about to sign a black foreign international. Later that week, a dummy gallows was set up outside the ground and a black cardboard figure in a team shirt hung from it. Needless to say, the player was not signed.

Thankfully, we do not have such a situation in this country and many doubt we ever will. But at a time when the relationship between the English game and the fans is at an all-time low and the exploitation of supporters' loyalty shows no signs of abating, consider this: football sells itself on the back of a big-game atmosphere. How long will it be before some of the more volatile groups begin to think about what their role in the creation of that atmosphere is actually worth to the clubs? Personally, I don't think it's very far away at all because for the fans there would be a very obvious trade-off: tickets.

At the majority of clubs, getting tickets for home and away games is a simple process. Season tickets take care of the home ones and if you need them for away games, you go down the club and hand over your hard-earned. In the Premiership, it isn't always that easy. Allocation by ballot seems to be on the increase, especially at the big clubs, which, while fair up to a point, does nothing to reward loyalty. It also does nothing for you if you go to every game with twenty other lads, because the chances are, many of you will not even get in, never mind you all sitting together. The clubs, of course, could not care less who gets the tickets just as long as someone pays – and neither do you, as long as you and your firm get yours. So, a few chosen words here, a threat or two there, and who knows what could be achieved? The hooligans already use violence against other clubs, so why not use it against their own? Especially when the club they love, or at least the people who work at it, think nothing of shafting them at every turn. And if it worked once, it would set an alarming and terrifying precedent (mind you, who's to say it hasn't already?).

If, or should that be when, football allows itself to get into this situation, then it will quickly find itself in real trouble. And this brings us back to my original point: football hooliganism exists because it *can*. And while the game allows it to exist, human nature dictates that the people involved will push their luck as far as they can, until someone decides to do something constructive to stop them. Until that issue is addressed, then we cannot be surprised at just how far the hooligans may be prepared to go.

7

Life's a Beach!

Eddy Brimson

Having been on their best behaviour during Euro '96, which was held in England, the English hooligans were back to their worst when France hosted the World Cup two years later. Thousands of English hooligans flooded across the Channel with the intention only to cause trouble.

Probably the worst incident of the tournament happened on 15 June, when England played Tunisia in Marseille. What began as a run-of-the-mill tussle between fans watching the match on a big screen set up on the beach soon turned into a full-scale riot, with the English and Tunisian fans in the streets, battling each other and the French police, while laying waste to the city centre.

Eddy Brimson was there and, in this extract from his book *Tear Gas and Ticket Touts*, he recalls exactly what happened on that infamous night.

The day starts early due to the fact that not one of us had managed to obtain a match ticket while out on our travels the previous night. One of the lads tells us that he heard a rumour about an American ticket agency based down near the port area behind an Irish bar. They are supposed to have a large amount of tickets delivered today, so it is decided that after breakfast we will head off in that direction.

Back up in the room we are getting ourselves together when Herne Bay enters and tells me that he has just been given the room number of a bloke who has a spare ticket for sale. I call the number to be told that he has one hospitality ticket going for £100. He goes on to tell me that the ticket belongs to his dad who has been put off by all the trouble and would now rather watch it in the hotel bar. One hundred pounds doesn't seem that bad a deal, but something tells me not to take up the offer. I don't like all that corporate stuff at the best of times, or paying the odds for tickets, so the combination of the two is never really going to appeal. I ask all the other lads, and surprisingly they also pass. Herne Bay thinks we're all mental.

We leave the hotel at the same time as a group of German tourists. They look at us as if we have just escaped from the zoo and make no attempt whatsoever to disguise their amusement at this freak show. "You typical English hooligans, ya?" Their interest prompts an "Invaded Poland lately?" retort from one of the lads as we return their stares.

The sun is already hot as we make our way back down the same main drag that provided us with last night's "entertainment". Even at this early hour we encounter groups of Tunisian fans making their way up to the ground. Most are in good voice with drums, whistles and hooters adding to their noise. I can't help thinking that with over four hours to kick-off they might just burn themselves out. We pass by the same bar that witnessed last night's violence. In the bright light of a new day the place is now calm, although the smashed windows and piles of broken chairs bear testament to the events of the night before.

We turn the corner and start to head off towards the main port. Suddenly every ten yards we come across someone asking for tickets – not a good sign. On the front we find a line of bars. A large group of Tunisians occupy one area while a larger group of English supporters, all in good voice themselves, have taken up residence next door. A few yards away sitting on some railing I spot another group of English. These lads are quiet, their eyes fixed on the two groups, waiting, watching. Not one is wearing national colours. As we pass, Mr B also points them out and we agree that very soon something is likely to kick off.

As our priority is finding tickets we leave the situation behind and hunt down the American ticket agency. Pretty soon we stumble across the Irish bar and go to make our way in. From nowhere appears a very large Frenchman who proceeds to block our path. I ask him if the bar is open, but he just shakes his head and tells us to go. Inside I can see more of the same, all eyes fixed on us, and I begin to wonder if we have come across something we shouldn't have. Suddenly a man comes over whom I recognize as the owner of the bar. He is the man who was shown on breakfast TV back home, the one who told the world that you could get tickets for any England match. For a split second I think of asking him whether or not he has any spares, but he soon tells us that the bar has been shut and ushers us away.

We wander aimlessly around in the vain hope of stumbling across the ticket agency, but have no luck, so we stop for a swift half. The bar lady tell us that she doesn't know of any such agency, and it appears that we have been chasing a red herring.

On finishing our beers we head back to the bars on the front. The situation is pretty much as we had left it, but I soon hear one bloke talking about things kicking off any moment. To avoid getting caught up we cross the road and sit on the roundabout. Within minutes, things turn nasty.

There are certain things that separate many English football supporters from their foreign cousins, one of which is a complete lack of tolerance towards any other country's fans showing patriotism. We all know that the English are loud, very loud, but whereas the English will sing their hearts out, many continentals like to gesticulate, blow horns and generally be a pain in the arse by running up and down while waving flags in your face. As much as it hurts me to say it, I have to state that if flag-waving and being a pain in the arse were an Olympic sport then the Tunisians would be battling it out with the Italians and Argies for the top spot. It was gestures such as these that finally brought things to a head.

As we looked on, one Tunisian lad pushed his luck that little bit too far as he rode his bike right in among the English supporters while waving his flag and generally giving it the large one. Pretty soon he found himself relieved of his vehicle, followed by a swift boot up the jacksy. As he made off some idiot threw a bottle at him, which prompted another ten or so like-minded idiots into doing the same thing. The Tunisians in the adjoining bar quickly ran for cover fearing the worst, but thankfully the majority of the English lads followed up their actions with a bout of singing rather than chasing after them. With the Tunisians making their exit I soon managed to pick out some of the faces that had attacked the bar we had been drinking in the night before, including the fat lad who had been leading their charge.

While this was going on the police seemed totally unprepared and just stood by as if waiting for someone to come along and tell them what to do. The whole incident was over in a matter of seconds, but once again it proved that wherever the two groups of fans mixed, trouble was always likely to flare up.

As calm descended Mr B shouted at me to watch out. I turned round just in time to see a small lad, no more than eleven or twelve, throw a beer bottle at me from about ten yards away. Standing right by my side were four coppers. I managed to avoid the missile and waited for the Old Bill to grab the lad and give him a stiff cuff around the ear, but they just stood still and did nothing. A few other lads shouted at the coppers as the young Tunisian just stayed put, but the best they could do was gesture to the lad to piss off. The bottle-thrower greeted their request by giving them the finger, then turned round and walked off while still looking over his shoulder and giving it large. You had to laugh, but it sort of hinted that the police were more interested in the English than the locals.

Not knowing what would happen next we quickly decided to move off in the direction of the ground. For all we knew the riot police could well have been heading our way at that very moment, tear gas at the ready, and we still had tickets to track down.

As we got closer to the stadium the crowds grew bigger. By now we were all starting to get worried as we hadn't yet come across anyone with tickets to sell. Tunisian fans were busy riding up and down the main drag in their cars and on motorbikes, making as much noise as possible, while the English just looked on as they drank in the street cafés and bars that lined the route. The closer to the ground we got the greater the number of English fans, until they totally outnumbered the Tunisians and the scene turned into a wash of red, white and blue. It was obvious that the number of fans without tickets was vast and yet all were still hopeful as the singing grew constant and louder.

A small group of French riot police moved in to push back one group of England fans as they threatened to spill into the road, thus blocking the way through for the traffic. Their actions were met with a chorus of "If it wasn't for the English you'd be Krauts", a song that, although very funny at the time, was never going to help win the local bobbies over. The riot police were then joined by more officers in plain clothes, although the bright orange armbands they were all wearing did give their little game away somewhat.

Over the last ten years many things have happened to football that, in my opinion, have seen our great game take a turn for the worse. One such problem for me is the growth in the amount of people who think it's funny to dress up like a cunt whenever they intend going near a football stadium. Of course, I blame the Dutch for inventing this kind of behaviour, which I can only imagine has stemmed from their rather lax drug laws, but unfortunately this disease spread and now, thanks to the Channel Tunnel, has reached epidemic proportions on our side of the water.

One group of lads walks by dressed like the Knights of the Round Table, which I can kind of understand what with King Arthur and all that bollocks, but when a couple cross my path dressed as Superman and Wonder-Woman I have to physically restrain myself while asking the Lord above why he allows these people to walk his Earth. OK, so the man upstairs must have a sense of humour, but he has already given us the Spanish, so why this? Do these people honestly think that by dressing up in such a manner the camera crews will pick them out and beam their little joke into the living rooms of the world so that Hans, Mustafa and Gregori can go, "Oh, those crazy English?" If so, they must also realize that many right-minded people are pointing at the screen and saying, "Oh look, a wanker."

As we make our way among the crowd Gary spots his mates from Gillingham and introduces me for the first time to their friend and our new room-mate, Tony. He looks about seven feet tall, is built like a rake and never looks you in the eye when he is talking to you, something I find very aggravating. He also has a very, very loud voice.

The search for tickets continues endlessly and becomes more desperate as the minutes fly by. I keep asking myself why I turned down the corporate ticket I had been offered earlier, and begin mentally kicking myself. It soon becomes apparent that the majority of the tickets up for grabs are in the hands of either the French, who have no interest in the game whatsoever and their one ticket to sell, or the local Arabs, who have tickets by the handful and are out to make as much cash as possible. Unfortunately for us, the asking price has stuck at around £100 due to people starting to panic. Like us many decide on waiting until the last possible moment in the hope of picking up a ticket on the cheap, while others are talking of steaming the gates.

One lad next to me suddenly strikes up a conversation with a Frenchman in his fifties who has one ticket to sell. The local is obviously not short of a few bob. He is well dressed and doesn't look the type to be touting a ticket outside a football stadium. He has with him a lady, whom I presume to be his wife, and another couple of around the same age, and for them this looks like an afternoon out rather than a football-watching day. Like everyone else this Frenchman is asking £100 for the ticket, so the lad hoping to take it off his hands does the sensible thing and checks that it is the real McCoy. To his surprise the ticket has no watermark, so he shoves it back in the palm of the Frog while also giving out large doses of verbal. The Frenchman looks as surprised as everyone else gathered around, and busily checks the ticket himself. The four of them then take it in turns to hold the ticket skywards as they enter into heated discussion. I must admit, he doesn't look the type to be palming off dodgy tickets, but as the English dish out more verbal he and his friends quickly decide to make a rather swift exit.

The local Arabs are themselves much more organized and are moving around in groups openly selling their tickets while the police stand by and watch them go about their business. With so many English lads on the lookout I am amazed by the fact that not one ticket tout is getting turned over before having his tickets lifted. This may stem from the fact that more stories about people being stabbed the previous night are now doing the rounds, and people just don't fancy the risks involved in finding yourself in an argument with a local gang, no matter how small their numbers are. It soon gets to the stage where every person you pass is asking for tickets.

Then comes the moment when I think I've struck gold. As I shout my request for the thousandth time a lad next to me offers one up.

"I've got a ticket you can have cheap, mate."

I can't believe my luck, and immediately another twenty lads crowd round.

"How much?"

'Well, I just paid eighty for it, but it ain't worth that."

His answer completely throws me until his friend explains.

"Dozy twat just handed the money over without checking it first."

"What is it, a dud then?"

"No, it's kosher. If you want to go and see Belgium play South Korea, that is."

The lad had only realized his mistake after he had been turned away at the first checkpoint. The local who had sold him the ticket was now long gone.

By now the rest of the lads have decided that they would rather watch the game on the big screen set up down on the beach as the ticket prices have continued to stay high. Pretty soon, one final encounter with a tout persuades me to join them.

I spot a group of three lads who are busy being the centre of attention, so I head over in the hope of securing a late result. As I get to them I see lads turning away in disgust, but I take my chance.

"You selling?"

"Yes, pal." Their distinctive accent instantly tells me they are from Merseyside. "How many do you want?"

"Have you got four?"

"Yeah. Two hundred each."

"Two hundred! Fuck off."

"If you don't want them then you fuck off."

Another lad who has joined the frenzy quickly voices his opinion. "You thieving cunts. We're fucking English, mate. We should be looking out for each other not ripping our own off."

The Scouser obviously doesn't share this patriotic stance. "Tell you what, pal, the beach is down that way."

Honestly, I didn't believe that even a Scouser would try to rip his fellow countrymen off that badly. Why people continue to hold them up as cheeky little chaps with a great sense of humour is beyond me. I have travelled hundreds of miles in the hope of watching England kick off a game in the World Cup Finals only to be ultimately ripped off by someone who calls himself a fellow Englishman.

With less than fifteen minutes to go before kick-off I finally give up and head off in the direction of the beach. I later find out that not only have I missed out on seeing the match in the flesh, but also that back home you are treated to the sight of Jimmy Hill wearing a Cross of Saint George bow-tie. I really hope Sir Jim dressed just to offend Alan Hansen. I stroke my fingertips against the end of my chin in appreciation. Jim-meeee!

In every city playing host to World Cup matches the local authorities had set up large television screens so that all those without tickets could still get to watch the games while enjoying the next best thing to the atmosphere generated within the stadiums. As every step brought us closer to the arena the noise grew louder and the adrenalin began to flow. We soon heard a big cheer go up and a quick check of the watch told me that the game had finally started. The whole area in which the screen was situated had been fenced around, and before you were allowed in you had to go through some gates so that your bags could be checked. We soon learnt that due to the trouble of the previous few days the local authorities had sensibly placed an alcohol ban within the arena. Gary and Mr B decided to wait outside and watch from behind the fences rather than surrender their recently purchased refreshments, leaving Tony and me to go in alone.

The arena covered an area about the same size as four football pitches. The screen was large, positioned high enough up for everyone to get a clear view, and it gave off a fantastic image. Around the edge of the arena were catering vans and merchandizing kiosks which all appeared to be doing good business, and at the back they provided a large temporary stand for the spectators to sit in. Every seat in that stand appeared to be occupied by the local Tunisian population, and the first impression I got was one of being totally outnumbered. I also soon realized that there was no form of segregation whatsoever, so the alarm bells started to ring. I knew there and then that the second the ball hit the back of the net this would turn into a beach party with a very unhappy ending.

The noise the locals generated was both loud and annoying with screams, whistles and shrill cries piercing my eardrums. As the sun beat down I began to look around for some fellow Englishmen, but only managed to pick out the odd three lions shirt, but pretty soon my eyes fell upon a highly amusing sight. Standing by the side of the seating area I spotted a woman trying to keep her three children under control. All four of them were wearing England shirts; she was looking slightly harassed while the kids looked hot, bothered and thirsty. I couldn't help thinking that her old hubby must have life completely sussed. He took his wife and kids on holiday, then bunged her a few shekels before telling her to go and have a nice day out on the beach, while he buggered off to football. Pure genius. Surely if that man could bottle whatever it is he has that enables him to live such a heavenly lifestyle, he would be a millionaire overnight.

Up on the big screen we could see the match was in full flow, and Paul Scholes very nearly put England a goal ahead. For the first time the Tunisians fell quiet, but their silence was short lived as their whistles soon filled the air once more. Within minutes Scholes missed an even better chance, and the cry of "Ing-er-land!" could be heard from the area immediately in front of the screen, the English fans making their presence felt for the first time. The sudden outburst, although music to my ears, was taken rather differently by the Tunisians sitting in the stand. Within seconds a few stones and bottles were thrown in the direction of the English fans, and these were followed by a flare that left a bright orange trail as it flew towards its target. I looked around to assess the reaction of the security only to see a group of riot police stand by as if nothing had happened. Tony and I agreed it was only a matter of time, then Alan Shearer scored and the place went ballistic.

The second the ball hit the net the Tunisian fans fell silent. There is nothing better than seeing a load of mouthy bastards being shut the fuck up in an instant, and as they had been giving it the large one since we had entered the arena I was in pure heaven. I must admit that for me and nearly every other football fan I know, that is always a magic moment. However, the trickle of missiles they had been throwing since Scholes missed soon turned into a barrage, and all of a sudden we found ourselves right in the middle of what could only be described as a battle zone.

As the English gave it loads the Tunisian fans began to throw everything and anything they could get their hands on into the crowd in front of them. They threw ripped-out seats, stones and bottles, many of which landed on their own kind as well as England fans. Their actions caused panic as families tried to gather themselves together and people ran in all directions in order to find cover. A quick look over my shoulder also told me that the area where the police were once standing was now empty, the men in blue uniforms nowhere to be seen.

The England fans were forced back up against the big screen and fences from where there was no escape as the Tunisians continued to unload their never-ending supply of ammunition. Pretty soon an area of no man's land opened up between the two groups of supporters as the locals kept enough distance for them to throw their missiles but avoid getting caught up in hand-to-hand fighting. Up on the big screen you could see the players walking off for their half-time cup of PG, while here bottles and stones continued to land on the grass around my feet as I kept a keen eye on the direction of their origin.

To my right the main bulk of the England fans were gathered, and once the shower of danger had slowed down they made their move. As a large group of English steamed forward the Tunisian turned and legged it. As they went, the English supporters were screaming at the tops of their voices. Their charge prompted many of those trying to escape from the stand to run back up, and many began to scramble down the scaffolding at the side or climb over the back. One Tunisian fan, in his desperation to escape, slipped and fell some twenty feet to the ground. Once the English had cleared the area they stopped chasing after the locals and began to gather themselves once more. The momentary calm that followed enabled many to go back and collect the belongings they had left behind before making a hasty exit.

At this point I honestly felt that calm would be restored, but as the English regrouped under the big screen yet another group of Tunisian fans appeared throwing more missiles, only this time they came from the far side of the arena. The English fans were now well tooled up them-selves, and once again they steamed off in the direction of the locals in order to give them a taste of their own medi-cine. This action was greeted by the sight of Tunisians once more doing the 100-metre dash. As the English ran at one group another mob of locals would appear from the opposite direction and start to unload their weapons.

Standing within the middle of the chaos I caught sight of something that will live with me for years. One lone England fan stood defiant as bottles flew around; he remained unmoved, beating out a rhythm on a snare drum. It always amazes me how people react in situations such as these, and the sight of the drummer only added to the unbelievable events that were unfolding before my eyes.

Suddenly I felt the dull thud of a stone hitting me directly in the knackers, so I thought it best that I try to make my way to a safer part of the arena. I looked around for Tony, but in the chaos we had already been split up.

As the dull thud of the stone turned into that familiar painful ache all men get when hit in the tender bits, I was passed by a black guy who was desperately shouting out for his mates. At first he seemed eager to get in on the action, but I soon realized that he was pointing towards a wound that had appeared just under his left armpit. I asked him whether he was OK or not, only to realize that he was in a mild state of shock and that the injury was in fact a stab wound. The poor bastard had just been plugged in the side by a Tunisian lad who ran past us. He didn't really know where he was, and the thought suddenly hit me that I could just as easily have been on the end of that blade. In the chaos I found it amazing that more people didn't get seri-ously injured, although the number of people walking by with head wounds and blood pouring down their faces was beginning to grow by the minute.

The mayhem continued between the two groups for what seemed like ages, before the cheer went up from the English to greet the arrival of a small group of riot police. At last I thought that order was about to be restored, but once again they stood motionless, appearing to wait for some kind of instruction. No more than ten yards in front of them was a group of Tunisians busy unloading their bottles and stones, yet they seemed powerless to act. Many of the Englishmen around me were calling out for them to do something, but even as their numbers grew the police stood by and watched the battle continue. On the far side another group of riot police appeared, so now they had the locals firmly situated between them, and there for the taking. We had been told so much about the French riot police on our televisions back home, yet when it came down to it and the shit hit the fan they didn't appear to have a fucking clue.

As we waited and waited for them to kick into action, what I assumed to be another flare landed twenty yards from me. Pretty soon the smoke smothered me and entered my throat, and I began to gasp for air while finding it hard to breathe. As we had stood back and waited for the police to round up the Tunisians, one of their officers in charge had taken us all by surprise and ordered his men to fire tear gas into the English fans instead. Soon we found ourselves under a shower of gas canisters. As the police fired at random, their actions caught not only those lads ready to mix it but innocent lads, women and children as well. The wind blowing off the Mediterranean only added to the stupidity of their actions as the choking gas was whipped around in all directions.

The police then moved forward, allowing the once trapped Tunisians to go unchecked, and the local mob found itself behind the safety of the police lines, from where they continued to shower the English with whatever they could get their hands on. Thankfully, by this stage some

England fans had managed to pull open a gap in the fences so that we could escape to the safety of a car park and fields situated behind the big screen.

The effects of the gas had now taken their full toll. As if getting air into my lungs wasn't hard enough, my skin had now begun to itch. The irresistible desire to rub my watering eyes soon gave them an added stinging sensation, until thankfully someone handed me a bottle of water with which to splash my face. All around me people of all ages were suffering in the same way as a sense of disbelief mixed with anger at the police's actions began to spread.

In all my years I can honestly say that I have never seen such inept police tactics being deployed in order to restore some form of control; their actions only spread this particular situation over a larger area. I am not saying for one moment that the English fans were angels, because that simply was not the case. There were plenty of lads down on the beach that afternoon desperate to have it away with the locals. I saw plenty of English lads grabbing at anything they could get their hands on, and then happily firing bottles and stones back at the Tunisians. And there were plenty of lads running in all directions hoping, above all else, to stick a size nine up the arse of some local. But it also has to be said that there were plenty of people in among them who had just found themselves caught up in a situation from which there was no escape. The main bulk of the England fans had been under the cosh for approximately three minutes before they finally took it upon themselves to retaliate and chase into the Tunisian fans.

Three minutes is a very long time to have potentially fatal weapons flying around your head. Three minutes of chaos must seem like an eternity when your kids are screaming, panic-stricken by the violence that is happening all around them. And three minutes is a long time to wait for the authorities to come and defend the rights of people who have suddenly found themselves under attack. Let me make this clear: the violence that erupted down on the beach that afternoon was started by the Tunisians. When that ball hit the back of the net putting England 1–0 ahead it was the Tunisians who started throwing their bottles, not the English supporters – we were too busy celebrating. The failure of the French police to protect those that had come under attack finally forced many of those people into defending themselves.

There were plenty of film crews taking footage that would clearly show the English fans chasing the Tunisians out before stopping and moving back towards the big screen into what they felt was a safe area. It is plain to me that those fans didn't continue after the Tunisians. They didn't trap them up against the fences in order to smash their heads. I never saw anyone run up into the stand to beat the crap out of those locals who still found themselves trapped. What the majority of those England fans did was to clear the area and then move back and wait for the police to finally make an appearance and restore calm. I have no doubt in my mind that that was the intention of most of those lads, and that was what I was witnessing down on the beach.

I have seen so much of this in my lifetime. Every time it happens you think the same thing. *This time they can't lie. This time they have to tell it like it was.* But deep down you know that will never happen. It is very easy for people to sit at home in their armchairs or in the Houses of Parliament and slag people off. It is very easy to stand back from, disown and pass judgement on people when you are hundreds of miles away. It is very easy to believe the loaded comments of people trying to pass the buck on television, or the journalist desperate for that sensational headline, but unless you are there and witness the event with your very own eyes, you only get a small slice of the true story.

It is impossible to understand the range of emotions that pass through the mind when you find yourself in situations such as these unless you are actually there surrounded by the noise, the heat, the smell and the chaos. You feel frightened, excited, angry and on edge. Your whole body is alive, buzzing as your brain tries to cope with all the messages your senses are picking up. It is also very hard to control those emotions. People will sit back and say you should just walk away and not get involved, which is easy when you're in the safety of a studio or your front room. But the reality of being there is something quite different. You can't help but be affected by what is happening. Some people will panic, while thankfully others will do their best to protect those around them when no one else will. Personally I've no idea how I would have reacted if I could have got hold of the Tunisian lad who had stabbed that black guy. Being perfectly honest, I imagine I would have tried to beat the shit out of him, whereas at any other time I would more likely have run a mile. People react to the circumstances in which they find themselves, and those passing judgement back in Westminster should take that into account before opening their ill-informed mouths.

As I milled around the car park the sense of anger continued to grow. From the direction of the main exit police sirens rang out and I could see people running in all directions as the violence continued. My first thought was of Gary and Mr B; then the image of that woman wearing her England kit along with her three children shot into my mind. God only knows what happened to them; they were right in the firing line when everything kicked off. I only hope someone managed to get them to safety.

Many England fans had decided that they had seen enough and were now heading off across the field behind the big screen in the direction of the city port. Suddenly a loud shout went up and I turned to see yet another group of Tunisian fans appear from inside the arena area. Once again they aimed a barrage of missiles in the direction of people heading away, wanting to leave this whole situation behind. The sight brought the anger felt by so many England fans to a head once again, and very quickly a hundred or so lads steamed off in the direction of the locals, who soon turned and headed back. As the English fans chased in after them the air was suddenly full of the sound of more tear gas canisters being fired. As the smoke rose it was clear that the English fans had become the target for the police, and this despite the fact that those local lads, so up for it just moments earlier, must have run directly past them!

Standing next to me I noticed a very old French gentleman. I looked at him and he just shrugged his shoulders. I couldn't help but apologize – but my apologies were to do with being a supporter of a sport that had come to his city and caused so much trouble. I wasn't going to apologize for being English.

Five more minutes passed before calm finally appeared to descend. The last I had heard England were 1–0 up, but a quick check of the watch told me that the second half was now well underway and so, like everyone else, I needed to find out what was going on up at the ground. Slowly, I made my way back to where the fences had been pulled open, only to be told by an officer of the law that the arena was now closed. By a small television van I could see a female reporter interviewing five lads with blood splattered all over themselves. Great TV, I thought, but where was the medical help? I took one last look down towards the main entrance, only to see the blue lights still flashing and people moving in all directions. It was time to move on.

My experiences were one thing, but what people had

witnessed outside was something else. Davy, Essex WHU, tells all:

From where we were you could just about see the screen enough to realize Shearer had scored. We started cheering, of course, and it wasn't too bad at first, then people started running out of the field totally shitting themselves. We couldn't really see what was going on, or the stand that had all the fans in, but when people started climbing over the back you knew things were getting bad. The police outside with us looked like they never had a clue, and then a mass of Tunisian fans came running out and we guessed they must have been done by all the England lads. They were well fucked off, and pretty soon they started throwing bottles and attacking anyone who had an England shirt on. Me and the lads I was with thought, fuck this, we better get away, as it started to get well naughty. There was no way you could have a go back as they would have killed you.

I took my shirt off straightaway and tucked it into my strides as best I could. That was horrible, that; I've never had to take my colours off before, ever, not in over ten years of going to football. But it was dangerous. Once they got hold of someone they were on them like dogs, loads of them. There was one lad we saw as we went by the roundabout who was well fucked. Not moving, nothing, and the coppers were trying to clear some space for the medics to get at him.

It's a dodgy one, being in situations like this. If you run you attract attention, if you try and walk you can get caught up – you don't know what to do. We headed back up the main road towards the ground and you had to have eyes in the back of your head. There were more of them coming down towards the beach so you had to get yourself through that as well. Any car with an English plate was getting trashed, and then we saw this bust-up between two birds that was amazing. This

French or Tunisian girl, I couldn't tell, just started booting this car, and straightaway this English girl jumped out and went loopy. At first she grabbed her by the hair and started whacking her. That then turned into a right cat-fight before all these other Tunisians turned up and started kicking the car as well. This poor English bird didn't know where to go next. They mullered the motor, put the back window through and just about dented every panel there was, but again there was fuck all you could do to help 'cause they would have turned on you. It was really bad, very scary, with people getting lumped left, right and centre. God knows how we all managed to get away without getting a slap. The coppers were shit, although I don't know what they could have done anyway. They were well outnumbered and it was going off all over the place. Most of them were just kids, nasty little bastards.

When we got up by the ground it was a bit different. Some English lads had managed to get it together and were up for a pop back at them, but they just fucked off back to where they were on top. There was more Old Bill up at the ground as well, which made it safer. But a load of the English fans were giving them some real verbal for not getting in there and sorting it out. We just headed off back towards the centre and found a bar on the way down. There was no point in staying around there as it just looked like getting worse.

I had seen enough too, and decided to head off and find a bar in the hope of catching the last twenty minutes of the game. After walking no more than a hundred yards I came across a French guy who had just been hit above the eye, blood pouring down his face. He was being comforted by a group of girls, and ten yards further on I could see the lad that had just hit him being restrained by his mates. What had sparked it off I don't know, but once again it proved that the relative calm could be shattered in the blink of an eye, and now that I was on my own I felt more than a little worried. Not least by the fact that I didn't actually know where the fuck I was.

Pretty soon I managed to find a bar that was crammed with England fans, and I settled myself down. I took a long look round and picked out many faces that I recognized from down on the beach. It was amazing to think that no more than twenty minutes ago these very same people had found themselves smack bang in the middle of a full-scale riot, and yet here they were enjoying a beer and acting as if nothing unusual had happened to them. Maybe I just have a happier home life than most, I don't know, but their desire to watch their national football team in action was all that mattered.

As Shearer and Co. battled out the final stages on the pitch we put all that had happened behind us and got behind the team. In the final minute our support was rewarded as Paul Scholes more than made up for his earlier misses by unleashing an unstoppable shot into the back of the net. As the England team clinched three vital points the bar erupted and the world in which I live became a much happier place to be as all my worries disappeared to the back of my mind.

Sitting next to me were two young lads from Canada. I had to ask them what they had made of it all, and I have to say that their initial reaction surprised me. They told me how they had joined the England fans in chasing off the Tunisians whenever they steamed forward. They had wanted to see the English beat the shit out of the locals, and I had no doubt they were telling the truth after one of them explained what had happened to them the previous night:

We had gone out on the drink and had a really good night out. We stayed away from the port because we had seen what went on during the day and didn't want to get caught up in that again, so we drank in some of the smaller bars. Every one of them had football fans in and we met some great people. We did get really pissed, I must admit, and we stayed in one bar till about 3 a.m. drinking with some locals who seemed really all right.

It got so late that we decided to go find a taxi, and left. We had only just got around the corner when this bloke from the bar came up and said he'd give us a lift to where we were staying, and you know what it's like when you're pissed, you just go with it. We got in the car and he drove real slow. Then we stopped at this corner and all of a sudden another four blokes piled in and started beating the hell out of us, then they stole our wallets. The driver drove us to Christ knows where and they kicked us out. We ended up walking for a while, because for all we knew we could have been in a real bad part of the city. Then we just found an alley and waited down there until it got light. We didn't lose that much really as we had already drank most of the money we had on us, but I tell you, there is no way we are leaving this city without giving some Arab shit a good hiding.

The lump on the side of his head seemed to fit in with the story quite nicely, and considering what had happened to them they appeared to be in surprisingly good spirits, but stories like this always scare me. It's not that I am worried for my own safety, but rather that of the person passing their experience on. I mean, how many sandwiches short of a picnic do you need to be before accepting a lift at three in the morning from an Arab you don't even know, while wandering the streets of Marseille suddenly becomes a good idea? What a couple of tossers. We all have moments of madness in our lives – I even bought a David Essex single once – but their particular tale took the art of being a fuck-wit to a whole new level.

After fifteen more minutes the bar began to empty, and the time had come for me once again to brave the streets of Marseille. I only had a vague idea of what direction I should be heading in, and so the butterflies rose once more as I gingerly made my way through the very expensive-looking back streets. A few yards in front of me were two lads, one of whom had an English Cross of Saint George flag tied around his waist. Immediately my brain reminded me of the old saying "safety in numbers", so I took a short jog and struck up a conversation. Just like me, they didn't have a clue as to where they were, so each crossroads we arrived at had us voting on which direction was the best to take. The two lads were both from the People's Republic of Yorkshire and followed Leeds United, and we spoke excitedly about what we had seen in the hope that talk would help cure our anxiety.

Finally we worked our way through the maze of back streets and found ourselves at the end of a road that led up to the main drag back to town. In the distance we could see the thousands of fans walking back towards the city centre, their leisurely pace suggesting that they were enjoying a walk unaffected by rampaging hooligans.

As one we breathed a sigh of relief and took the first few steps in the direction of safety, then suddenly some hundred yards ahead, and between us and the main street, a group of Tunisian lads came jogging into view. The looks they were firing over their shoulders suggested they were doing their best to get away from someone else, but unfortunately it was in our direction that they were heading. Quickly we turned and headed up a road that ran at right angles from the one we had wanted to travel on in the hope that we could avoid getting trapped.

This area of the city must have been one of the most wealthy as the houses and apartments looked magnificent.

As we passed by a school all three of us broke into one of those "I am not really scared and trying to get away without you noticing me" walks that most football supporters come to master during their time. The people wearing their designer clothes and waiting to pick up their children must have wondered what the hell was going on, but soon the mob came into view and started up the street after us. A quick glance over my shoulder confirmed to me that we had been spotted, and now a couple of their lads at the front had broken into a full-blown sprint. A gut-wrenching feeling that only occurs at such moments shot through my body as all of a sudden we found ourselves in a pretty dodgy situation.

Now, like most blokes, I don't like being run, but I also don't pretend to be some kind of hero ready to take on all comers. I had already seen one bloke stabbed today and didn't fancy becoming the second. I already know my wife didn't marry me for my looks, but I don't need to make a poor job any worse, so it was time to do the off. I was quite pleased to see that even at the tender age of thirty-four I still had the running on the Leeds lads, and within seconds I was heading the race. It's amazing what your legs can do when your arse is about to give way. The Tunisian lad leading their charge soon found himself alone as his friends gave up the chase, and from somewhere deep down that overwhelming urge to give him a right-hander suddenly entered my mind. Maybe it was due to the fact that I had simply had enough of being run down side streets, or that now the odds were even, I fancied my chance – I don't know, but I hate being run. It leaves an awful feeling in the pit of my stomach, as it does in most other blokes I know, and I would have loved to stick one on that lad, just one. He couldn't have been more than eighteen, no more than a kid, but in the back of my mind stories of people getting stabbed were still ringing the alarm.

Once again we found ourselves at a junction and swung a right which took the road back towards the main drag and safety. Just a few yards down from that junction and hidden from view we came across an entrance to a block of apartments, down which a woman was driving her car. As we scooted past she shot forward, just as the lad chasing after us appeared, and he went crashing into the side of her vehicle, halting him in his tracks. All three of us couldn't help but piss ourselves laughing. Dozy twat. Suddenly, all thoughts of confrontation disappeared from my mind, and as the rest of his mob came to pick him up we broke into a final little jog and made it to the safety of the main drag.

As I joined the throng of supporters making their way from the stadium, a feeling of relief swept over me. It was as if everything I had witnessed that afternoon shot through my mind in a matter of seconds, only to be quickly followed by the knowledge that I had managed to get through it all without suffering anything more than a slight pain in the groin. The people walking next to me must have thought I was off my chump as I walked down that road laughing happily to myself, but I didn't care – I was alive.

Within ten minutes I had said my farewells to the Leeds lads and was back in my hotel – and boy, was I happy to be back in that hotel. Sitting in the bar area were the rest of the lads who thankfully had also managed to get through the afternoon unscathed. We had been joined by Gary and Mr B's friend from Gillingham, and we soon began to swap stories surrounding the day's events. Whereas I had been ripped off, tear-gassed and run, their experience had been slightly less traumatic.

The Gillingham fans had travelled down on the TGV overnight, arriving in Marseille during the early hours of the morning. As they were travelling back and forth for each England game they were prepared to pay whatever it took in order to purchase tickets, and so getting hold of them hadn't proved much of a problem. They had actually been approached by an American guy who had tickets by the fistful to sell. They couldn't believe how he had managed to get hold of so many when there were so many desperate English fans. At the time they thought his asking price of £120 each was a fair deal and so took him up on his offer and bought four. He told them to keep a look-out for him at the rest of the England games as he would be getting tickets for all of those fixtures as well. All of their tickets were stamped with one company's name.

One of the people in the group was a young lady called Sharon and she had obviously had a top day out, describing the atmosphere in the stadium as the ultimate buzz. Now they were just winding down, enjoying a few beers and killing time until they needed to head off back to the train station in order to catch the TGV back home. They hadn't had any hassle or seen any trouble. For them it had just been a fantastic match and an unforgettable trip. Lucky bastards!

As we sat around talking I quizzed Sharon about her love for the great game. In the past I have taken the odd dig at women who follow football, but this particular filly soon left me in no doubt about her feelings about the sport:

I've been going to Gillingham for years. They're my local club and I would never have supported any other team. At school we had all the lads in their Liverpool and Arsenal kits, and they would take the piss out of us lot wearing a blue shirt, although we soon made them shut up. The thing is I know that they never went to see the team they say they supported, and still don't go today. You still see the same lads walking around town in the latest shirt as though they are the greatest fans in the world, but they are not football fans. A football fan is someone who goes every week, home or away. I don't see the point in supporting a team you never get to see.

One thing that really gets to me is when I see people at Priestfield supporting the Gills but wearing another team's shirt. I would rather they stayed home listening to Radio 5 and wearing out the Ceefax button. They can stick the Premier League up their arse for all I care. There is no better feeling than turning a big side over. All that money and the greedy bastards still get beat every now and then, just like we did at Coventry.

Following England is the business, there is nothing like it. We all stick together and help each other out. If someone hasn't got a ticket everyone will try to bunk them in. If someone is getting grief everyone else will help them out. I don't regret paying £120 for a ticket because watching England abroad is the ultimate, and after all, this is the World Cup. It's a long way to come just to stand outside.

There is no doubt that Sharon is as passionate, loyal and obsessive a football supporter as any person you could hope to meet. She knew more about the game than I could ever hope to store within my tiny head, and I am sure she could sing for just as long and with just as much passion as any bloke I have ever met. The problem that I have is that not every woman that goes to football is like Sharon, and at this stage I have to be honest: I thank the Lord that they are not.

I really like being a bloke. I like having a laugh with a mob of blokes, and I like doing blokey stuff. Moaning, swearing, farting, ranting. Man's stuff. As is turns out, most men's behaviour in the cold light of day is idiotic, highly stupid and very embarrassing. Fortunately for me, and many like-minded blokes, the football stadiums provide the perfect place in which to act in such a manner. Or at least they used to. There can be no doubt that football is a male-orientated sport. It's mainly played by blokes, watched mostly by blokes. There are people who will hit the roof at the opinion, but I couldn't give a toss, because I only have to open my eyes to confirm that I am right. Go down any park on Sunday and you'll see hundreds of blokes enjoying the game they love. Take a panoramic view of any football stadium on a match day and you will see many more blokes than women. It makes me angry that football panders to the minorities in order to widen its fan base, and that such pandering is done largely against the desires of the majority, which no matter what they try to do or say will always remain blokes. Blokes, blokes, blokes. Blokes everywhere. But only man-type blokes please. No girlie ones.

However, here I would like to point out that I am not one of those people who think women have no part to play in the game. Obviously women have just as much right to enter any football stadium as I or any other blokes does – someone has to heat the pies up. But that shouldn't mean that the majority should change their habits. I do get pissed off when some lad brings his girlfriend along for the first time and then starts asking me to sit down, not to shout and to watch my language because his loved one may get offended. Every football ground in the country has in the past had a traditional area where the main bulk of support has been vocal lads. This is the part of the ground where the atmosphere is generated, and always has been. Slowly but surely these areas are being eroded by chief executives and administrators who have little or no sense of history. Some even have no traditional support for the club, it just happens to be their current employer. As those people tighten their grip around the neck of the game, these special areas within our football stadiums have begun to disappear, and the atmosphere along with them.

A football team is the focal point for a display of loyalty

that cannot be found in any other walk of life. The bond between supporter and club is handed down from generation to generation and remains lifelong, and if the game wants to sell, sell, sell then those are the money shots. Tradition, loyalty and passion, not the half-time entertainment, plastic seats or the catering at the United burger bar.

The people in the game that are so desperate to appear politically correct should get into the real world and understand that, for the vast majority of their paying punters, going to football is like nothing else they can experience. For them going to football isn't an excursion for the family unit. It's not a day trip to the local swimming pool, or like taking the kids to the pictures. The football stadium is a place for letting off steam, a place to bond with people who share your passion and who share your dreams. If one member of the group finds the experience alien and fails to understand the emotions being shared by all those around them, then that person can have the effect of killing the thrill for everyone else. When that golden moment arrives and your centre forward hits the back of the net the feeling is electric. It's a feeling you want to share, a magical moment when you become united with your fellow believers. But that moment can be shattered, utterly shattered, by the sight of some sour face who doesn't understand. If you have just one non-believer, one person along for the ride who fails to grasp the bonding that is taking place among the people all around them, then their effect can be devastating for the rest. Yet there are still those that run football who fail to understand; people continue to seek them out as though they are the golden key to everlasting success. The reality is quite different, of course. For those types of people, going to football is seen as an occasional day out rather than a lifetime's obsession. They will always remain mere spectators rather than supporters, and if that special bond isn't there then pretty soon neither will they be. My only worry is that they will have taken many more with them.

We sat in the hotel bar and watched Romania beat Colombia 1–0. The good news from England's point of view was that both teams looked shite, but in Romania the match provided a far more sinister reaction. Pavel Veber was so incensed at his wife when she switched the television over during the first half of the match that he beat her to death. Mr Veber was arrested by police moments later in his local pub while watching the second half!

As our hotel bar slowly began to fill up, we were soon joined by Colin from Gloucester, the guy who had offered me the corporate ticket earlier in the day. After being introduced to me by Herne Bay he started apologizing for asking £100 for the tickets by saying, "Sorry. I know it was over the odds, but it had to be worth a hundred, didn't it?" Well no, not really. If you want to rip me off that's your choice, but please don't apologize while you're doing it. You're either on the make or you're not, matey. The ticket was worth the face value as I saw it, which happened to be just £30. I had already shelled out over £250 on this trip and didn't really like getting ripped off by a fellow Englishman who then tried to make himself feel better with a poor excuse for being a money-grabbing arsehole. There are many people who would gladly have paid that price, especially after travelling all that way, but as I said at the time, there was that little nagging voice in my head that told me to pass it up. Pretty soon I found out that I was right to follow my instincts, as Colin told me what had happened:

> I ended up selling the ticket to this lad from Birmingham for
> £100, but it turned out to be a nightmare. I didn't just want

to sell the ticket to anyone because I was going to have to sit next to them at the game and I didn't want to end up sitting next to some meat-head, so I hung on to it until I got drinking and talking to a few blokes who I thought were OK before letting them know I had a spare. This lad and his mates were all right and I had a good laugh with them. I sold him the ticket and we carried on drinking until just over an hour before kick-off, then we all walked to the ground together. It made sense to stay with him because we were sitting next to each other.

He was all right, this bloke, just your typical England fan. I must admit he did look a bit of a handful – cropped hair, shirt off, a Cross of Saint George hanging round his neck – but so what? There's nothing wrong with that. We had a good old sing-song at the bar with everyone else, and the lad I sold the ticket to had an air horn which helped start most of the singing.

We decided to leave the bar about an hour before kick-off, and once we got up there his mates went their separate ways and we went off to our section. Getting through the first couple of checkpoints was no problem, but once we got to our section it all kicked off. I've gone through first, no problem, but as he went to go through after me this copper stopped him and just said no, he weren't going in. I am standing there wondering what the hell is going on, then I see him showing the ticket to another and he is obviously getting a bit worried about getting in. It didn't matter what he said, the policeman was still not having it, and pretty soon more police gathered round him. One policeman takes the air horn off him, then they start unwrapping the flag and just giving him a hard time. There was no reason for it. He wasn't drunk, playing up or anything like that.

The lad from Birmingham suddenly realized he might not get in and started shouting to me to come back and tell them he was with me. But as soon as he started shouting this other policeman cracked him on the side of the head with his truncheon and he went down. Then the rest of them were on him like a shot. It was totally unjustified and out of order. He was shouting his head off and putting up a right old fight and all this happened right outside the hospitality bit with everyone looking on. They quickly had him handcuffed, and then kept him pinned up against the railings for a few minutes and were being really heavy-handed with him, kicking and punching. In the end it took about ten of them to carry him off. I felt terrible, but there was nothing I could do about it. He probably now thinks I sold him a dodgy ticket or something.

It was mad; one minute we were just about to go in and enjoy the game together, the next that happened. I think the police just took one look at him and thought, no way, he isn't getting in here. What kind of police are they to do that? Maybe because it was hospitality or something, I don't know, but when I got inside there were plenty of other lads with England shirts on and flags. He's probably been deported now or something.

As we sat around, stories started to circulate that the local police had put on a special train in order to get as many English out of the city as possible. According to the rumours, the train was departing the main station late that night and heading straight for Calais, so Herne Bay headed off to the room and began to pack his bags. At this stage the temptation was certainly there for joining him, but as the room was already booked I thought better of it, so a final night out on the streets of Marseille was soon planned.

Once again we found ourselves at the bar opposite the local Old Bill station, only this time the police had blocked off the road to traffic and were telling us that it was not wise to go any further as the locals were out for more trouble.

They went on to explain to us that that the port area had been closed off as it was not safe for the England fans, that the best thing we could do was go back and drink in our hotel. On hearing this I was more than happy to follow their instructions, but as ever Mr B and Gary fancied taking a little walk "just to see for themselves" whether the Old Bill were telling the truth or not. Personally I believed them; I wanted to believe them as I'd had enough already. As I sat in the bar talking to a group of lads from Liverpool (well, I'd have been on my own otherwise), small groups of local lads walked past at various times, obviously scouting the bars for England fans and the possibility of more trouble. Gary soon returned without anything to report while Mr B couldn't make out why no one was selling drugs on the street corners "in this of all cities". Having to keep an eye on the street at all times soon became too much of a pain, so the second the whistle went to signal the end of Germany's 2–0 win over the USA we decided that Marseille had little else to offer and made our way back to the hotel in order to get some much-needed kip.

The German team had suffered some terrible press back home in the build-up to this tournament: players too old, no inventiveness in their play, all that kind of stuff. And so some had taken it upon themselves to install television sets in over three hundred churches so that they could watch the match and pray at the same time! I can't help thinking that somehow the prayer "Please Lord, help Jurgen cheat his way to another penalty" seems a little misguided.

Back in the room we flicked through the television channels hoping to catch some news reports, and soon became aware that the English fans were mainly being held to blame for the trouble that had erupted that day. Deep down we all should have realized that things were never going to be any different.

8

At Home

Dougie and Eddy Brimson

During the eighties and nineties there was increasing media coverage of English football hooligans. Our supporters were under the spotlight whenever they went abroad for matches, such was our reputation and history. However, when the national side hosted foreign teams at Wembley, the hooligan element seemed to be largely absent.

Writing in their book *England, My England*, the Brimson brothers, Dougie and Eddy, look at the confrontations that still go on away from the stadium.

While the media and the authorities, labouring under the notion that trouble is inevitable, go to town on England fans when they travel away, there is little or no acknowledgement that the reverse is true when England play at Wembley. There are a number of reasons for this, of course, and as far as the media and FA are concerned, it is because the stewarding at Wembley is first class and the police do a superb job in controlling the hooligan element. While there is some truth in this, there are a number of other, and far more significant, reasons why Wembley is usually a trouble-free zone for supporters. These factors stood out clearly during Euro '96, and we need to look at them to see if any lessons can be learnt for the future, and for other venues.

The most important thing is that whatever your opinion on the matter, Wembley is, to the England team at least, home. As a consequence, it is revered by players and tolerated by supporters, but the underlying fact is that when England play, it becomes *ours,* the focus for English supporters for those ninety minutes. This, in essence, means that fans have a duty to defend it, if the opposition have a hooligan element, just as they would their own ground. But in truth, the reputation of the England fan abroad, combined with the fact that most "foreign" supporters who come to Wembley either live here anyway or are shit-scared of what might happen to them, means that trouble is invariably the very last thing visitors want. The fact that everyone knows this means that unless the opposition is fairly high-profile, or active on the hooligan front, or the match is important, the crowd will almost certainly largely consist of mums, dads and kids while all the geezers will be watching the game in a pub either at home or near the ground.

There are, of course, a number of other reasons why crowds for friendly matches at the national stadium are so small, and to us the most important is that with the exception of the odd performance, England games are meaningless. At club level, we can make our feelings known every Saturday, but the fact that England games are infrequent means that there is very little we can do to influence the thoughts of the FA or the manager. We just have to live with what they do and leave any whining up to the media who, with few exceptions, seldom disappoint in that respect.

As we noted earlier, there are also huge numbers of supporters who could not give a toss about the England side because they want nothing to do with any team other than their own. If you talk to supporters at England games or examine the flags around the Wembley pitch, one of the questions that comes to mind is how many of the fans are only there to watch *their* lads play. Dougie freely and happily admits that the only time he ever cried with joy at a football match was when the great Luther Blissett scored a hat-trick at Wembley against Luxembourg. What for Luther was the culmination of years of hard work and the pinnacle of a great playing career was shared by every Watford fan who was at that game, but to this day, Dougie couldn't tell you who else scored because it isn't important to him. And if Luther hadn't been playing, the game would have faded into a long-distant memory.

Confirmation that we are not the only people who share these beliefs can be seen not only in the low attendances at England games, but also in the fact that when England play, the local pubs, as we've mentioned, are packed solid. This is in itself a strange thing because it shows that many people do travel to Wembley, only to stay in the pubs nearby to watch the game on the box. But as anyone who has done this will tell you, it is by far the best way to watch England's friendly games. It is also important to note that it isn't just fans from around London who travel to Wembley to visit the pubs on match days, but fans from all over the country. During a friendly against Portugal early in 1996, we spent the evening in a pub full of Southampton and Sunderland fans, less than one mile from the twin towers. They were there because they wanted to travel with their mates, walk up Wembley Way, have a laugh and a drink and watch the game – but they positively refused to walk through the turnstiles.

The usual theory here is that if you mix drink, men and football, it is inevitable that trouble will occur. While this is indeed the case on many occasions, in and around Wembley, when England are playing, it seems that the opposite is true. Quite why this camaraderie arises is not easy to pinpoint, but it does seem to us to be an extension of the "service station" mentality, where fans only want to mix, talk and have a laugh among people like themselves. A sort of neutral ground, if you like. But while we may be painting a rosy picture of Wembley pubs, it does not mean that these drinking houses are always nice places to be. They do tend to foster male aggression, and the usual "get-your-tits-out-for-the-lads" type of sexism enjoyed by many males at some time or another. So strenuously avoid taking a woman to one of them on a first date!

The fact that during an England game you can often play "spot the crowd" does little for the credibility of the English as supporters; but there you go, we have to live with that. However, if the opposition are active, well-known historical rivals or attracting a big support, the crowd's English contingent will be larger and the noise more vociferous, with a far deeper, and more aggressive, tone. In 1988, during the build-up to the European Championships to be held in Germany that same year, the FA invited the Dutch to Wembley. The English fans wanting trouble couldn't have picked a more volatile "friendly" themselves, while the reputation of the Dutch only helped to fuel the fire.

The account below came during a pint with Jamie, a follower of Tottenham.

Holland

We were desperate for this match because we had been waiting for Holland to visit for some time. At club level we have had a few run-ins with the Dutch, something that goes back to the seventies, when we did the Feyenoord mob over there. I was much too young to remember that, but I do remember seeing the pictures on the telly, loads of Spurs lads coming back from Amsterdam after having the shit kicked out of them in 1981. Three lads were stabbed at that match, so as you can see we have every reason to hate those wankers, and this was a good chance to give them a good hiding on our own ground, especially as we had heard on the grapevine that their main mobs were coming over to set things up for Euro '88. At that time there was loads of trouble at Dutch League games, and in particular with the mobs from Utrecht and Feyenoord. Both these clubs had links with firms in London and that's how we got to hear about it. They were meant to be up for it and coming over to have a pop at us.

We would have liked to have got down to Liverpool Street Station in order to pick off any that had come in on the train from Harwich, but we didn't have the time. Anyway, West Ham should have taken care of that, so we decided to meet up at Baker Street, as most of the Dutch would have to come through there at some time if they were using the train. Some of the lads were able to get into the centre of London early to do a bit of scouting and they told us that a mob of around forty Dutch had been taking the piss down Carnaby Street most of the afternoon. Nothing had really gone off but they were taking liberties, there were no other England lads around at all and our boys had the right hump.

By half five there were about thirty of us in the bar opposite the Baker Street tube station. A few other lads were obviously there to see if anything was going off – you recognize some of the faces, but who they supported, I wasn't too sure. Word soon spread about what had happened in the daytime and the mood was starting to change, the old buzz was starting to kick in. Someone put forward the idea that we should move into the tube station to see who was coming through, and a total of around fifty blokes moved off. The Old Bill were all over the place and on every train that came through. Loads of England fans were also passing through the station; some joined us, others continued on, saying that they were going to wait at other stations and pubs along the way. Not one person said they had come across any kind of Dutch mob and we were seeing only the odd orange scarf. The Old Bill were on to what was happening, and some dogs soon arrived, which seemed to indicate that something was about to happen. Most of the lads were getting restless and wanted to move on to the stadium and wait around there, as time was getting on.

We got the tube up to Wembley Park Station, then walked down to Wembley Stadium Station, as we knew the Dutch were being put in that end of the stadium. The Old Bill wouldn't walk them up Wembley Way, as that would be too risky. The walk up to Wembley saw a few slaps dished out and flags taken as the odd Dutch fan was spotted, although most of those hit were your family types – nothing serious. Still, the hype around the match, and the fact that the Dutch mob had not been found, had got to some of the lads. They didn't give a toss who they were hitting, they were all fair game anyway. Anyone is at a game like this. There were plenty of lads hanging around and the word was that the Dutch had been brought into Wembley by bus from Harwich as the Old Bill had been warned that there was going to be trouble at Liverpool Street and Baker Street.

The mob that had been in Carnaby Street had been escorted by the police up to the ground much earlier and were now inside. It was clear that the English lads were well pissed off, and their numbers were growing all the time, especially as many of those milling about had only come up for the trouble and didn't have tickets for the match. There were some Dutch giving us verbal from behind the gates, looking down on us, and we were singing back at them but the Old Bill were getting a bit heavy as we were getting near to kick-off. As ever, the Old Bill handled it in the worst possible way. The dog handlers were brought in and the horses started to try and push us back, which of course just triggered it off. Loads of the lads streamed up the steps and tried to get to the gates, and the riot police started hitting out, and it went mental.

Everyone had now turned on the police and they were getting a bit of a hiding until they regrouped, and the dogs were in there. I saw this one bloke with this dog hanging on to his leg go to the floor, and as the copper went in to nick him he got the shit kicked out of him. The dog was set free but wasn't letting go, and this poor bloke was screaming his head off, and there were blokes booting this dog to get it off. In the end it let go: they always scare the shit out of me, but that one was well fucked. The Old Bill steamed back in and nicked the geezer just to get someone for it probably, and he took a whack on the head and was out cold. There was a bit of a stand-off then and the Old Bill got it under control, so we moved off to get into the ground, as did most of the other lads. I was surprised that the Dutch didn't have more fans really, they hadn't done badly on the turnout, but didn't seem to have a mob of any kind anywhere. In any case, Wembley is a hard place now to have an off inside.

The Old Bill had them well sectioned off, and unless you are sitting in the sections that are right next to them you haven't got a chance. After the match, the place was swarming with police and the Dutch were being kept in. Some of the lads wanted to go back into town after the game as there were bound to be a few Dutch around the West End and there was no point in hanging around Wembley as we would only end up having it away with the police again. We hung around the West End for an hour or so, but once more the Dutch didn't show and there were plenty of Old Bill around keeping an eye on us, just in case; but nothing happened. I suppose the mob they had in Carnaby Street are going around saying how they did the English but really they just bottled it, the tossers.

★ ★ ★

At games like these, supporters simply have to attend and put on a show and at Wembley, front is really all you can do. The reason for this is, as we have already mentioned, because visiting teams rarely bring anyone capable, or willing, to have a pop at the English fans. In fact, only on one occasion has Fortress Wembley been taken.

Inevitably, that occasion involved Scotland. In 1977, during the Home International fixture, the Scots came to town and took London over lock, stock and barrel. They were all over the capital that year, and the photographs of tartan-clad sweaties taking liberties on the hallowed turf and pulling down the goalposts are a shaming sight for most English supporters. The fact that this invasion was repeated, albeit on a smaller scale, until the English finally got their act together and took the battle to Glasgow, so that the competition was scrapped, still rankles with most Londoners, who remember only too well the hordes of drunken, kilt-wearing Scots staggering around the tube or lying unconscious in gutters. Over recent seasons, there has been a great deal of discussion behind the scenes regarding the possibility of resurrecting the tournament at some stage – something that fills many of the established firms on both sides of the border with glee. For the English, the chance to exact revenge for what was, in effect, total humiliation, would surely be too good to miss; and for the Scottish, the opportunity to build on what has become a legend among supporters would almost certainly be most appreciated, too.

This was certainly the big fear following the draw for Euro '96, when the two sides were drawn together. But as we all know now, nothing significant actually happened at Wembley and the same can be said of every game held at the twin towers for many years now. Before the tournament, if anyone had come out and said that England would play

Scotland, Holland and Germany and that there would be no trouble, most people would have laughed. But that was exactly what happened. There were also genuine fears not just that the countries coming to the tournament would import their own problems, but also that mobs up and down the country would indulge in massive campaigns of violence against the many thousands of visiting supporters. There had been a threat, made on television, that the Derby Lunatic Fringe would make an attempt to force the abandonment of the tournament halfway through, for example. However, apart from a few minor occurrences, there were only two serious incidents of note, and they both involved England fans in London. In the end, the tournament was remarkable for the trouble that never arrived.

There are a number of reasons for the relative lack of hooliganism during Euro '96. The main one is that the rival mobs, with the exception of the Scottish casuals, didn't show. Either they had no interest in their national side, or at least not enough to induce them to travel abroad with the team – and there is some evidence to support that theory – or they simply did not have the bottle to cross the Channel. Quite which of these it is difficult to say, but the fact that they didn't show irreparably damaged what reputation they, and particularly the Germans, had previously built up. They will never live that down with the England mobs. Have no doubt about it, though – if they had shown, as was proven after England were knocked out, then serious problems would almost certainly have occurred, because the England groups were more than willing and ready to kick things off.

This leads on to another factor. There had been massive amounts of pre-tournament hype surrounding the so-called meetings between the hooligan ringleaders who were, by all accounts, planning the Third World War. However, as anyone who spent time among the fans or at certain pubs in London during June will know, this was obviously complete bollocks. The evening of the Scotland game, the two of us walked all around the West End and it was obvious that there were mobs from clubs all over England looking for it to go off; but thankfully, no one was talking to each other. At one point, while we were standing on the corner of Trafalgar Square by St Martin-in-the-Fields, it was like the opening scene out of the film *The Warriors,* but no one knew what to do next and it was left up to individual clubs to kick things off on their own. Heaven knows what it would have been like if they had been organized, because that was certainly the biggest potential mob either of us has ever seen.

The following diary of Euro '96 was sent to us by someone we have corresponded with for a number of years. It is fairly representative of a number of accounts sent to us since the tournament ended.

Euro '96 Diary

At last the waiting was over. We had been waiting for years for this chance to come our way and here we were, with the biggest tournament for thirty years in this country just about to start. All the top targets were coming: the Scots, the Germans, the Italians, the French, the Dutch, even the Turks. The only ones really missing were the Paddies, but we had only just turned them over big-time anyway. All the foreign mobs were making the right noises, they were all coming to turn the English over. Well, let the fuckers come because England were ready and waiting.

The domestic season had really picked up, the casual scene was on the rise again and even the media couldn't cover up all the activity that was taking place. The network was full of the mobs who were going to work every week, who had done who and all that, and it was obvious that football violence was back. We were going to target London because for us it's within easy reach and with it being the base for the England games, it was the obvious place to be. We had taken the time off work just in case things kicked off elsewhere and were phoning around to keep up with the news at the other venues.

We caught a train down to Wembley for the first match with the Swiss. None of us had tickets for any of the matches, except the Scotland game, for which we had four seats, but Wembley seemed really subdued. Most of the fans were your scarf-wearing types and the Swiss had brought over a family following, not the type we were looking for. We wandered around for a while, ending up at The Torch. This was more like it – loads of lads on the piss – but still not what we were after. We were told that all the pubs around Wembley were going to be shut at one o'clock, which really pissed us off, so we decided to move off to The Globe, a pub opposite Baker Street tube station, and see what was happening there. This was obviously the place to be. The pub was rammed with pissed-up English lads singing their hearts out. Lovely! The police had swarmed the area and were on the lookout for known faces, so we went into the bar to start drinking, keep our faces hidden and catch up on the news. We were told by some of our acquaintances that the police were taking people out, giving them the full search and photographing them, and were also videoing the pub from across the road.

After about an hour, the fans started to arrive from Wembley but apart from the odd bit of verbal, there was no trouble and we actually ended up in a bar which was full of Swiss. We had a great time talking about football with lads from all over the place. That is how it should be.

The next day, the Germans were due to play their first match in Manchester. We were informed on the news and in the papers that 600 to 1,000 neo-Nazis were coming over to do what Hitler never managed, and rumours were also flying around that the British far right and the far left were going to descend on the match to settle old scores. In reality, it was all far-fetched. There had been the odd incident in Manchester involving Germans the night before, but nothing worth travelling 200 miles for, despite the fact that the press had played their part in building the Germans up to be the main threat of violence in the tournament.

The next night saw Scotland play Holland at Villa Park. There had been the threat of trouble the last time these two had met, but once again both sets of supporters were intent on displaying their better side. The media were giving out hype that English fans were going to attack both sets of supporters, but Birmingham had been quiet so far, even though they were doing their best to start things moving following England's opening match, which they viewed as a disaster. Nothing to write about.

For us, all our attention was on the Scotland match. Everyone thought this would be the one to really start it off, and come Thursday night they were proved right. In Camden Town in North London, following the Holland–Switzerland match, fighting broke out in two pubs. A group of Scottish casuals, believed to be Aberdeen supporters, had started and finished the trouble. At last the first sign: the Jocks would be up for it. We travelled into the West End on the Friday night to suss out the atmosphere and hopefully get our first piece of Euro '96 action. We met up with a few exiled London supporters and scouted around, but again the police had the area covered. We moved around in twos and threes a few yards apart, looking out for each other, but still nothing. We couldn't believe it. Two more lads with us got collared by the police, but that was about it. Trafalgar Square had a few hundred Jocks running around, but no Scottish or English mob was to be seen.

We found a bar, got pissed and stayed the night at our mate's house. The next day we went straight up to The Globe, and it was heaving. Rumours were flying about of small offs and people getting done during the morning and there were a few Villa Combat-18 making themselves known. "England expects" seemed to be the vibe. Luckily, I was one of the lads that had a ticket, so we headed off to Wembley expecting the action to start any moment, but everyone seemed focused on the game. I didn't fancy getting nicked before the game myself, but I still couldn't believe how quiet the whole thing was. There were plenty of Scots around but I didn't see anything that looked like a mob. We were sitting on the grass bank outside our section when this German comes and sits down next to us. We got talking and he told us that the German hooligans were only coming over for the second part of the tournament. He said that they were sure to qualify and that due to the tickets being so expensive they were waiting in the hope of meeting England or Holland, or hopefully both, and then they were coming to prove that the English were no longer top dog. We would see about that later. He may have been a mouthy German wanker with that stupid haircut and denim shorts but we had one thing in common, he thought the FA were ripping people off as well and he did give me a bottle of beer!

In the stadium there were Scots in our section but it was all just down to taking the piss out of our poor relations. There was this one Scot all on his own, about forty-five, face painted, wearing the football top and kilt and when Seaman saved the penalty his face was a picture. Hundreds of Englishmen taking the piss and laughing right in his face, and when Gazza scored he was off before I looked around, just an empty orange seat. I hope those moments give him nightmares for the rest of his life.

After the game, walking back to the station, you would

never have known that England had just won. We were mixed
in with the Scots and maybe it was all an anticlimax, but
everyone was just getting on with it and taking the piss. We
just could not understand these people. This was England–
Scotland, for fuck's sake, what was wrong with everyone? We
headed back to The Globe, but when we arrived, the police
had closed it down and were moving people on. At least we
were where the England mob were and not with the wank
supporters. The pub had been closed because of trouble
among England fans, and some were saying it was Chelsea
and Spurs, others that it was Forest fans playing up. Anyway,
we had to move on. Word was out to meet up at The Porcupine
on Charing Cross Road, as this would give us the chance to
get into Trafalgar Square if the Scots were going to turn up.
The Porcupine was rammed, police were everywhere and the
atmosphere was buoyed up by the result and news that
actions were taking place all over. The Scots were in Trafalgar
Square and were having running battles with the police, so
we didn't go in to the pub. We wanted to be able to move if
things kicked off big-time. This proved to be a wise move.
This was the buzz we had been waiting for, and looking
around you could start to pick out the faces we had been
looking for all week.

Mobs from all over the country were here – Leicester,
Stoke, Forest, Plymouth, Chelsea, Spurs, Exeter, Middlesbrough
and plenty of our lot – which gave us a right buzz. I would
imagine that around 50 per cent of the clubs in the country
had some lads in the area at some stage. We walked the short
distance to the Sussex Arms and things were looking dodgy.
Everyone was trying to suss each other out, who was English,
who were Jacks. We saw a group come up from the direction
of Trafalgar being followed by about twenty police that
looked totally confused. I think they were Burnley fans and
they had certainly seen some action as they were well

buzzing and one had a cut head, but they were laughing and had obviously had a result of some kind. This seemed to be the way things were working out. Each individual mob was out for their own result. We went back towards The Porcupine just as an off started, which we were later told was Chelsea and Spurs playing up with each other. This sort of shit should have been put aside today, as this was about England and Scotland. It was nothing much, but the police thought this was the start of it all and came flying in from every direction. We quickly crossed the road and it was then we realized just how many different mobs were here. The tourists had been waiting for something to happen and were totally engrossed in what they were seeing, although I think a few were a little surprised to see the friendly British bobby whacking the fuck out of anyone that looked like a bloke and telling them to get out of the fucking way, else they were going to get a truncheon over the head as well!

With the police preoccupied, this suddenly left the route down into Trafalgar Square wide open. There was one mob from Sunderland and a few of the Leicester boys trying to get everyone together, but it was each man for himself, really. It's funny that the Northerners were prepared to fight alongside each other, but the Cockneys were not, wankers. We made our way towards the Square with caution. People were coming in the opposite direction and we didn't know who was who or how many Jocks we were likely to come across. When we made it, there were already plenty of English lads around. Most of the Jocks had been forced out by the riot police, and only a few were left. The English were trying to get into the Square to get at them, leaving the police well stretched. We were told that the Jocks had been playing up all afternoon and more came straight down after the match, and they now had about three hundred to four hundred lads well up for it. I found out later that night that their mob was made up mainly of Aberdeen, Hibernian and Dundee fans, and they had spent the last hour having battles with the police that had provided good entertainment for those that had been following them all day.

The media has always managed to do a good job on covering up the problem of football violence in Scotland. Many of the clubs are well active, week in, week out, just as the English clubs are, and it must be said that they had gained a lot of respect from those that had been watching. Not only had they come down, but they were ready and willing to fight, so fair play to them. It would have been some battle if we had managed to meet up, but the police had taken them down into the tube and got them out of the way. Fuck knows where they went. A few bottles were flying around and slaps dished out, but nothing major, and eventually we got into the Square. Stories were going around about individual mobs having it away with groups of Scottish casuals during the day, and a few lads had been slapped, but other stories of more successful meetings were also coming through. Middlesbrough had it at Charing Cross Road, and another mob were talking about something at Tottenham Court Road. After an hour or so we decided to move on. Things were dead here, and maybe we were missing out on events elsewhere, but as it turned out the action was all but over as far as we were concerned. Still, at last the tournament had got started.

There were a few things about the day that got me thinking. First, we had the Scots to thank for two things. They had the bottle to come down and to a certain extent they went home with a result, and also the team took the piss at Wembley. Secondly, the day was noticeable for the absence of a few of the larger mobs, such as West Ham, Millwall, the Scousers and Rangers and Celtic. Maybe they were up to other things elsewhere, I don't know, but they didn't make themselves known in the West End. Thirdly, the crowd and the atmosphere at Wembley were very different from those at Trafalgar Square. They did sell those tickets very carefully, didn't they? Finally, by all accounts the battles between the police and the Jocks in Trafalgar Square were pretty good, so I was told, yet all you saw on the television the next day were pictures of England fans outside The Porcupine, where nothing very much happened. The friendly Scottish fans didn't get a mention. Everything would now focus on our match with the Dutch on the Tuesday.

We headed into London around midday, going straight to the West End. There was orange everywhere, but no lads. We had not really expected the Dutch to bring a mob, but you never know, it only takes five or ten of them, and you can have some fun if they want to join in. They never cease to amaze me in the way they dress. It's funny, and fair play to them if that's what they like, but it's all very strange if you ask me. One thing is that you can't really get it going with a bloke dressed as a woman looking like the Tango man, and I wouldn't want that anyway. If it's their way of saying they are not into fighting then fine, enjoy the game. We headed to the Dutch bar just off Chinatown, which was rammed and well protected by the police, but there were no boys around. We were refused entry when we told them we were English – another case of them being allowed to show their colours, and the English being refused in every other bar. Going to Wembley was a non-starter, so we made our way up to The Globe for a few beers. Again, the police were pulling people out and there were a few Dutch coaches that got loads of verbal, but that was all. We watched the match in the same West End pub as before, which was packed again. I can honestly say that I've never seen England play so well in all my life. They were superb. Just to top the night off, they showed the last few seconds of the Scotland game and we got to see the Jocks get knocked out. When the whistle went, everyone else seemed disappointed the Scots were out, but we went fucking barmy. What is wrong with these people? They were looking at us as though we were mad. Later, in Leicester Square, there were plenty of relieved Dutch around and Trafalgar was starting to fill up with England fans celebrating. We left to find a pub but later found that the police had moved in to get the England fans out, and they were really starting to piss everyone off. I mean, if we can't even celebrate a victory like that, what can we do?

The next night saw Germany play Italy. Before the start of the tournament, this game had been highlighted as a potential big one. Rumours that groups such as Combat-18 and Anti-Fascist Action were supposedly up for the Germans and the Italians had been going around for weeks, but when we got in touch with our northern mates they told us that nothing was happening and that it would be a waste of money travelling all that way just on the off chance.

Saturday was the quarter-final with Spain. We had hoped that they would bring a mob of some kind over, as they have had loads of trouble in their league this year and had a history with the English anyway, but like everyone else they bottled out. Again, we did the West End and The Globe. For me, the best moment of the whole tournament was when Seaman saved that penalty. We went mad and the buzz around the West End was fantastic that night. The next day we found out we were to play Germany at Wembley in the semi-final. The whole country was buzzing and the press were stoking the match up to be the Third World War.

Once again we set off early. Remember, the Germans had done the business in Holland and Belgium recently, and had been giving it the big one about coming over here to kick our arses. Well, now was their chance. Surely they wouldn't bottle out, they couldn't. We did Carnaby Street, Soho, Leicester Square, Trafalgar, the lot. Nothing. We decided to split into

smaller groups and keep in touch on the mobiles. One lot
went to The Globe, we went up to Wembley. Up at the
stadium, there were plenty of Germans around, but no lads,
and even The Torch had some Germans drinking in there. I
never thought I would see that, so we left. Apparently The
Globe was packed, but the lads were keeping their distance
because the police were on to everyone, and some of the lads
with us today didn't need their photos taken. They said that
plenty of the top lads were around and that they heard the
police had started on the crowd again in Trafalgar Square
after the Spain match. We made our way down to West
Hampstead and watched the match in a pub down there
which would make it easy to get to Wembley if something did
kick off.

Fuck knows how we lost. Once again, the team did us
proud, but the second that bastard scored that penalty, we
downed our pints and left for Wembley. On the way to the
Tube, a vanload of police had pulled up and had three lads
pinned up against the wall and were frisking them. They had
obviously had the same idea as us, but luckily we passed by
unnoticed. The phone rang and the rest of the lads told us
they were staying down in the centre and would keep us
posted. They also said that the atmosphere was heavy.

I couldn't believe what I saw at Wembley. We were expecting to see things going off big-time, but again – nothing.
Maybe it was the shock of defeat or the realization that the
tournament was over, but the English were walking next to
Germans as though they were the same. We thought they
must be holding the main lot of Germans in to avoid trouble, so made our way up towards that end of the ground
going up past the Conference Centre. Wrong, the Germans
were gone. Down to Wembley Central Station: nothing.
Then the phone rang. We were told to get down to Trafalgar
quick because things were now kicking off with the police. I

fucking hate the police and they hadn't really done themselves any favours in the public relations department so far
during this tournament, so a chance to gain a bit of revenge
would be most welcome. There is nothing worse than knowing things have kicked off and that you might miss the lot,
but luckily the trains were on our side, although it took the
longest forty-five minutes of my life to get to the Square,
and that is saying something for a football fan. Things were
in full swing. The atmosphere was electric and the riot police
were steaming in and out hitting anything they could. Cars
were being smashed and kicked and I saw a police car that
had been kicked to fuck. Excellent. God knows what would
have happened if England had been knocked out earlier.
The police made the mistake of forcing people off into the
side streets, and you could hear windows going and alarms.
It was fucking great, we had the bastards on the run and it
proved to them that no matter how much in our faces they
are, we will always take them on when we want to, and take
the piss. After a few hours, the thing was starting to fade out
and when the numbers get low the police usually start beating the fuck out of anyone that looks remotely like a bloke,
so we did the off. We had enjoyed our run around and the
English had proved their point.

The tournament was over as far as everyone was concerned.
Saturday was the last real night of the holiday, and we didn't
expect the Germans to bring their mob now, even though
they had reached the final. We went into the West End that
night just in case, but no such luck. The pictures from
Trafalgar Square would be shown all over Europe, in every
country taking part. All those wankers who bottled out would
see what they would've been up against if they had been
brave enough to turn up, and their failure to do so was the
only reason the tournament was so quiet. I think that if
England had been knocked out earlier, the whole thing would

have been the biggest non-event ever. The football was fantastic and England did us proud. If it wasn't for the Jocks having a go and the German game, we would have wasted our whole year's holiday – but those two games made it worthwhile.

Cheers then, and fair play to the Scottish, but to the rest, well, wish you were here but you haven't got the bottle so we will have to come to you as always.

See you soon.

Many of those who indulge in violence at domestic football were borne along with the euphoria of the England team's good performance, and this was another major factor in the lack of violence. As our correspondent stated, if England had gone out in the early stages, then Euro '96 may well have gone very flat, as was proven after the Germany game, and the supporters may have started a tournament of their own. But there was another, more important factor in the relative peacefulness, as far as we were concerned, and whether you think the FA were very clever or just very lucky, it was an interesting phenomenon.

We have in the past spent a great deal of time talking about countries who have serious problems within their domestic leagues, but very few with their national side. Denmark is one, but the most obvious is Holland. The famous (or infamous, depending on your opinion) "Oranje" experience is one of the more intriguing aspects of the Dutch footballing culture, and one which was very much in evidence during Euro '96. They certainly know how to enjoy themselves, and nearly every game is played in a carnival and, well, orange atmosphere. For many people, this is the way that watching England should be and having been around Wembley for all the England games and watching the crowds and the obvious enjoyment, it is possible that we saw the start of the St George experience at Euro '96 and if so, just how and why did it occur?

It is clear to many, including us, that the arrival of the Premier League heralded a whole new chapter in the growth of football in England. The way that it was marketed attracted a whole new audience to football. The male terrace environment we grew up with was gradually eroded within the top flight, and this process is continuing to this day as the Premier League goes on changing its fan base. The corporate boxes and half-time cheerleaders are all symptomatic of the change in the way the game is being watched. And these developments, coupled with improvements in facilities at stadia and the inevitably increased prices, ensured that certain elements were positively discouraged from attending because they simply were not wanted or needed any more. The Premier League also won its battle to fill the grounds with families quite quickly, and the increasing numbers of women who go to games are proof of this.

All this has meant that the game at the top end is very different from the rest of the professional game, especially in the way it is watched, and this has been a key element in their success in reducing the amount of hooliganism. However, this has a down side. The removal of certain elements within the home crowds has led to significant problems for a number of Premier League clubs, centring on the fact that the new breed of fan simply does not know how to create the right atmosphere. Arsenal, Tottenham and even Manchester United have had to appeal for more noise from the fans – a pretty good indication of how bad it can be.

Now where the Premier League has changed, or developed if you like, the England team have followed, and what we saw at Euro '96 was the result. Whether this was part of some kind of master plan which evolved out of Lancaster Gate is impossible to say. But if it wasn't, the FA were very, very lucky and if it was, then they were very, very clever, because it is obvious to anyone who follows the game that the support at Wembley during the tournament was very different from the support usually seen at home fixtures. Football coming home? In reality, it never left; but what a great slogan and superb marketing device, instantly associating the game with the new breed of supporter. That is not to detract from their performance in generating atmosphere at Wembley in any way, because as anyone who attended games at the twin towers knows only too well, all the England matches were notable for the noise. But we have to wonder how many of those people will turn up for the next home game. If they do, that's great; but if they do not, and we see a rapid return to the crowds of around 20,000, that will be a major concern.

Of course, it is important to realize that many people who bought tickets through official sources bought their full allocation and took the wife and/or kids, which may not normally be the case. After all, it was a once-in-a-lifetime footballing occasion. This did, however, have the knock-on effect of diluting the male content within the ground. The cynic, of course, would say that this was part of the FA plan to beat the hooligans by keeping them out – a plan that also included giving away masses of tickets to corporate empires. If that was what they wanted, and still want, fine; but if it continues and we do join the face-painted generation of international fans, it will upset an awful lot of people. As English football continues to chase its new breed of fan, some of the behaviour emerging from this contingent is beginning to seem rather disturbing. The following opinions came to us via a good friend during Euro '96, and while we must state that these opinions are not ours, we would like to add that we agree with them 100 per cent.

Down the Pub

Just what the fuck is going on? Am I losing the plot or missing out on something here? There does seem to be a rather large number of blokes walking around with inflatable clogs on their heads and others with their faces painted all sorts of colours. Some are dressing up like a bad version of Bart Simpson's mum, some as orange (not red) Indians. Now don't get me wrong. I like a laugh as much as the next man, but there is a time and a place for everything and to me, dressing up like a complete prick is not part of going to football.

I love being a bloke. I love being English and being an English bloke is the dog's bollocks because we are different from the rest. The sweaties can wear their kilts (which to me are only a small piece of fabric away from a dress and person-ally I find that a bit scary) and the rest can paint their faces, dress up in silly costumes, wear their scarves around their heads and wrists and can then stick them up their arses and sing their national anthems as far as I am concerned but don't ask me or the English to join in. I remember in Frankfurt during Euro '88 watching the lads get stuffed by the USSR. All the supporters were taking part in the Mexican wave but whenever it came over to the English section, we just gave them the old wanker sign. I mean just who the fuck do they think we are? The girl on the PA system kept asking us to join in, but bollocks, the rest of Europe are welcome to make themselves look like wankers, just leave us out of it.

Here I am, eight years on, and the Championship is here in England. I couldn't get any tickets so I watched all the games in London with a load of mates down their local. All the foreign supporters are doing their dressing-up bit – fine, no problem

– but what I saw on the way home following the Dutch match made me sick with anger and embarrassment. I was on the train back to Watford and it stopped at Wembley Central. Loads of English got on and among them was this bloke and his bird and they came and sat right next to me. They had obviously been to the game. She was talking complete bollocks about football and the match, going on about what player she liked, that sort of stuff, and the pair of them had their fucking faces painted. Now this bloke was in his thirties, not a little kid but a bloke. I wanted to wring his fucking neck. What is happening to the English football fan? Is this the future following of the national side? Will we all start dressing up as women or, worse still, Morris dancers? Please no.

What made me angry was the fact that these people had tickets and were keeping the real fans away from the ground. They should be banned from football, not encouraged. If you want to dress up like a wanker, then follow a wanker's sport like basketball or American football, and if you want to paint your face then go to the circus with all the other clowns. We're in danger of losing our sport to these wankers and I think it is the duty of every England fan to tell these prats to grow up, get a life, or fuck off.

What has happened to the traditional football fan and the traditional songs? Why have we suddenly adopted "Swing Low, Sweet Chariot" as a song? It's bollocks. I'll tell you why, it's because all those that attended the England games got their tickets through corporate packages, that's why. They're not the sort to follow their side to Shrewsbury on a Tuesday night, and d'you know why? Because they haven't got a fucking side. They're there because football's trendy at the moment. That song is a public schoolboys' wanky, head-up-your-arse rugby song. It's nothing to do with us, but these bastard trendy, designer fans have dragged it into our game.

Football is busy developing its own class system, and it is

dividing the support of the country. The average supporter that travels the country every week in support of their team couldn't get a ticket for the Germany semi-final for love nor money, but if you just happened to have a spare £450 on the day, you could buy yourself a nice little hospitality package with beer, meal and match ticket – bargain! One match for the price of an average season ticket. Well, let the wankers have it if that's what they want. Don't they understand that we get that same buzz every week because we support football? We support football all our lives, not just for twenty-five days every other year. The FA must love their designer fans, just the image they wanted the world to see: your average face-painting, fun-loving, boy-meets-girl, loves-football, go-every-week English fan.

Let's see what happens when the crowds go back down to twenty thousand for the next friendly, shall we? Then they'll ask where the loyalty has gone. Well, I'll tell you, it's gone down the pub where you placed it, you greedy fuckwits. There's your loyalty and that's where it'll stay. Then we'll get all the stupid adverts telling us, "There's nothing like being there" and all that bollocks. Well, sorry mate, I need my money to follow the lads to Cardiff on Saturday so you can stick Wembley and your prices up your arse because we remember when we were not worthy. Your true supporters at England games are easy to spot because they're the ones not dressed up like complete pricks, although you won't find too many true fans at the really big games – the tickets would have found their way elsewhere.

When will the trendy bastards realize that we are not like the rest of the world when it comes to following our sport? Losing is not something to be taken lightly and washed down with a pint of Guinness. England expects and it hurts when we lose. We don't want to dress up in bright colours. We like the element of fear and of being different, something that is hard to carry off when you look like Barbara Cartland's worst nightmare. Not only that, but dressing up all jolly can make you look really pathetic when the despair of defeat is written all over your face. I love laughing at people when they look like that, it brings great joy to my life. Kids are best, just as the tears start rolling down their cheeks. Football is a serious way of life. Welcome to the real world, now grow up.

The upshot of this move away from the more traditional type of fan is that while the Premier League has moved on (and that's not necessarily a good thing for many people), those clubs outside the top flight have been left languishing in its wake. The changing fan base, as well as the success of clubs who now enjoy sell-outs, has seen the hooligan problem pretty much solved at the top end, and it is now very rare indeed for trouble inside grounds to occur. However, this has left the hooligan problem firmly in the sphere of the smaller clubs where, as most people know, it has usually been at its most dangerous in any case. It is also true that some of those supporters from the top flight who do indulge and cannot get tickets or are banned will simply adopt a smaller club where they can get their fix of violence. As regards the national team, the same thing will occur; but whereas many could not get into Wembley for Euro '96, they'll have no danger next time, or the time after that. The great worry for us is that the FA will begin to believe that the trouble with the national team has finally been solved at home, but as we have seen, it never really existed in the first place. The real threat, and the real test, will be the next time England travel, because then we will see how far we've come.

Euro '96 was a great time for both football and its supporters and was thankfully notable for the absence of the hooligans but the fact that they weren't there does not mean that things have changed. Sadly, that is far from the case. Football may have come home but the hooligan elements never left.

9

National Pride

Colin Ward and Chris Henderson

The England football team is a symbol of national pride, but sometimes the fans' patriotic sentiment goes a little overboard. There has been a historical link between hooligan firms and fascist groups, and in the eighties many of those in hooligan firms were also involved with the National Front.

The Chelsea Headhunters were not famed for their racial tolerance, and made up a large percentage of England's travelling support. Taken from the book *Who Wants It?* by Colin Ward and "Chubby" Chris Henderson, one time leader of the Headhunters, this chapter focuses on their travels with the England side, giving a new twist on George V's aphorism: "Abroad is bloody."

Chelsea were big on the England scene. Some said Chelsea followed England because they were so bad that they couldn't get into Europe, but the real reason was simple – it was great fun. Twenty-four-hour drinking and foreign trips with your mates. Nothing much had changed since D. H. Lawrence wrote this on 18 August 1914:

The reservists were leaving for London by the nine o'clock train . . . They were young men, some of them drunk. There was one bawling and brawling before the ticket window; there were two swaying on the steps of the subway shouting, and ending, "Let's go and have another before we go." There were a few seeing off their brothers, but on the whole the reservists only had their own pals.

"Well, so long!" they cried as the train began to move. "When you see 'em, let 'em have it."

"Ay, no fear," shouted the man, and the train was gone, the man grinning.

I thought what it would really be like, "when he saw 'em."

In the early eighties it was common to see loads of England lads dressed in dark-blue Admiral tops. Admiral were the England team's sponsor at the time. With the three stripes, it could have been a contingent of sailors direct from HMS *Invincible*. Instead, the lucky foreigners had an undisciplined rabble letting them have it whenever they saw them.

Without doubt, the benchmark for foreign travel was the France v England friendly match played in March 1984. The fighting started with the French skinheads on the Paris metro, where both sides had armed themselves with CS gas, and continued throughout the match with seats being smashed all around. As the Paris riot police came through the crowd, Paul Penny from Kilburn skimmed seats into the front row of the riot police like frisbees. They bounced off the front of their protective clothing, hardly even making an impression, yet every time one connected people cheered. At the fairground, for such accuracy, he would have won a whole row of cuddly toys but for his trouble that night he got a good whacking with a police truncheon.

At Dunkirk, some of the lads disembarked from the ferry to find rows of brand-new British Leyland cars ready for export on the quayside, complete with ignition keys. An impromptu game of bumper cars ensued in front of startled, open-mouthed French onlookers. British Leyland estimated the damage at £30,000.

Another landmark match was Denmark away in 1982. Copenhagen is a wonderful city, full of gentle Danes offering you polite advice and friendship – unless you are a travelling England fan. The local youths wanted to pick a fight, like they do everywhere. One of the lads walked out of a Copenhagen bar to a smack in the teeth: "They don't print that in the guidebooks, do they!" Everywhere you go, English fans set the standards for toughness. Mix it with us and you've got credibility. A smack in the teeth doesn't need translation, it's a universal language.

Guppy from Brighton loved Copenhagen until he stepped in the dog shit which seemed to be everywhere. "Wonderful, Wonderful Copenhagen, Your Streets Are Full of Shit" became his theme tune after that.

Inside the ground, the local police hadn't heard of segregation and fight after fight broke out. The locals were up for it. In fact, they were thriving on it. Plain-clothes policemen mingled with them and got stuck in because it was fun, like a boxing booth at a travelling fairground. For a short while, one end of the ground resembled a punch-in-the-face contest.

In one comical exchange, two large coppers in plain clothes set about an England fan near the front. Hickey charged down the terracing and delivered a kung fu kick which sent the larger, blond-haired policeman bouncing against a fence. The momentum knocked Hickey to the ground. Another police officer stepped forward and lashed him with his truncheon around twenty times. The riot police snatch squad arrived and the two policemen flashed their badges at them, so they proceeded to give Hickey a good bashing. As he got up to run away, blondie gave him a beauty of a punch to the side of his head which knocked him sideways, then sent him on his way with a kick up the backside. Everyone laughed, especially when he retreated up the terrace still getting a whacking from the retreating police. The wind was knocked from his body, but he was half-laughing at his escape from Thumpsville and at everyone's incredulity at his stupid bravery. "Just my luck to pick on the police."

The two plain-clothes policemen were now unmasked. Instead of melting away, they stood there like latter-day John L. Sullivans in the classic old boxers' pose: both arms out in front moving up and down, while slightly bouncing on the spot. "Come forward, English hooligans, we are ready to fight." Very politically correct, very Danish. Forward went the lads, ready to take up the challenge, but there was a very polite afterthought which the Danes had conveniently left out: "We are offering you a fight which we cannot lose. If you beat us in a fight we will have you nicked and battered by our best riot police, not necessarily in that order, Mr Englishman." Hickey had found that out the hard way!

All the while, this was going on to a backdrop of thousands of Danes singing a happy oompah song while they swayed from side to side in unison. When the huge blond copper took a particularly good right-hander and staggered backwards, the Danish crowd let out a huge "ooh" roar, swayed at a higher speed and sang a little louder. Oh, what fun these English hooligans are providing us with. Afterwards, in a bar on the Nyhaun, the Danish equivalent of Covent Garden: "We really love you English hooligans. You certainly know how to have a fine punch-up."

Seems that the police getting a whacking is popular wherever you go. Leaving Copenhagen station the next day, the locals and police waved goodbye. "Come back again, boys." Unreal.

Denmark '88 was just as much fun. The only difference was the level of organization we needed in order to keep away from the police. By now, the police were using the press as a propaganda weapon, telling the public that they had circulated details of the hooligans to all Danish airports so that all known troublemakers would be denied entry. Despite being told that for years, I never knew of anybody who had been denied entry to a country. Scarrott used to get off his face at Dover and continue to drink on the ferry and train until he arrived at his continental destination, but was never once refused entry. OK, so he used a false passport, but using the names Elvis Presley and Al Capone, among other aliases, should have alerted a criminal intelligence unit.

Anyway, the lads all met in the centre of Hamburg. Neo-Nazis or not, the local pimps and rougher class who hang around the red-light district, the Reeperbahn, soon came into conflict with us. In the centre of the Reeperbahn there was a series of bars where the local black population hung out. On the Monday evening, Angus had been on an all-day session and stopped in one of the bars for a drink. Apart from the German girls in there, his was the only white face. "What the hell, it was so dark in there I didn't notice all those darkies," he later said. He kept trying to chat up the girls. Eventually he went to the toilet and fell asleep. After ten minutes, the door was kicked in and he was hoisted off the pan by two black men. "Fuck off, Sambo, I'm having a shit," he shouted. They threw him into the street.

The next night, Angus waited at the station for his pals to arrive. As he stood there he was recognized by the Pompey 6.57 mob, so called because that was the time of the train they always left Portsmouth on when they travelled away. Normally the rivalries which happen in club football don't spill over into Europe, but this time one of the Pompey lads whacked Angus – he owed him one from a few seasons back. When Angus's pals turned up, it developed into a brief fight with a few punches thrown, causing the police to run over before all of them moved away mouthing threats at each other.

Later Angus, with his pals in tow, went back to the blacks' bar and sat on the same stool he had the night before. With him was Marcus, who was half-caste and had long dreadlocks. The German blacks, who all spoke with pseudo-American accents, asked Marcus what he was doing with white boys. "These are my Chelsea pals," he replied, which confused them even more. Nothing came of it, mostly because Angus couldn't remember any of the guys who'd thrown him into the street the previous evening.

Later that night, some of the lads tangled with a few pimps and other blacks. The Germans pulled out gas but Salford was faster on the draw and gassed them out before they could fire theirs. "Our gas is better than yours, eh, Fritz?"

One German was down on the floor. Just as he was about to get paid out, another German pulled a gun. As soon as the word "shooter" was heard, everybody got on their toes. No shots were fired.

To Salford, that was a defining moment. Hamburg was gas city. Lady canisters (lipstick-size, very handy, make a nice Xmas stocking filler for the wife), jumbo canisters, truncheons with gas. His eyes lit up when a friendly smiling Turk produced imitation firearms like magnums, which fired CS capsules. He was in heaven when he saw his favourite plaything – the exploding gas canister: "Just right to set a whole bar moving." "Yeah, Abdul, we're gonna gas out some Germans," said Salford gleefully, rubbing his eyes and giving it the "aargh" sound that people make when the gas hits them, the irony of which was not lost on the Turk.

By Tuesday, the firm numbered sixty. The lads who had flown in via Pan Am had nicked the entire contents of the duty free shop and the carrier bags. We chinked as we jinked as we moved.

All the main faces were on board: Tony Cavelle, Giles, Skitsy Carl from Tooting, Steve Rolf, Pete Tate and Braddy Dave from Southampton (many years later Braddy was to end up in prison in the USA for drug running), Peg Leg and Damian Brown from Southend, Jock, Paul Gee and his pal Pete Vokes from Fulham as well as Gatwick Steve, Stuart Glass, John Bailey, a geezer called Bucket, and Paddington.

"*Ou est le hauptbahnhof*, Fritz?" was Salford's favourite line for most of Tuesday morning, after he'd demolished a large amount of the stolen duty free. "Multilingual and cunnilingual" was how Giles described him after his performance in the red-light district the previous evening.

Our idea was to get a train from Hamburg on Tuesday, arriving in Copenhagen just after lunchtime on Wednesday. After the trouble with the Pompey lads nobody wanted to hang around the station, so the plan was to get to the station just before departure. That way, the police would also be caught unawares. Unfortunately, we cut it a little too fine and as we approached the barrier the train was pulling away. The quicker lads made it easily but I was struggling, running while carrying my bag. Unlike some who travel light I always like to dress well, so my bag was quite heavy. A Scouse lad held the door open for me. "Come on, mate, throw us your bag," he shouted. Not on your life. I've seen that trick before. Throw 'em your bag and the door slams shut, leaving you with nothing, standing on a railway platform looking like a right mug. After all, they were Scousers. The thought of them wearing my clothes gave me the impetus to catch the train. On the train they were all "Well done, mate". "Yeah, lads, well done, indeed." I smiled at them.

The train journey saw Salford consume the rest of the Pan Am duty free before passing out. Bad move, mate. By the time he alighted from the train, Salford was receiving some very funny looks – the other lads had borrowed lipstick from a lady passenger and had painted a red swastika on his forehead. It stayed there for hours.

We had arranged to meet everyone at the Spunk Bar, in the centre of Copenhagen. By the time our firm arrived, it was so crowded you couldn't move. While we were waiting outside, a beer lorry pulled up to make a delivery. The driver and his mate went across the road for their dinner break. If they had printed invitations stating "please thieve from our lorry" they couldn't have done any better. Within minutes, half the lorry was being unloaded and carried up the road. People inside the bar left their drinks and came outside to help themselves.

In the centre of Copenhagen is the Carlsberg Brewery. Every day it has guided tours and at the end of the tour you are invited to sample the beer and to enjoy the Danish hospitality. As fast as you drink it, they provide you with more: "You like our Danish beer?" Of course we did, but free methylated spirits would have been consumed by that mob. A one-legged York fan got so pissed that when the fresh air hit him he fell flat on his face and his false leg fell off, leaving him lying in the gutter, literally legless. Everybody fell about laughing, with nobody helping him up. The Danes going about their work and shopping looked on and smiled, as Danes do.

Outside the ground, some Scousers were selling tickets, doing their best imitation of needing to work to earn money. They were certainly getting plenty of scowls. Touting is OK, but taking money from travelling England fans is frowned upon. Near the ground was a sentry box, and inside was the archetypal friendly Dane selling tickets.

Salford kicked in the side, while someone else grabbed fist-fuls of tickets. Salford got his foot stuck and was shouting for help. Sod that. Everyone thought it was just another wind-up and shot off down the road. "Don't leave me, lads," he howled. Everybody half-expected him to pull his foot out, shout, "April fool", then run off. The last we saw of him he was under arrest. Around the corner, we put the Scousers out of business. Tickets for sale became tickets for free to England fans, leaving the Scousers out of pocket.

Inside the ground, there were no plain-clothes policemen offering a stand-up fight, but row after row of riot police. This time all the fans were put straight back on to their trains after the match, Salford excepted – he had an extended holi-day in Denmark when he received two months for robbery at a special after-match court. When he returned he told us that the Danish prison was cleaner than his London flat, which wasn't surprising when you saw the food stains on his clothes. By all accounts, it was the best he had eaten in years. He looked almost healthy, a frightening thought.

Paul Scarrott was thirty-two and at the height of his drink-ing and fighting abilities. The year 1988 was the finest hour for some, and the few were vilified by the many pressmen out to capture the battles in every minute detail. Euro '88 was being held in Germany, and for two months Scarrott had been telling anybody who would listen about how England would be renewing its acquaintance with Rommel. Manfred Rommel, none other than the son of Field Marshal Rommel, the Desert Fox, was the mayor of Stuttgart and the English hooligan army would be descending upon his city. Manfred, like all Germans, held out a hand of friendship and waited to welcome us. Scarrott, like many other fans, didn't under-stand this mentality. He never did make it to Stuttgart – the Ministry nicknamed Scarrott Public Enemy Number One and the German authorities arrested him after street disturbances in Düsseldorf and deported him. What was in reality a brief skirmish between German and English youths became blown up into the "Battle of Düsseldorf Railway Station" with Scarrott leading the English charge. It conjured up images of Richard the Lionheart and General Montgomery. It was the stuff that legends are made of.

There was a lot of talk of travelling out to Spain for the international in February 1987. February is a crap month for football unless you are challenging for the League title, and there wasn't much chance of that with Chelsea at the time, so a trip to Spain by coach would be fun. By the time we left the Hand and Flower pub on 15 February, the coach was full of fans from different teams tagging along, just for a laugh. Altogether, sixty-six were on board. Chelsea were the largest group on the coach with Stuart Glass, Darren Crewe, Andy Rutledge and Dell Boy from Battersea and Mickey Smith from Darlington. There were also Scarrott and Gary from Nottingham, a couple of Pompey lads, Craig Allison from Aston Villa, some Palace chaps, Chris and two Shrewsbury lads, Peter Vokes and Paul Grover from Fulham.

As the coach pulled away, a huge cheer went up. Next stop Paris, we hoped. First, though, we had to get through customs at Dover. The coach driver was paranoid about getting tugged by the police for having alcohol on board, so he asked us not to drink between London and Dover.

One of the lads had made some calling cards up and had them translated into Spanish: "Congratulations, you have met the Chelsea Headhunters, No. 1 in England." We saw that as a nice touch. Everybody wanted one of those.

The tone of the journey was set by Giles Denslow. It was a typically horrible February day with an east wind driving the sleet into your face, making you scrunch up your eyes to keep it out, and that damp type of cold which gets right into your bones. Travelling to Spain for the football, it was enough to make you think about emigrating to the sunshine permanently. Unperturbed by this, Giles Denslow turned up for the trip in shorts, a huge sombrero, an Ibiza T-shirt and those Clarks-style summer sandals with no socks.

"Wearing socks is very uncool and typically English," he informed us. As if to make himself immune to the cold, he stood outside for a few minutes while we remained inside and shivered for him.

As if it was an eccentrics' convention, Eddie Mills arrived with a giant Paddington Bear-style suitcase. Since that day he has been known as Suitcase Eddie. Salford was dressed in his usual trampish manner in his regulation donkey jacket, DM boots and jeans that had a life of their own. Alongside him was his regular England travelling companion, the Manchester City Bin Man, Dave Blezzard.

Salford was an uneasy travelling companion because he was so intense about his political beliefs and was unpredictable – although he made most people laugh, others were nervous around him. He was good fun and humorous but you had to accept the package as a whole. His claim to infamy was of one of his pilgrimages to watch Glasgow Rangers, this time in Dublin, which added an extra edge to the match. During the journey between Holyhead and Dublin, Salford achieved his usual state of complete intoxication. This resulted in him punching a priest as they disembarked. In the mayhem that ensued, an Irish garda hit him in the face with a truncheon, blinding him in one eye. Whilst this prevented him from being charged with a very serious offence (punching a priest in Ireland would have copped him a long prison term had he not lost an eye), it meant that he now looked at people with a slightly sideways glance, making even those who knew him a little nervous as it gave him the look of a madman.

A fellow traveller, that complete madman Paul Scarrott, turned up complete with false one-year passport in the name of Al Capone. (Scarrott definitely started a fashion. During Euro '98 guys named Freddie Krueger, Frank Sinatra and Robert de Niro were thrown out of Germany.) Making the clickety-click noises of the Prince Buster tune, he informed us noisily that Al Capone's enemies don't argue. "What is this, a bleedin' madmen's convention?" shouted one of the lads from the back of the coach.

We arrived without incident in Paris early the next morning. The coach parked just underneath the Eiffel Tower. It was crisp and clear, very cold, with white wispy snowflakes blowing around. Giles looked up at the tower: "Where are we, Blackpool?" he exclaimed. By now he had decided that the Spanish uniform would have to give way to something more sensible, so Suitcase Eddie was relieved of some of his warm clothing while he was asleep.

Small groups headed off in different directions, with instructions to be back at an agreed meeting time. Giles tagged along with a group of twenty lads heading for the Latin Quarter. For some reason, they thought that meant they were going to bump into groups of Italians looking for it. What they did bump into in the early morning as they walked along the banks of the River Seine were two African street cleaners. "I wonder if it's true that blacks can't swim," someone said, so without further ado they chucked both of them straight into the water. The water was icy cold and it was incredible that they didn't die of shock. After a few seconds they struggled out on to the bank. "No," said Giles, "it's a fallacy, they can swim after all." "Paris is full of black immigrants, the rest are middle class" is a quote I remember.

The Latin Quarter was all art shops, poncey stuff, so after a cursory glance the lads caught the Metro a few stops into the Pigalle. What else is there to do in Paris except for finding an English pub and settle down for a serious drink? Why else would you come to Paris, except to drink in the Rose and Crown? After all, Paris is a city that does tours of its sewers.

After an hour or so, Giles got bored and got a small crew together for a river cruise. Everywhere they looked, people were pissing into the Seine – and to think that the French look down on the English. As they cruised up the Seine, a boatload of Japanese tourists came the other way. "Get a load of this, Nippon," Giles shouted and dropped his trousers to flash his bum at them. One of the Japanese shouted and then the whole lot of them raced over to snap it, making us think that the boat was about to keel over. The sound of the camera shutters whirring, along with the funny squeal Japanese tourists make when they see something unusual, was quite incredible.

As they disembarked, Giles did his party piece and ran out with the contents of the boat's till. Seconds later a Vietnamese guy came rushing out. Everybody sprinted for it and ended up in a restaurant laughing and joking. A couple of minutes later the boat owner's face appeared at the window. "You very handsome man, my wife love you long, long time," shouted Giles in a mock-Vietnamese accent. With that, the guy held a gun at the window.

"I shoot you. You are a very bad man," he shouted.

"Sod that, he's got a gun," shouted someone. With that everyone was off, through the kitchen and out the back alley, never stopping to look back. Everybody was waiting for the sound of a gunshot and the pain in the back but it never came.

As evening fell, the lads became the focus for the groups of Africans and Arabs who were hanging around and were getting heaps of abuse, most of it because they didn't drink. "You can't be a real man if you don't drink, can you?" was the considered reasoning. Being able to hold your drink as well as fight was what being English was all about. What started the trouble, though, wasn't the level of abuse, but the fact that someone touched up one of their girls as she walked past. All hell broke loose, but Salford was well armed with his gas canisters, and this as well as a barrage of bottles put them to flight. Yet everywhere we looked they were there lurking in the shadows, waiting for one of us to venture somewhere we shouldn't.

As we retreated into the bar, a large police presence turned up and a number of them came in. One of them saw a gas canister on top of the table. He picked it up, shouted something in French then squirted himself in the face with the gas. It took a few seconds, then he ran out of the bar. He obviously told his colleagues what had happened because they didn't attack us. Instead, the head of the police wanted us back at our coach and they piled us into vans. As we drove away, we suddenly realized the enormity of the problem we had created – there must have been half of African/Arabic Paris waiting for us in the sidestreets.

Back at the coach, we caught up on the gossip. One of Scarrott's Nottingham mates, who was very quiet on the coach journey down, had been arrested. He had been sitting in a bar when he was insulted in French by a waiter when he demanded a beer: "*S'il vous plait est un langue international, Anglais.*" He didn't understand exactly what was said but didn't like the tone so he jumped up on to the table. "This is what I think of your country," he shouted, then dropped his trousers and deposited a steamy one on the table. For a few seconds the whole bar was stunned. He jumped down and sprained his ankle, which is how he got himself caught and arrested.

He should have known better than to travel with Scarrott. This was a man who seemed to have a habit of getting fellow travellers arrested. On a trip to Switzerland, Binman tagged along with him. En route, they got off the train in Austria for a beer. As they were sitting in the bar they saw some locals depositing money in a wall safe. Scarrott slipped out, went into a hotel and took the fire axe, then went across the road and tried to axe the safe off the wall. Binman, sitting in the bar faceless drunk, copped a three-month stretch for his part, despite telling the Austrian magistrate that he'd only known Scarrott for a few hours.

The police watched us leave Paris, minus the six of us who were being held for "theft, assault and associated offences", as they put it. The coach sped south with none of us giving a second thought to those who had been arrested. It was an occupational hazard. Most people slept. At the Hendaye/Irun border crossing, the coach pulled into a service station. Inside, one guy was serving. While one of our party went into the restaurant to eat a meal, the rest helped themselves, practically looting the shop.

Back on the coach Scarrott had fifty reels of film but no camera. He had reasoned that somebody would have brought a camera, but he was out of luck. Also on the coach were a large number of sombreros, as well as liqueurs covering every colour you could possibly imagine, plus some you couldn't. Scarrott and Salford were tasting them all.

The further south we went, the worse the weather became. As we pulled into Burgos it was snowing heavily. Thirty of us went into the old town, a fort, for a drink. We ended up in a bar full of medieval armour and artefacts. Giles got hold of a crossbow. The owner came rushing across and had one of those Spanish-English conversations.

"No, no," he went. "Pow, whoosh malo." He intimated that it worked and could kill someone. With that, Giles picked up the crossbow and pretended to fire it. Accidentally, the catch went and the bolt inside was fired off. It shot past those at the bar and thudded into a suit of armour. The owner went spare, grabbing the crossbow and shouting, "Loco Anglaisy, loco Anglaisy."

"Just what is his problem?" retorted Giles.

Once again we had attracted the ire of the locals and a scuffle started outside the bar. Meanwhile a fight had broken out at the disco in the town, and a local Spaniard had pulled a knife. One of the Chelsea lads saw him do it and hit him with a chair. In the ensuing mêlée two of the locals ended up getting stabbed, and the Chelsea lads got a pasting. Back they came to the bar we were in. Once inside, fighting broke out again. This time, though, Salford let off a gas canister after we had all gone outside, then we held the doors closed. The people inside were up against the glass coughing and spluttering, trying to get out. Then we let go of the doors and made a run for it. They staggered out on to the street and fell on to the pavement, holding their stomachs and eyes, staggering around, vomiting, the full works.

The next morning, the police arrived at the coach and arrested everyone. The senior police officer made a solemn announcement: "We are going to have an identity parade and hold for trial those identified." One by one we filed past the police and the two witnesses, who were sporting marks to the face. One of the chaps who had been in the thick of it pulled his hood up and put a scarf over his face. Unbelievably, he was allowed to pass. Paul Grover, however, was immediately spotted. Perhaps it was his poor complexion which made him stand out. That was the end of the Fulham Two, as Peter Yokes had been arrested in San Sebastian for looting a Burberry and Lacoste shop.

Paul Grover received a six-week sentence. He was one unlucky chap, because in Marseilles in 1998 he was the only one of six English people jailed after the trouble between the English and the local Tunisians. The witnesses

picked out another four who, despite protesting their innocence loudly, were driven off at speed with the car's blue
lights flashing.

The snow was getting heavy now and it lent the Spanish
landscape a surreal quality. Not that it bothered Scarrott,
who was wearing his sombrero and singing "Si Si Senora"
for the umpteenth time.

A few hours later we entered Madrid. The cold air was
reflected in the faces of the Spaniards, who looked discom-
fited by it. It was obvious that this weather was a shock to
them. They were well wrapped up but somehow it didn't
look quite right, as if they were more used to bright summer
clothing. Salford was contemptuous of the architecture and
the people in general, shouting derogatory comments about
their heritage.

The coach pulled up outside the magnificent Bernabau
Stadium in Madrid. It was an impressive sight as it seemed
to tower almost into the clouds, but that didn't bother
Salford, who immediately led a raid on the stand outside,
looting it of T-shirts and badges, most of which had been
thrown away by the time we reached the first bar.

Eventually, we set up camp in a small bar two stops down
on the underground, and had San Miguels all round. As we
prepared to leave, Salford stood up on a table: "Right, you
lot. This is Spain and they are all filthy Catholics here.
Remember that the Pope is the Antichrist and that you
must never, ever trust a Spaniard. If it wasn't for Drake
defeating the Armada, we would be a colony of these
morons. We burned their boats off Cadiz and now it is time
for us to show these heathens once more that we are all
good English Protestants. We'll go out of here and roar
straight into the first mob of dagos that we find. Is that
understood?" He had a manic look in his eyes. For those
who didn't know him, listening to him must have been a

sobering experience. Everyone nodded, although there were some perplexed looks among us. "Is he for real?" someone whispered.

We left the bar. Coming out of the restaurant opposite at the same time was Terry Venables, now managing Barcelona and here for the match. "Behave yourselves, lads," he chirped in a bouncy voice, as if he was our best Cockney mate.

"Fuck off, you yid," shouted Salford in a reference to him having left Chelsea to play for Spurs. Terry hurried away, shocked at the reception he had received from his fellow countrymen.

Further down the road were a group of Spaniards. Salford roared into them, letting them have it with both barrels of his gas cartridges. They scattered but then regrouped and it became a running battle all the way to the ground. At least it kept us warm.

When we had finally arrived at the ground it was 18 February and we'd been travelling since the evening of the 15th. We had lost a few souls along the way, but this was what we were here for – to support our country. We were welcomed by unsmiling police as we went through the entrance. Inside the ground, the cold started to come up through our shoes, into our feet. We were positioned on a terrace behind the goal, with Spaniards spitting at us from above. At half-time, what someone thought was rain was in fact piss coming through the concrete above our heads. I experienced the worst feeling in the world as falling piss went down the back of my neck in the gap between my scarf and hair, sending a horrible cold shiver down the length of my spine. The knowledge of what caused the feeling made it even worse.

England played well and won the match 4–2, but the cold made this seem like an afterthought. As we left the ground there was a huge mob of Spaniards, at least 2,000 strong, waiting for us. You're scared at moments like these, but you know your mates won't lose it, and you hold it together because that's the way it has to be. Two thousand against sixty doesn't look like good odds on paper but, surprisingly, the numbers in this sort of scenario are irrelevant if every one of your firm decides to have a go. The Spaniards started advancing, but we started chanting and in the dark corners the sound echoed and reverberated, making it sound as though there were thousands of us. "We're the north stand, We're the north stand, We're the north stand Stamford Bridge."

"Come on, let's do it, let's fucking do 'em," someone frantically shouted in the midst of the grunting, roaring and shuffling sounds a large crowd makes exiting a ground. Then, the most vile blood-curdling roar from the depths of hell was uttered by Salford and a few others and the entire group charged. The Spaniards had already been backing off from the noise of our chanting, but the charge made them scatter. Small irregular fist-fights broke out. Dell Boy from Battersea saw one Spaniard with a brick advancing towards him. He was just about to pitch it when Derek lurched forward and caught him flush on the jaw. His lights went straight out, and he went down still holding his brick. Dell Boy picked it up and launched it into the retreating mob of his mates, causing one of them to go down. None of the Spaniards waited to help their mates, but legged it while the two on the ground copped a kicking. This was no poseurs' battle, waiting for the police to arrive and save you – it was every man for himself, a fight for survival and the Spaniards knew it. They backed right off, shocked at our ferocity, then waited at a safe distance for any single stragglers to leave our group.

Eventually the police arrived and we returned to the

coach in high spirits, only to be greeted by the sight of smashed windows. The thought of the cold journey chilled everyone, but there was nothing we could do. Just as we were about to leave, some West Ham boys came up and asked if they could get on our coach. "Clear off, you've been sneering at us for years. Now piss off and take your chances elsewhere. You think you're so bloody hard. Now go and prove it," shouted Dell Boy at them. When it suited them, they wanted to be all English together, but any other time they'd be whacking out our guys. Well, now they had their just rewards. They slunk off – good riddance.

We left Madrid huddled together for warmth, advancing slowly up the motorway in the worst blizzard Spain had seen in forty years.

The coach crawled north along the E25, with visibility of no more than a few yards. We passed the sign for Aranda de Duerro and after that the terrain became even more mountainous. The blizzard seemed to worsen. The Spanish landscape just didn't look right covered in snow. We felt like Buzz Aldrin looking across the Sea of Tranquillity for the first time. The snow reflected an eerie light.

I was sitting at the front and, like most people, I fell asleep. Suddenly, I was awoken by the most almighty crash, and found myself flung out of my seat. There was a horrible grinding of metal and smashing of glass, and after what seemed like an eternity, the coach shuddered to a halt. Shouts and groans filled the air. All the lights were out in the coach, but there was a faint glow from the snow. I looked around. The coach had hit a lorry which was parked up in the right-hand lane and had skidded to a halt. No lights were visible on the lorry.

By now, people were staggering out of the coach covered in cuts and bruises. The only explanation for the crash was that the driver of the lorry must have fallen asleep at the wheel. He climbed down. "There he is, get the bastard!" someone shouted. With that, the driver ran across the road to the other side and sprinted away across the fields.

The scene was one of utter devastation. Then there came a sound I never want to hear again as long as I live – out of the darkness came a lorry. The driver saw us, hit his brakes and pressed his horn. The sound of that lorry braking and skidding out of control made me feel sick to the pit of my stomach. I thought for a moment it was going to take us out like ninepins, but the driver regained control and continued on his way, not even bothering to stop. With that, somebody rushed forward and got a torch from our coach driver then ran down the road waving it frantically. We heard the sound of lorries honking as they saw the torchlight being shone. Whoever did that deserved a George Medal. They were risking their life, especially as the Spanish lorry drivers were speeding like maniacs in the dangerous conditions.

Then came the terrible realization that one of our mates was trapped in the wreckage. All we could see was a pair of trainers, not moving.

"That's Andy's red Adidas," said a voice in the darkness. It was Andy Rutledge who was trapped in the mangled wreckage of the coach. Looking at the state of it, I couldn't believe how many of us had got out without any damage.

"Andy, Andy, can you hear us?" Nothing, not a sound, not even moaning.

"Pull him out," shouted someone. So everybody tried to pull him free, but he was firmly trapped – pull as we might, he didn't move. "Stop pulling, we might damage him further if he's not already dead," I shouted. Still they tried. "No!" I yelled at them until they stopped. We stood there waiting in the freezing cold.

Eventually, the emergency services turned up. At least we now had a red light further down the road to stop any lorries crashing into us. They got out, looked at the coach, had a discussion in animated Spanish and stood there.

"Do something, then, you dago wanker," shouted Dell Boy. One of them intimated that he had no cutting gear, while his mate got on the radio. By now every emergency vehicle in Burgos must have turned up. The cutting gear finally arrived and Andy was cut out and placed gingerly in an ambulance. He looked close to death. The ambulance sped off while we were put into vans and bussed into Burgos.

When we arrived we were met by the mayor: "Welcome to Burgos. I am so sorry that you are coming to my wonderful town in such circumstances, but we will put you up in the Hotel Fernan Gonzalez where you can have free accommodation, food and drink and telephone calls back to your families in England. Those of you who require medical attention will be taken to hospital and returned here after treatment, or kept in if necessary."

Scarrott was moaning about his arm and went off in an ambulance. What a sight he looked in his stupid sombrero, by now crumpled and smelling of piss. He was right proud of the fact that his sombrero had prevented piss from landing on him. "*Touché*, dirty dago," he had shouted up at the Spaniards while others swore and cursed as the piss fell on them.

An hour later, he was brought back to the hotel by two very stern-faced policemen. As he walked in, he winked at me: "I've got just the thing to do the machines with." I had no idea what he was talking about. He told us what had happened. While he was in the hospital waiting-room, he had slipped out, smashed a window and stolen a magnum of champagne then started drinking it. He had got halfway through when he was called for treatment, so he stuffed it down his trousers and walked awkwardly in. Thinking he had damaged his leg, the staff tried to get his trousers off and realized he had a bottle stuffed down there. They then told the police to throw him out.

During the journey back to the hotel, he spotted a tool kit in the back of the car and stuffed that up his jumper. All he seemed worried about was the fact that the police had confiscated his unfinished champagne. "There's Schubert and now Scarrott with an unfinished one," I said to him. Scarrott looked perplexed then told everyone how he was going to do all the machines in the hotel as he now had "the equipment".

Within ten minutes, the two policemen were back at the hotel spitting blood. The manager got us all into the lobby and translated the policeman's stern words: unless the emergency tool kit was returned, everybody was going to be kicked out of the hotel. Without further ado and as calm as you like, Scarrott produced it, walked forward and placed it at the feet of the two policemen. They looked at him in complete incredulity. You could see it in their eyes: "What sort of person are you?" They barked something in Spanish at the hotel manager, then walked away with a shake of their heads.

I don't know what sort of bush telegraph they have in Burgos, but within a short while a hostile crowd had started gathering outside the hotel. That precluded any of us from revisiting the disco we had earlier gassed out. Someone even had the daft idea of going to see the lads who were in jail because of our previous visit a couple of days ago.

The next morning, while everybody congregated in the breakfast room, the *Sun* informed England what we had been up to: "GARY SCORES 4 AS YOBS SHAME ENGLAND; 500 GO ON RAMPAGE." In the same report, it stated that four England fans had been stabbed before the match. Ted Croker, the FA secretary, was devastated. Not about the four stabbed fans – no, he was devastated about the violence caused by English fans.

Suddenly, as a few left the breakfast room a huge commotion broke out. People walked out to see what was going on.

"I don't believe it, he's given us a bill for £1,500 for food, accommodation and telephone calls."

"Tell him to stuff it up his arse."

It was all arm-waving and remonstrating while we just shrugged our shoulders. A short time later a representative from the British Embassy, Vice-Consul Mike Murphy, turned up along with the mayor. He was ushered into a room and the door was shut. It looked like he was being held hostage until the money was paid by either us or him.

The £1,500 bill wasn't deterring us from ordering at will. The barman refused to open up a tab for Scarrott at the bar, so he obviously had some sense. Scarrott was ordering plenty of beer and persisted in calling every Spaniard Julio and Juan.

Some time later the British Embassy man, looking very white-faced, came over and addressed us. "You will be escorted by the police to Madrid via the train then taken to the British Embassy."

Sure enough, we were soon on the train. As we pulled into Madrid, half the Spanish army was there to meet us. They directed us into buses with metal grilles over the windows. The way the locals looked at us was amazing. You would have thought we were Basque terrorists. I half-expected them to start pelting us with rotten vegetables. One old lady with more wrinkles on her face than an Ordnance Survey map and no front teeth stared at us. "Do us a blow job," shouted Scarrott.

We disembarked off the bus at the British Embassy only to be met by nobody and found the doors firmly shut.

Someone pressed the buzzer. "We are the England football fans who were involved in the coach crash. Please open the door."

The answer that came back on the intercom stunned us: "We are not letting you in. Go away."

"Open the fucking door, you dago nonce." Then silence. Someone pressed the buzzer again for about twenty seconds. "Wanker!" he shouted down the intercom. He could have been shouting "Mayday" into a force ten gale. Nobody was going to answer.

We stood there, stunned. After a few minutes we retreated to a bar and took stock. Then someone had an idea, and back we went to the door and buzzed again. "Hello, my name is Alan Cartwright and I am a backpacker who has lost his passport. I need to see the British Consulate about getting a replacement." All spoken in a very posh and correct English public-school voice.

The buzzer sounded, opening the door, and through we surged, past the startled security guard. "Hello, Juan," said Scarrott with a stupid grin as we flew past him. We then staged a sit-in, demanding to see the British Ambassador. There was nothing they could do about it as we were on British territory. When they threatened to evict us someone retorted, "What are you gonna do, shoot us or watch us starve to death in Madrid?"

Eventually, someone came down to meet us. He looked very posh in his short-sleeved white shirt. Top of our list of demands was bacon rolls. They duly appeared about thirty minutes later. The man explained that as we had no insurance cover the British government was prepared to help us get back to England, but that we would be expected to pay the money back. He asked about those who had money and a few fools told him they did have some money, while everybody else kept quiet about whatever money they had in their pockets. The British Embassy representative then turned up and we gave him the bill.

A short while later a bus arrived to take us to the airport. It resembled one of Hickey's luxury coaches. "Bloody hell, are we gonna be in another crash?" asked one guy.

Eventually we got to Madrid airport and traipsed over to the British Airways check-in desk. The man from the Embassy became involved in a long discussion with someone there. He walked away, saying "Wait here." He returned about ten minutes later. "British Airways are refusing to have all fifteen of you on board their plane." A couple started shouting and swearing at him, while others shook their heads: "Why?" He held his hands out. He seemed to know something more, but he wasn't saying. To give him credit, though, he asked us to stay put and then got ten of us on to an Iberia plane, but he couldn't get us all on.

The choice was another night in Madrid or a coach for the others. The five lads who chose the coach wished they hadn't. It took them three more days to get home. They arrived starving hungry and exhausted. For the lads on the Iberia plane, myself included, the wait on the tarmac seemed to go on for ever.

As the plane took off we all let out a collective cheer, part happiness, part sigh of relief. As the plane climbed steeply, the landscape looked even more unforgiving. It was certainly a trip to remember, but for all the wrong reasons.

When we arrived back home, we were followed by hostile newspaper headlines from all over Europe, but we didn't care what they thought of us. Here are some examples:

France: The sickness of hooliganism comes from England like a scourge from the Middle Ages.

Italy: Barbarians live among us.

Germany: The English rowdies are no longer people – they are animals.

Spain: Some Britons cannot be controlled.

Belgium: Madness of hooligans. Keep the English out.

On Friday, 20 March, the *Sun* had its say:

NO MERCY FOR SOCCER YOBBOES IN BUS SMASH

A "Thugs Special" coach waited in the snow for help for 80 minutes. No Spanish drivers stopped because they were too frightened. The travellers were reported to be skinheads and National Front. Andrew Rutledge, 18, was last night in hospital with head injuries in a critical condition.

Amazed Consul General Trevor Llewellyn came face to face with several fans, including one who was wearing an SAS style mask.

"It's not our fault. We were just passengers involved in a coach crash," said Chris Henderson.

Then came the sickening part. While our friend lay in hospital fighting for his life, we endured the dubious distinction of being featured in "The *Sun* Says" leader column:

"Do you wonder that the Spanish wouldn't help the English soccer hooligans lying injured in the snow after their coach crashed? The yobs had only gone to Spain to beat up the locals. Many of them carried visiting cards in English and Spanish . . . It would have served them right if they'd died in the snow."

You had to read that at least twice to take it in. Of all the excesses ever indulged in by the press, that had to be up there in the top ten worst.

Upon our arrival back in England, the *Sun* newspaper vultures were waiting. No sooner had the lads walked through customs control than the photographers were snapping away and stuffing microphones under everybody's noses. No one said anything, just gave them the withering looks of contempt which are all you're capable of when your body has gone beyond fatigue. One of the scribblers stated with real conviction, as if he believed it himself: "Talk to us, we won't stitch you up . . . it's your chance to put the record straight." Right, mate. Not that it made any difference, because by Monday they had another story and didn't bother printing anything more about us.

We heard through the grapevine that another tabloid paper had paid for the air ambulance to fly Andy home. He and all of the other sixteen injured made a full recovery. It was a fitting tribute. In the world of the tabloids, we were leader-column material on Friday and a non-event by Monday. Not that we expected anything else. That summed it all up, really.

10

No One Likes Us . . .

Dougie and Eddy Brimson

Known as "The Lions", Millwall Football Club are more famous for hooliganism than any on-the-field footballing achievement. There seems to be something intrinsic in the psyche of the Millwall faithful that lends itself to violence, and despite being a relatively small club they loom large in hooligan history.

From their book *Capital Punishment: London's Violent Football Following*, which looks at the football clubs and hooligans in London, Dougie and Eddy Brimson look at the history of this much-maligned club.

For those who do not like or who have no interest in football, the mere mention of the subject of football hooliganism provokes the inevitable question: "Are you a Millwall fan, then?" Because as most people know, the supporters who have inhabited The Den over the years – both Old and New – have never been the best behaved.

For some, this is hardly surprising. The bulk of Millwall's support has always originated from the East End and the docks, traditionally the roughest and poorest parts of London. The combination of the two has seen the supporters develop a sort of "patriotic" pride in both their local area and the club, and they have been more than happy to defend this should the situation arise. Any attack on Millwall Football Club has always been regarded as a personal attack on the fans, but in some ways the problem runs deeper than that.

Like West Ham, when the club was formed (in 1885 as Millwall Rovers) it soon became an integral part of the community. Subsequent name changes (to Millwall Athletic and then plain Millwall) and a number of different grounds merely cemented this relationship, and by the time they moved to Cold Blow Lane in 1910, Millwall FC were as much a part of East London as the docks themselves. The club became a focus for those who lived in the area and, for many, their only escape from the poverty in which they lived. Thus it assumed major importance for them, and the success of the club became paramount. A more alarming aspect of this, however, was that those who visited Millwall were not always welcomed with open arms, primarily because they were seen to be "knocking" the East End, and there were numerous incidents of violence before the second world war. The first major outbreak happened in 1920 when, during a game against Newport, missiles rained down on the opposition keeper from among the home support. Unfortunately for him, he then steamed into the crowd to apprehend those who were throwing things at him and was kicked to the ground and beaten up for his trouble. The club were forced to close the ground for two weeks as punishment, something that was to happen with alarming regularity over the next fifty years. Indeed, the next such occasion was only fourteen years away. In 1934, the referee came under missile attack during a game against Bradford, which resulted in another two-week ban, while in 1938, the club were again fined for persistent crowd trouble involving their fans.

During the war, the docks and the local area received a

horrific pounding from the German bombers and [...]
many people were forced to move out of the area into the
surrounding suburbs. Once hostilities were over, however,
the rebuilding of London provided a great deal of employ-
ment, especially at the docks, enabling many of those who
had left to return. The club had retained a sentimental link
with the East End population and was still regarded by
many as a vital part of the community.

It was not long before the crowd violence returned. In
1947, the ground received yet another closure notice and
a £100 fine was imposed following trouble against
Barnsley. As was normal in those days, in the absence of
any real travelling support the focus of the crowd's anger
was the officials; in this case one of the linesmen was shot
in the chest with an air-gun. The next ground-closure
came just three years later, in 1950, and again it was the
officials who came under attack. Following a game against
Exeter City approximately 200 fans ambushed the referee
outside the ground, resulting in another seven-day closure
and a £1,000 fine.

By the early sixties, things were changing in Britain. The
rebellious youth of the "Teddy Boy" era were causing problems for society in general, and with transport becoming
more readily available, travelling supporters were beginning
to become a normal feature in football. From among that
element, there quickly grew a minority intent on confrontation, and Millwall soon developed a reputation as a rough
place for opposing fans to visit. Certainly the other London
clubs, who had always taken fans down to Cold Blow Lane,
were coming under increasing attack from the local supporters. The scale of this violence, and the nature of it, was never
more evident than in 1965. Early in the season, a policeman
was attacked by supporters on the pitch during the
Wrexham fixture, and this rattled the police more than

usual. They were now very concerned at the way things were going at the club and made sure that every game at The Den received their close attention. But the fans were now taking the trouble on the road as well, and the November London derby against Brentford saw football hooliganism touch a new low. There had already been fighting before the game, but during it, a hand-grenade came out of the Millwall enclosure and landed on the pitch. As it happened, the grenade was a dud, but no one was to know that at the time.

In April the following year, it was to be a player that bore the brunt of the fans' anger. Derek Dougan, having scored a last-minute equalizer for Wolves at The Den, turned to celebrate with a fan who had run on to the pitch. Unfortunately, the fan in question was from Millwall and promptly punched Dougan in the face before being apprehended by the police. In the year that England were to host, and eventually win, the World Cup, it was the last thing the FA needed; but there were no major repercussions for the club following this incident.

Millwall were now regarded by many as having the worst followers in the country, and for many visiting fans, the trip from New Cross station to The Den would provide one of the more scary interludes of their supporting lives. Violence involving Millwall fans continued almost unimpeded and with increasingly available and affordable travel, they were to indulge in hooliganism almost wherever they went. The wrecking of tube trains and "specials" became almost routine. It was a rough time for the club, but also for the game in general. It is important to note that while Millwall were undoubtedly one of the worst offenders, there were numerous clubs who were finding themselves saddled with this problem, not least because of the huge amounts of news coverage being devoted to it.

By the mid-seventies, the reputation of the Millwall

followers was all but carved in stone, but 1975 was to see another attack on an official – a linesman after the match – and also the stabbing of a Cardiff City supporter. Then in 1976, a Peterborough United player was punched in the face by a Millwall fan during a match. The supporters also staged a mass takeover of The Valley, running Charlton ragged and swamping the local area. While the exploits of the Millwall fans were common knowledge among the foot-ball-loving public, they were now thrust into the television spotlight in 1977 when they were featured on BBC Television's *Panorama*. The Millwall mobs were suddenly household names and assumed a level of infamy previously unimagined. Inevitably, they began to play up to this new-found image even more, if that were possible.

In 1978, the club received yet another ground-closure as a result of hooliganism. With the team already 3–0 down during an FA Cup quarter-final tie against Ipswich Town, the fans invaded the pitch in an effort to get the game aban-doned. After an eighteen-minute delay, the game continued and Millwall lost 6–1, but the fans had not finished. During disturbances inside and outside the ground, twenty-two policemen were injured. The FA immediately closed the ground for two weeks, fined the club £1,500 and banned them from staging FA Cup ties for the next two seasons. The Ipswich manager, Bobby Robson, went on record in the press to say that he thought that flame-throwers should be turned on the Millwall fans, while the Ipswich players confessed that even before the match they had been very concerned for their safety because of the intimidating nature of Millwall's ground. In truth, this was far from a rare thing at The Den. Numerous players of the period refused to take corners when they played there, because they simply did not know what would happen, be it abuse or even something worse. For the visiting fans, things were even more dangerous. It was bad enough inside, but getting in and out was a nightmare.

In April 1980, the Easter holiday saw Millwall visit Southend. Many of the fans travelled down on the Good Friday to make a weekend of it and it was not long before trouble erupted, not just involving Millwall and Southend fans but also groups of punks and skinheads who had all converged on the town. Thankfully, this trouble was fairly sparse but on the Monday of the game, the town was flooded with youths. The police, fearing the worst, split the groups and took as many football fans as they could find up to the ground. Meanwhile, they marched the other groups around until they got bored and left of their own accord. Trouble surrounding the football match was not far away, however. A small pocket of Millwall fans wrecked a pub in the high street, and another small mob fought with police at Pier Hill. A massive police presence ensured the game itself was fairly peaceful, but later that night a mob of sixty Millwall fans smashed up a pub on the seafront, putting every window through and attacking a policeman with bottles and ashtrays. In all, 118 people were arrested and although not all Millwall fans, the latter had hardly endeared themselves to the local population.

Back at The Den, things were still on a downward spiral. In 1980, a lump of concrete thrown from the terraces hit a linesman during the game against Shrewsbury, and the fans were involved in incidents throughout the country as they battled their way through the Third Division. In 1982 things took yet another turn for the worse. During an FA Cup tie against Slough Town, Millwall fans went on the rampage and fought with local fans as well as, it was rumoured, Chelsea supporters. The Millwall chairman went ballistic and threatened to close down the club if the fans' behaviour did not improve. The rest of that season was relatively quiet, but 1984 was to see the beginning of a steady rise in the number of incidents and a sharp increase in the number of high-profile ones.

The first of these took place on the night of a Milk Cup tie against their old foes, Chelsea. The West London club brought thousands to The Den and proceeded to swamp the area, in their favoured tactic. A concerted police action drove numerous pockets of fans from both clubs out of the side-streets, but eventually everyone ended up in the Old Kent Road, resulting in a massive off. Many people were injured, almost all by flying glass, as the police somehow managed to keep the fans apart. In the end, the home supporters managed to keep on top, and as far as they were concerned, the pattern was set. With trouble at football on the increase throughout the country and numerous mobs on the rise, the Millwall fans decided that if they were to enhance their reputation even further, they would have to go for it in a big way. Seeing off challenges from the likes of Chelsea was an essential part of that process.

The next incident involved another club Millwall were familiar with, Bristol City. City had always been a bit of a thorn in the side of the East End club because they were one of the few sets of supporters not afraid to have a go, either at home or away. The feud had started the season before, when City came to London and their fans wrecked one of the Millwall pubs. This led to the Millwall supporters exacting revenge when they next travelled to Bristol. They began this as soon as they got off the train, wrecking a pub three miles from the ground, then launched a series of ambushes and attacks on Bristol City's pubs. A number of Bristol fans were stabbed, while another suffered a broken back after a frenzied assault. The City fans then began to go on the offensive, mobbing-up and attacking Millwall supporters wherever they found them. Two Millwall fans were seized and thrown over a railway bridge; many more were attacked and suffered serious injuries. Inside the stadium, the situation was manic. The Millwall fans had infiltrated almost every part of the ground and trouble erupted almost immediately, before the police somehow managed to gain control.

A few weeks later, the City fans decided to take their own revenge for the broken back suffered by one of their number, and planned an attack on one of the Millwall firm's pubs. The Bristol pub that had been wrecked by Millwall next to the station had a huge wooden sign outside, and this was "liberated" by the City fans and taken to London the next time Millwall were at home. The City fans then sprayed "BCFC" on it in red paint and at half-past two, with the Millwall pub packed out, they pulled up and threw it through the pub window before doing the off. The Millwall fans were furious and decided that they would finish this once and for all.

When it came, the attack was almost unprecedented. The next time Bristol City travelled to The Den, their supporters' coaches were directed down a dead-end nine miles from the ground and totalled by a huge mob of Millwall supporters, using all sorts of missiles and weaponry. Everyone at both clubs was astonished at the ferocity of the attack, while the police were furious that they had been unaware of anything being planned. However, the fans weren't finished yet because worse was only a matter of months away. Millwall fans were soon to be involved in what has become not only one of the most infamous episodes in hooligan history, but also a turning point for football fans everywhere.

In March 1985, the Millwall fans travelled to Kenilworth Road for an FA Cup quarter-final tie against Luton. The club took thousands to this match and this led to many of the problems on the night as the police, already on full alert, were taken aback at the excessive numbers. The fans had already been involved in numerous incidents in the town, but the police forced them up and into the ground as quickly as they could. The problems inside began as the Millwall fans were crammed into the away enclosure which was clearly too small for them. Just after the start they spilled out on to the pitch, delaying the game for twenty-five minutes. Once the match restarted, a number of fights broke out in various parts of the ground but were soon dealt with by an increasingly nervous police force. With Millwall losing 1–0 and only ten minutes to go, several hundred fans spilled on to the touchline in an attempt to force the abandonment of the game. They forced their way through the police cordon on to the pitch but were repelled twice before the referee, himself a police inspector and determined to finish the game, blew for full-time. A soon as the whistle went, the Millwall fans flooded on to the pitch. The police had no chance. The fans went for the seated enclosure, ripped out seats and attacked the police with them. The police then regrouped and baton-charged the Millwall fans, who first pulled back and then attacked again. Other Millwall fans poured on to the pitch and astonishing scenes took place as the police, stewards and Millwall fans fought for control of the pitch. Eventually the Millwall fans began to calm down, but as they were driven out of the ground they kicked things off again, causing untold damage to houses and cars outside the stadium and wrecking the train taking them back to London. It was an episode that left forty-seven people, including thirty-one policemen, injured.

Football was shocked and the very next day, UEFA awarded Euro '88 to Germany, something the FA attributed directly to the Luton riot. However, of more importance was the fact that the violence had been screened on television and the entire country had watched open-mouthed as the events unfolded before their very eyes. That did it as far as the government were concerned, and Mrs Thatcher made it clear to the FA that if they did not sort things out, she would. The FA, reeling from this, hit the club with a £7,500 fine and made all the following season's Cup ties involving Millwall all-ticket affairs. For the hooligans, though, it was simply a massive result as they had shown everyone what they were capable of and they continued their activities. There was more trouble at Southampton and also at The Den, where seventeen fans were arrested and five injured during fighting when Millwall played Leeds United.

With the club now under attack from all sides, the fans continued on their path of destruction. In 1986, a football fan was stabbed by Millwall supporters during an attack at Charing Cross, and in Hove they caused mayhem before the Brighton game, smashing windows, fighting with locals and wrecking a pub. Later that season, a group of about forty Millwall fans staged a daring attack on a train carrying Charlton fans at New Cross station. They used bottles, bricks and even benches during the assault, as they attempted to fight their way on to the train to get at the opposing fans.

By now, in the post-Luton, Bradford and Heysel era, football was under intense scruntiny, with Millwall in particular under the watchful eye of the FA. As a result, things calmed down a little and the number of major incidents began to decline. Yet the hooligans still played up on their travels and it was clear that something more radical would have to be done. The key was to come up with the right idea – but sadly the matter was resolved for Millwall in 1989 by events at Hillsborough. As a result of the tragedy and the subsequent Taylor Report, the club decided that they would have to move to a new ground if they were ever to comply with all of the recommendations. When this was announced, fans everywhere let out a collective sigh of relief at the thought of the walk to The Den being no more. However, another three seasons would pass before the move was complete, which left plenty of opportunity to play up in the old spiritual home. In November 1990, the Millwall fans did battle with their local rivals West Ham, in what the local police described as "a flashback to the seventies". Four hundred fans fought with each other outside the ground, damaging property and injuring a number of policemen before order was restored. In 1992, the Arsenal striker Ian Wright was hit by a coin thrown from the Millwall enclosure at Highbury during a Coca-Cola Cup tie, and in the second leg his team-mate Nigel Winterburn suffered the same fate. In the following January, the Millwall fans went to Southend for an FA Cup tie and again caused mayhem, resulting in twenty arrests.

The last ever game at The Den in May 1993 was always going to be an emotional occasion but the club were ill-prepared for the events that unfolded as the team took to the field against Bristol Rovers. The longer the game went on, the more problems there were in the stands, with supporters tearing out seats and eventually invading the pitch. They then began ripping up the pitch and causing severe damage to the ground. In the end, it all degenerated into ugly scenes which did a major disservice to all of those linked with the club. It was a deplorable episode even by Millwall's standards.

The club now took up residence at the New Den and set out on the new season in optimistic mood. However, things didn't start very well as the fans went for it again in September, when there was severe crowd trouble at The Valley. Police were forced to separate fighting mobs inside the ground and made ten arrests, while the Charlton chairman was attacked by a fan supposedly from Millwall. More fighting erupted outside the ground as Charlton fans, furious at the events inside, fought back. This incident caused dismay at Millwall. Having moved into the smart new all-seater ground only weeks before, they were convinced that they had created an environment to calm the fighting hordes, yet this episode had made it abundantly clear that little had changed. It certainly made many at the club wonder if it was all really worth it. However, on the pitch at least, the season was finishing on a high. The team reached the play-offs and were all set to entertain Derby County at the New Den.

Such was the importance of this game, the police made it known that they would be all over the fans to ensure that things went peacefully – but the increasingly organized violence associated with the football mobs saw the two sets of fans indulge in a massive off in Rotherhithe more than an hour before kick-off. Police called in reinforcements to calm things down, but this was only a prelude to the events surrounding the game.

Derby

I have to say in all my years following Derby, I have never experienced anything like that game at Millwall. Outside was bad enough but once the game was underway, it was ridiculous. We all know Derby are no angels and certainly have a mob who look for trouble but those lot . . . mental. Totally mad. When the game started, the black players on our side were just given so much racial abuse it was disgusting. I really thought we had seen the last of all that, but these lot were really having a go. It was obviously getting to our players, especially Paul Williams who looked a bit shaky. Well, they were everywhere, fighting and giving out abuse, it was really scary. Near the end, when we knew that we'd won, we were all going mad but it was obvious that they were going to go on the pitch. I just didn't expect to see what I saw.

Just before the end, the two black lads were substituted, more for their own safety that anything else, but once the whistle went, the Millwall fans came flooding on. I saw one of them punch our keeper in the mouth, and then another load attacked Mark Pembridge as he ran off. How they all got off I'll never know, it was outrageous.

After the game, we were scared shitless. They were everywhere outside and were really looking for us. The police kept us in for ages but managed to get us on the coaches without much happening. We knew, though, that they would attack them and they did, even though we turned the lights off and closed the curtains. Bricks were bouncing off the windows within a couple of minutes, but we got out OK. I won't go back there though, ever. They were mental. Even women stood on the doorsteps were giving us two fingers.

This was an extraordinary incident. At the pre-arranged off at Rotherhithe, both sets of fans were using mobile phones to call up reinforcements before the police could get there. There were also groups attempting to ambush coaches carrying Derby fans as they came into London, while others were hiding in a council estate that they knew the Derby fans would have to cross. Similarly, after the game the Millwall fans rampaged through the car park for over ninety minutes, rolled a Radio Derby car on to its roof and fought with riot police. They then moved away from the ground into the tube, where fighting erupted again as Derby fans attempted to get away from East London. The FA immediately charged the club with failing to control its supporters and eventually hit them with a £100,000 fine, docked them three points and ordered them to play two matches behind closed doors. Incredibly, in spite of the history of trouble involving the fans, the FA suspended this punishment for three years.

The Millwall supporters were themselves coming under increasing attack from the fighting firms of other clubs, who saw them as not only fair game but prime targets as they sought to boost their own reputations. In 1994 there was a good example of this when Stoke City supporters smashed up and then fire-bombed two pubs in the Old Kent Road frequented by Millwall fans. It is fair to say that, by this time, the Millwall supporters, although still highly active on the hooligan front, were no longer the force they once were. The declining (playing) fortunes of the club, together with the advancing ages of many of the more volatile fans, saw their number of active hooligans markedly decrease. However, the undercurrent of hooliganism remained with the club and it surfaced again the following season when they were drawn to play Chelsea at the New Den in the FA Cup.

[. . .] There is no doubt that their supporters came in force and were determined to take over Millwall. Trouble began early on the Saturday morning as fans fought on the underground and in local pubs, but inside the ground it erupted just after the start of the second half when Chelsea supporters who had infiltrated the home fans began chanting and dishing out abuse. This led to a number of minor offs, but near the end of the game, Chelsea supporters in the away end began a concerted effort to get at the home fans, who responded with fists, boots and flying seats. With the game drawn, the replay at Stamford Bridge was always going to be emotive. Again fighting erupted before the game, but it was clear that the trouble at Millwall had stopped many of the East End fans from travelling. While the game was actually underway things remained quite calm, but once it went into extra-time matters got progressively worse. An attempted pitch invasion by the Chelsea fans was averted by the police, but they were soon under attack from the fans who were using seats as missiles. Then things really turned nasty when Chelsea's John Spencer missed his penalty to hand the tie to Millwall. The Chelsea fans poured on to the pitch and attacked two Millwall players, and with the pitch covered in furious Chelsea fans, it took mounted police to keep them away from the Millwall end. Large-scale violence was avoided by this police action, but outside things went from bad to worse as fans fought with bottles, bricks and missiles. The Millwall fans also used CS gas in an attack against the police and, at the end of it all, twenty policemen were left injured and thirty-three supporters had been arrested. The FA, again, were outraged, but this time it was Chelsea who took the blame and not just from the football authorities: the Chelsea chairman congratulated the Millwall fans in the stadium on their behaviour in the face of extreme provocation.

From that point onwards, the large-scale problems associated with the club began to decline, resurfacing only sporadically. The excellent work done by the club following the move to the New Den was beginning to pay dividends, as increasing numbers of family supporters were attracted back to their local club. On their travels it was often a different story as the aggressive attentions of the police usually ensured that the mood among the Millwall fans soon became an ugly one, and when things happened, they usually found their way into the papers. In August 1995, Millwall travelled to Reading, itself a club with a small but hostile following, and after the almost obligatory trouble before the match, things really got nasty when a 8½-inch spanner was thrown at, and narrowly missed, the Reading keeper. The police went crazy and made a nasty situation inside the ground even worse as they sought to arrest the individual responsible. The following day, the FA were furious and the papers were full of it, calling this yet another new low in the history of the club. Later that same season, a Millwall fan got on to the pitch and threatened the Sheffield Wednesday keeper Kevin Pressman, in full view of the television cameras. With many saying that it was only a matter of time before a player was seriously injured by a supporter getting on the pitch with a weapon, there was talk of bringing back fences. Thankfully, that came to nothing.

The reputation of the fans, although in decline following their relatively trouble-free recent history, still made them an attractive target for opposing firms and in April 1996 Stoke City supporters decided that they would attempt to turn the club over big-style. By all accounts, they put together a massive mob of around 300-400, with the idea that most of them would meet up and travel with the main bulk of fans while others would travel independently. However, the police had received information on their plans and arrested twenty-five known Stoke City hooligans in Dundee and another twenty in Cheltenham as they set out to travel to the game. They also managed to separate another 160 members of the Stoke firm from the main bulk of the support and kept them under close observation. The plan worked, but outside the ground, the Millwall fans, frustrated at the lack of opportunity to take these interlopers on, mobbed up and threw missiles at the 300 policemen on duty, seriously injuring a mounted officer and his horse.

At the end of that same season, Millwall went to Ipswich for the final game staring relegation in the face after a spectacular run of poor results. Some 2,500 travelled with the club and trouble erupted early on the morning of the game, as Millwall fans began to arrive in the Suffolk town.

The police, staging a massive operation to deal with the anticipated trouble if the club were relegated, attempted to keep the Millwall supporters in specific pubs, but this plan failed as the fans came into the town from all directions in a concerted show of strength. A 0-0 draw, and results elsewhere, left the club in the relegation zone and the fans went for it big-style, ripping up seats in the ground and hurling them at the police and rival fans. Despite the presence of 200 police and security guards around the pitch, the home side's end-of-season lap of honour was prevented, which caused more problems among the Ipswich supporters. When the Millwall fans were eventually let out of the ground, they clashed with rival supporters and again with the police, who by this time were in full riot gear. The trouble continued as the Millwall fans were escorted to the railway station and at least seventeen of them were arrested.

With the club now in the Second Division, the activities of the fans received little or no attention from the media. However, things were far from over and the reduction in overall support meant that the hard core formed a larger percentage of the travelling fans. For the police, this should have meant that they were easier to control, but that was not always the case as events at various clubs were to prove.

This is, of course, merely a brief history of the club's notorious supporters and it is fair to say that almost every time they travel away, things will happen. They have long-standing rivalries with numerous other clubs, but in particular Portsmouth, Birmingham (which we will look at later) and West Ham. Indeed, Millwall's East London rivals have been at the forefront of their attentions over the years (in one incident at Surrey Quays station they were ambushed by a mob of Millwall fans "armed" with pitbull terriers) and as far as Portsmouth are concerned, the list of incidents is endless. There have been attacks at Waterloo station involving almost 200 rival fans, and mobs of Millwall supporters terrorizing shoppers in Portsmouth city centre. More bizarrely, during one of Millwall's enforced absences from The Den, the club were forced to play their games at Fratton Park, which meant that every time they played there, the two sets of fans would have it away. One such, particularly violent, episode took place in 1978 and involved not only Millwall and Pompey but also Bristol Rovers and the newly formed Anti-Nazi League, who were intent on taking on the East London supporters. The city was overrun with people intent on fighting and it took a massive effort to keep them apart, one that only partly succeeded as a number of pubs were wrecked. Yet another crazy incident involving the Millwall fans took place at Reading when, following a 4–0 defeat, they began attacking Reading fans outside the ground. As they moved down into the town they began baiting groups of black youths, who themselves mobbed-up and attacked the Millwall fans with missiles and wooden stakes. This fighting continued for over forty minutes before the police could get a grip on it and severe damage had been caused to property in the town centre by the time the Millwall fans left. They were also implicated in a brutal attack on a man on a moped who was studying "The Knowledge". He stumbled across the Millwall fans while wearing an Arsenal shirt, for which he was dragged off his bike and slashed with a knife. When he called for help, another group of Millwall fans came over and gave him another beating for exactly the same reason.

It is important to stress that what we are talking about at Millwall is a minority of supporters, but it is also necessary to remember that it is a sizeable and very vocal minority. The financial problems associated with the club since early 1997 have caused severe unrest among the club's supporters in general, but the hooligan elements have been the ones who have responded more vehemently. The pitch invasion and subsequent trouble surrounding the Bristol City game at the New Den in February 1997 was evidence of this. These east London fans have always been regarded as among the worst-behaved in football, and that is a label they richly deserved. They have systematically taken violence around the Football League with them, and it is astonishing that they have been able to continue almost unchecked for so long. The FA, while happy to hand out fines and ground closures to clubs, seem unwilling to tackle the attitudes of the fans, and have left it up to the police and the club itself to control. Time will tell whether the club can sort out its financial problems, but if the evidence of its failure with its hooligan following is anything to go by, it is in severe trouble.

11

Robson's Boys

Colin Ward

Sir Bobby Robson was one of the best loved men in English football. He managed England from 1983 until the end of the nineties, and was one of the country's most successful managers, galvanizing the team on the field.

In his book *Steaming In*, Colin Ward looks at the hooligan element that followed England during this time when they had some success on the pitch, a team we could be proud of and an English manager who knew what he was doing.

After the World Cup, Ron Greenwood, the England manager, retired and Bobby Robson took over. Robson's first game as manager was in Copenhagen. England drew 2–2 but that fact was forgotten as the England fans created absolute havoc. It is a fact that is not well known that the Danish street gangs wanted to get in on the action right from the start. The general behaviour of the England fans, though, was quite despicable. I wasn't there, but all those who were present will tell you the same. Here the hooligans turned up because they knew that the Danish authorities would merely deport any fans found guilty of misconduct at the match. And so it proved.

The next big game for any England fan worth his salt was in Budapest. The game was played on 12 October

1983, and was generally regarded as the best punch-up ever had on the Continent. It is not yet common knowledge but football fans behind the Iron Curtain most certainly do have punch-ups at football matches. The Budapest fans who caused the aggro were supporters of Ferencvaros, the local Budapest team. England fans turned up on the train and as they all got off at the Nep stadium station the Hungarians were waiting for them. The England fans, and especially the Chelsea supporters, thought this was great fun and an almighty confrontation ensued. It was fist and boot, and for those present a great time was had by all. The police turned up and broke it up, but it has still gone down as the number one punch-up.

This was also the game when Hickey and his pals stitched up the Football Association Committee. The FA people, and especially Ted Croker, the Secretary, are really extremely patronizing and do not like England fans travelling. They have never bothered to try to sort out the genuine fans or make them feel welcome. Hickey and the Chelsea fans were not popular, partly because of their blatant racist views (with which I do not agree) and partly because of their anti-social behaviour. Chelsea fans have the habit of drinking in the bar of the particular hotel where the England team are staying. This infuriates the FA officials who, in my opinion, take a completely pompous attitude. It is also a great way for fans to try to pick up tickets. Sometimes a naive player will organize some complimentary tickets – usually a small-club player who doesn't really know he is supposed to be above a travelling fan.

On this particular day one of the Chelsea fans approached the FA people, who were in the foyer of the Intercontinental. They had a table set up and the system was that people who were on the list could pick up tickets. The Chelsea fan went up to the desk and enquired whether there were any spare tickets. He was asked his name and the FA man went through his list. When the name was not found on the list he said gleefully, "No, and you won't get in because the match is sold out."

The Chelsea fan had noticed a name on the list and he walked back to the bar and said to his friend, "Go up to the desk and say you are V. Brown." He did this and got V. Brown's tickets, at the same time picking out another name on the list. This went on until all the Chelsea fans in the bar had tickets. The drink flowed all afternoon and when Ted Croker came down into the foyer looking smug he was greeted with the Chelsea fans waving the tickets in the air with shouts of "Look what we've got, Ted!" The FA officials were left with red faces.

After the game the fun continued. The Ferencvaros fans wanted to have a go at the England fans but were stopped by the police. The England fans, led by Hickey with a map, walked around the streets and came out behind the Ferencvaros fans and everyone had a really good punch-up again. Hickey was nicknamed "General Hickey" by some northern fans. His reputation was made. As well as this there was also the scene of scores of England fans storming out of the Intercontinental hotel for a punch-up, then returning casually to the bar for a drink.

The climax of the European Championship's qualifying competition was coming up. England were playing Luxembourg away. The same day Denmark were playing in Greece and if Denmark won they would qualify for the European Championships in France in the coming summer. Both games were being played at the same time on 16 November 1983. I had made plans to go to the England match with Keith Chitty. The Luxembourg authorities were very nervous about having thousands of England fans in the tiny principality, especially if Denmark won – although the media were predicting that Greece would win. A lot of England fans were going to travel. The scene was set for a confrontation.

Dave Kelly is a nutter, Leatherhead's equivalent of Smiler, but at that time I didn't know this. I learned his nickname was "No Marbles", due to his conspicuous lack of brains. Keith had decided to travel to Luxembourg with his fiancée, Sandra, so I decided to travel alone; but Dave Kelly made up his mind to travel with me. I didn't know how crazy he was until the night before I left and Sammy White approached me in my local pub.

"Are you going to Luxembourg with Kelly?"

"Yes, why do you ask?"

"Because he'll get you both locked up."

I had arranged to meet Kelly at Leatherhead station and we were travelling down to Dover for the overnight ferry to Ostend. The train journey to Dover was uneventful. I met a few people on the train and from what I could see every thug in England had decided to travel to Luxembourg. Kelly and I bought some beer and he started drinking as soon as the train left Victoria. The police, mindful that trouble might erupt, were waiting at Dover, and some also got on to the ferry. The ship departed and as usual everyone made their way to the bar at the front. But the captain had decided, under police advice, not to open the bar. I could see this as counterproductive, because the duty-free shops would still be open and the idiots would be drinking spirits instead of beer. I even went down and spoke to the captain, but he had made up his mind. Sure enough, the idiots went into the duty-free shop and bought plenty of spirits. Kelly bought a litre bottle of Bacardi and half a bottle of gin. This was on top of the six cans of McEwans Export he had bought in Leatherhead.

The boat berthed at Ostend, to be met by a huge

contingent of Belgian riot police. The British police felt smug and clever because they had kept the bars shut and, they felt, avoided trouble, but most people had slept on the ferry anyway. There was plenty of time for drinking over the next forty-eight hours, so why get pissed on the ferry and be refused entry to Belgium?

Everyone boarded trains under the watchful eye of the police. Next stop Brussels. The train arrived at about 7 a.m, and by this time Kelly had teamed up with a particularly odious character called Peter, who had no money and no gear and was intending to live on his wits for two days. At Brussels there was a bar on the concourse, and a lot of people went over and had a drink while waiting for the train to Luxembourg. Kelly went over with Peter and ordered a beer.

"Oi, you Belgian whore, give us a lager," shouted Kelly.

"Yeah, slag, pour the beer," joined Peter.

The Belgian woman spoke back in Flemish, but she knew what they were saying. They continued in the same vein, thinking it was really funny, and other England fans soon joined in this great sport. It is not unusual for England fans to act like this abroad, but I find it distasteful in the extreme.

I went for a walk round the station to see who was about. I noticed a big group of Scousers milling around, and I spoke to one of them. They had been thieving in Brussels and they knew that it would be even easier pickings in Luxembourg. I walked back across to the bar and heard Kelly being very loud. Just at that moment Keith and Sandra walked up to me. They had purposely avoided Kelly and didn't realize he had come with me. Kelly also spotted Keith and Sandra and came over. "Hello, Sandra, give us a kiss," he shouted. Sandra flushed bright red with embarrassment and told Keith she wanted to sit down somewhere. They made their excuses and left. By now Kelly was getting extremely loud. I was pleased when the train arrived and we boarded. I made my way through the carriages and found two seats. Kelly sat down.

"Oi, Kelly, don't drink all that drink or else you'll be out of the game by Luxembourg."

Kelly took no notice, but opened up the half-bottle of gin and started mixing it with orange juice. "This will dilute it," he said.

The Belgian people already on board the train looked at us anxiously. This was the cream of English hooliganism. Kelly finished the gin and immediately opened the Bacardi, swigging back the bottle. "I'm going for a walk down the train," he said.

"All right, mate, see you later."

He walked off and I started playing cards with four Southampton fans. A young England fan climbed on to the luggage rack, stretched out and went to sleep. The Belgian passengers looked at him in absolute horror. The guard walked through but did not notice him. Half an hour later Kelly staggered back. He had demolished a third of the Bacardi and was very drunk.

"Go easy, Dave."

"Stop worrying, Ginger, you sound like my mum."

Two pretty girls were sitting across from us and Kelly spotted them. He leaned over them; God only knows what his breath smelt like.

"Hello girls, fancy a drink?" They looked frightened. "Come on girls, have a drop of this," he said, offering them the Bacardi bottle.

"Leave it out, Dave," I said.

"What's the matter, girls, don't you fancy me? You think I'm pissed, don't you?"

"Dave, they don't think, they know you're pissed. Now leave them alone and go back up the train," I said.

Kelly staggered off again with all the other passengers whispering as he walked past. Occasionally he would stop and offer some poor Belgian a drink. One of the Southampton fans turned to me.

"Your mate is going to be in a right state by the time we get to Luxembourg."

I agreed and decided to walk up the train and have a few strong words with him. I entered a carriage through the automatic doors and Kelly was standing on a seat in full flow. He was providing the entertainment for the whole carriage of England fans. I went up to him and grabbed him. "Kelly, now listen here. I'm warning you, if you drink that whole bottle then I'll have nothing to do with you." People in the carriage were jeering at me; after all, I had ended the cabaret. One guy with a Manchester accent shouted at me, "Don't be a spoilsport, pal, let him get on with it." I stormed over to him. "You can piss off. If you enjoy his company so much then you look after him when we get to Luxembourg."

I turned and walked out of the carriage, with Kelly shouting, "Come on, Ginger, I'm only having a little drink. Fellow Arsenal fans shouldn't fall out." I could hear the roars as Kelly took another swig at the bottle while I walked away.

Once back in my seat I continued to play cards. I forgot about Kelly and just concentrated on my poker hands. Just before we got to Luxembourg I saw an incident which summed up the English fan mentality. We were sitting in a non-smoking carriage. Notices were everywhere, but still English guys lit up. One was puffing away as the guard came through, and a Belgian woman sitting with her husband pointed it out. The guard walked over and asked for his ticket, pointing out to him in Flemish that it was a non-smoking carriage.

"I don't speak that foreign crap. Speak in English, you

moron," shouted the England fan. The guard looked at his ticket, snatched it from the fan, and walked away down the train.

"Oi, you wanker, that's a return, bring it back!"

Two Leeds fans sitting further down the train grabbed the guard and took the ticket off him, returning it to its owner. The guard retreated, but the England fan did put out his cigarette. (When the train did finally arrive in Luxembourg, the woman who had complained was spat at by the England fan.)

"Right, lads, final hand," said the Southampton guy.

"Well, deal a good one," I replied.

The train was almost in Luxembourg when someone tapped me on the shoulder. I turned round and standing in front of me was someone I didn't know. "Your pal Kelly has collapsed and is unconscious."

"What happened?"

"Everyone bet him he couldn't drink the last third of the Bacardi bottle straight down – but he did, and he collapsed. You'd better come and get him."

I grabbed him by the lapels on his coat. "Listen here, you had the fun out of him so you get him up the station to an ambulance. Now clear off."

He turned and walked away, and I looked for Keith and Sandra.

"Keith, Kelly's collapsed."

"Bollocks to Kelly! He's a nutter," he shouted to me, and hurried off the train and up the platform with Sandra.

Kelly was carried off the train and thrown on a luggage trailer, then pushed along the platform. I stayed at a discreet distance, just to make sure I was not pointed out as his pal and asked to pick up the hospital bill. The guys pushed him up to a large contingent of riot police who had met the train. One look at him and they quickly summoned medical assistance. Kelly was rushed to hospital to have his stomach pumped. The look on the faces of the riot police told the whole story: their nightmares were coming true, the savages had arrived. Luxembourg was under siege. What would the next forty-eight hours hold for them?

I proceeded out of the station and up the road. I stepped into a bar and met a couple of interesting guys. One was called Paul, the other Bud. Paul was just twenty-one, worked in Berlin and was, like myself, an Arsenal supporter.

Bud was six feet tall, swarthy, and had a Zapata moustache.

He had been to Luxembourg the last time England had played there, and he said that the place to go was Barbarellas, but it was shut and during the time we were there it stayed shut. The three of us sat at the bar ordering beer and chatting. Paul had nowhere to stay and suggested we share a room. We walked about the streets but most hotels and guest houses had "full" notices in the windows. I couldn't believe they were all full, and indeed, one guest house proprieter who spoke perfect English confirmed my suspicions. He told me that the Luxembourg people had seen on TV the destruction England fans had caused everywhere, and a prominent newspaper had condemned the Luxembourg authorities for allowing the match to go ahead in the city. I said to him, "Not all Englishmen are the same."

"Come back and tell me in forty-eight hours; we shall see." We tried another hotel. I could see all the room keys hanging on the board so I knew they had vacancies. I rang the bell and a woman appeared. "Vacancies?" I asked.

"How many?" she replied.

"Just a room for two."

"Do you want to see it?"

"Yes please."

Suddenly the expression on her face changed to one of complete terror. I heard English voices coming from outside.

"In here lads, looks like a result."

I turned and saw about twenty guys coming in the door. "No vacancies, full up!" she screamed fearfully. I walked out quickly and turned to Paul. "We've got to lose that lot or else we won't get anywhere."

We were lucky in that Paul spoke German, and we got a room on the strength of that. A lot of England fans had got into hotels somehow, but now there seemed to be a block on any more. We had a quick wash and went out on the town, returning to the bar where Paul and I had been drinking earlier. Peter, the chap who had been abusing the Belgian woman with Kelly, was in the bar. Paul knew him and they began to drink together. I found Peter obnoxious because of his love of abusing foreigners, so I left and decided to visit Radio Luxembourg. I didn't have a match ticket but I went into a newsagent's and they were selling them across the counter. I bought one, but as I went to leave the shop I saw two England fans come in the door, grab a load of confectionery and run out again. It was all over in a flash, but I felt extremely embarrassed. The shock of seeing such blatant thieving made me wonder what the local people would think of us.

As I walked past a restaurant I heard a bang on the window. I looked up to see Keith and Sandra, so I walked in and up to their table and sat down.

"Where's Kelly?" asked Keith.

"In hospital, having his stomach pumped."

"How much did he drink?" asked Sandra.

"Six cans of McEwans, half a bottle of gin and a litre of Bacardi."

Keith burst out laughing.

"I think his luggage has gone to Switzerland," I said.

"What about his passport?" asked Sandra.

"That's in Switzerland too."

We decided not to talk about Kelly and left the restaurant to go and see if we could have a look round Radio Luxembourg, but when we got there, the girl on reception would have none of it.

"I am a famous disc jockey in England," I said.

She passed a sticker through the hatch. At that moment a real English disc jockey who worked on the station came in the door. "All right, mate?" I said.

"Hello. Here for the match?" he asked.

"Yeah. Any chance of a tour of the station?"

"Any other time perhaps, but not until all the England fans have left. The Luxembourg authorities are frightened of trouble."

We walked out into the cold night air. It was mid-November and there was a definite chill. The city looked grey and bleak, and the colours of the buildings seemed to sum up its mood. It was a city living in fear. We walked down to the ground and popped into a bar. A few England fans were sitting on bar stools. A few of them had had a lot to drink and were explaining that they had nowhere to stay. Keith had discovered a middle-aged Portuguese guy and was doing his party piece with him. He was reciting the England 1966 World Cup team and laughing at the older man's pronunciation. I have seen Keith do this on many occasions and it can be quite funny.

"Gordon Banks!" shouted Keith.

"Bobby Charlton!" shouted back the Portuguese.

Keith pulled a face to insinuate ugliness, and shouted, "Nobby Stiles!"

At this point the foreigners usually burst out laughing and gesticulate to indicate that Nobby had no teeth. Of course we know this, and it makes for a bit of fun. Keith always does it in good part and once he gets a bar full of foreigners going it really is pure theatre. After the name recital he will then go through a goal that Bobby Charlton has scored. On this particular night the other England fans in the bar thought this was the funniest sight they had ever seen – one of them even fell off his stool but was still laughing when he hit the ground.

The Portuguese chap went out to his car to fetch a football. He wanted to show us the goal that was scored in the 1966 World Cup Final in extra time – the famous one from Geoff Hurst that possibly didn't cross the line. Chalk was used, and everyone joined in the argument, including some people walking past. Keith shouted out "Paul van Binst!" (a famous Belgian footballer), and everyone wanted to shake his hand. The Portuguese guy left the bar gesticulating wildly, but returned ten minutes later with his wife. He asked us to go with them, so Keith and I, along with Sandra who is frightened we will get our throats cut, left the bar, which was still in uproar.

The Portuguese guy took us to see his son, who spoke good English and lived in a very attractive house. He explained to us that his father would consider it a great honour if we would dine in his house. I accepted gladly, but Keith had to talk Sandra into it. We arrived at his house and his wife cooked us a meal while we all consumed large quantities of wine. The poor woman was not amused, as her husband, Keith and I went through every footballer who had ever put on a pair of boots. Sandra was getting filthy looks from the wife and began to feel uncomfortable, so we decided to leave. It took us about fifteen minutes to say goodbye, and Keith promised to take him to the match the following night. I had been around his house, met his family, eaten at his home and still I didn't know his name. As we left his house and made our way across the freezing ground back to the centre of town I suddenly realized that his wife had not bothered to say goodbye to us. I bet the man took some verbal abuse that night.

Keith and Sandra headed for their hotel. It was gone midnight, but I didn't feel like sleeping yet. Although it was late and the temperature had dropped below freezing, English fans were standing around talking. I struck up a conversation with some fellow Londoners.

"Anywhere to get a drink?" I asked.

"Most places are shut," they replied.

A shifty-looking guy approached us. "Looking for a drink? Woman perhaps?" he asked in accented English.

"Yeah, where?" I replied.

"Follow me," he said.

"You coming, lads?" I asked the Londoners.

"No, Ginger, you go ahead. I bet it's rubbish."

I followed the small guy up a narrow street, surveying him from head to toe. He was about five foot eight, slim and reasonably well dressed. I looked behind me in case it was a set-up, but I didn't think it was. He walked up to a door and banged on it twice. The door opened and I was ushered in. Once inside I noticed a small bar with two women serving beer to about thirty or so England fans. There were small lamps on the wall giving out a dim light, and sitting in the darkness were three women and a guy. As I looked at them the man beckoned me to go over. I ordered a beer and went across to him. He spoke English, but not well, and looked a typical Belgian with the customary moustache.

"These are my girls. Want to join them?"

"Depends how much."

"Three thousand Belgian francs."

"Fifty quid? You must be joking."

He smiled at me. "English not so rich; you stick to drinking, eh?"

I returned to the bar and struck up a conversation with two overweight Yorkshiremen. They were Huddersfield supporters, and had nowhere to stay. They told me that they hoped this bar would stay open all night so that they could prop it up. I didn't blame them, for it was freezing outside. They spoke to me loudly and I took the Mickey out of their accents.

"You bloody Cockneys are all piss-takers. I suppose you're Chelsea. I bloody hate Chelsea."

A couple of young guys were drinking next to us and heard the remark. They walked over.

"What did you say, you northern div?" one asked.

"Leave it out, they were having a joke," I said.

"I do bloody hate Chelsea," said the Yorkshireman – but in fun, not aggressively.

The two Chelsea fans, for that's what they were, squared up. They were barely nineteen years old and didn't look very tough, but one of them was holding his hand inside his coat as if he had a knife. I looked at him. "You aren't going to pull a blade in here, and we both know it," I said. The other young fan punched the Yorkshireman but it barely brushed his head. I grabbed him and pushed him back. "I said leave it out."

The two Yorkshiremen didn't want to fight – they were just friendly big-mouths – but if a fight had started they would have slaughtered the two young Chelsea fans. I don't think they had an ounce of malice in them, but the woman behind the bar had seen the punch thrown and decided to shut the bar. The two Chelsea fans left in a huff, glaring at the three of us. I turned to the two Yorkshiremen. "Sit tight, they might serve us a beer in a minute."

The guy sitting in the corner with the three girls stood up and came over. "No more drink. Englishmen want to fight."

"Come on, mate. The two hotheads have left."

We pleaded with him to serve us some more beer, but he wouldn't listen. The three of us were the last to leave the bar. I scurried back to my hotel feeling a bit peeved,

leaving the Yorkshiremen to sort out the best way of finding accommodation. The next day I bumped into them
and they told me that they had found a strip club, gone in,
bought one beer and fell asleep. The owner had let them
sleep until seven the next morning. When I got back to my
hotel there was chaos. Some England fans had thrown a
wardrobe down the stairs and police were in the hotel
arresting and arguing with everyone. I finally got to bed at
three in the morning.

I was rudely awoken at seven the next morning by Peter,
who was washing his face in the sink next to my bed. "Oi,
what are you doing in here?"

"Paul let me jump in the room."

"Piss off, you ponce, you have just woken me up."

I was annoyed, mostly because I didn't like him. He
didn't offer me any money for staying in the room – but
that just summed him up.

I got dressed and left Paul and Peter to their own devices.
On the streets the police and army were putting on a show
of strength. I walked down to the railway station where
England fans were still arriving. I stood on the pavement
talking to different people, trying to find out what had been
happening. Rumour was that a jeweller's shop had been
done, and also that if England didn't qualify then all hell
was going to break loose. I knew that a large contingent of
West Ham fans was in town, but I was most surprised when
I saw other London fans with them, even a few Millwall.
Most of them were drinking further up the town in Club
42. I decided to give it a wide berth and settled down in a
little bar with some other Arsenal fans, where I heard that
there had been trouble on a train between Cockneys and
Manchester United supporters.

This is the part of away travel that I enjoy the most – sitting
in a bar and just spending time in small talk. There is no rush

to down the beer and you hear some wonderful stories and meet some real characters. As you may have noticed, I have a tendency to nickname people, and when a guy who looked like Tony Woodcock (the Arsenal footballer) walked into the bar, it wasn't very long before everyone was chanting "Woody, Woody". The bar we were in was very popular, and about mid-afternoon Hickey turned up and stood outside where a big crowd was gathering. The army and police thought it was time to shut the bar, and came in. "No more beer in this bar," the army captain said, and told the proprietors to shut down. Everyone went outside and was milling around. The army, looking smart and carrying big truncheons, were very nervous. The captain of this particular group had a pair of specs; he came over to the group. "You must all disperse. We cannot allow big groups to hang around the streets."

"You shouldn't have shut the bars then, you stupid pillock," someone shouted.

A few army men walked past; all had at least one stripe, some two. A sharp-eyed Londoner spotted this. "Oi, captain, don't you have any privates in your army?" he shouted out. Everyone burst out laughing. A few people started saluting the army and shouting "Attention!" and "*Sieg Heil!*" It was a tense situation, but all of a sudden everyone just walked off in different directions. The army stood perplexed, not knowing which group to follow. I went for a walk on my own and bumped into a few faces I knew and people I'd met the previous night. Fat Graham approached me. He was an overweight Chelsea fan who went to all England games.

"All right, Ginger?"

"Yes, fine. Where's everyone drinking?"

"Near Club 42."

"What's up there?"

"A few of the guys are going to do the Giorgio Armani

shop later on. They've already cased it out. Are you coming
up there with us?"

"No, it's not my scene."

I left, found a quiet bar and had a drink with a couple of
other people who, like myself, didn't like the mood that was
spreading among the England fans. If we didn't qualify
then this city would be wrecked; win or lose, certain groups
were going to use the occasion to loot and steal. I left the bar
at about 5.30 and decided to go for a stroll around the city.
The faces of the Luxembourg residents told the story. They
were nervous and fearful of the coming night. The army
didn't seem to know what to do. Most England fans had
been drinking and were in a good mood. Everybody knew
we would beat Luxembourg, and we just hoped Greece
would help us out against Denmark.

As I approached the traffic lights near the ground I spotted a huge group of fans. They were the "wild bunch", and
were walking across cars, helping themselves to food in
shops and generally terrorizing the inhabitants. A security
van pulled up at the lights and stopped alongside them. In
a flash a young England fan opened the back door. The van
was stuck, as there was a car in front of him. The driver
suddenly realized what was happening. He quickly manoeu-
vred to his left and accelerated through the red light. Cars
coming in other directions were forced to brake and swerve.
He shot off up the road with his door banging away, wide
open. I don't think anything was taken but this seemed to
inflame the mood of the fans, who smashed the window of
a petrol station when the owner would not let them into the
shop. I moved away from them and cut across some waste
ground. Again I bumped into Keith and Sandra.

"Hello, Keith."

"Hello, Ginger. Kelly's dead."

"Don't be silly. Who told you that?"

"One of the blokes who was with him on the train."

"I don't believe it."

I felt awful. What would his family say to me? I felt responsible and hoped against hope it wasn't true. We walked down the road to the ground, and there, standing outside the entrance, was Kelly, looking dreadfully pale. For the first time on the trip I was really pleased to see him.

We entered the ground together. The ground itself is very small, and the England fans were all gathered at one end surrounded by barbed wire, metal fences and riot police. Parts of the terraces were shut off and were full of police. The back of the terraces has a walkway, and we walked to the far end and stood next to the fence in front of the corner flag. Some people had radios and were listening for news of the match in Greece. Denmark had scored two goals. It didn't matter what happened here; England were out.

The mood on the terraces became violent. Despite England scoring two early goals, people started trying to pull down fences at the front. I went to the back of the terraces and saw a large group of England fans leave the stadium. It was at the back of the terraces that all the action was happening. All feuds and battles were back on; inter-club rivalries would not now be forgotten. I stood at the back of the terrace on my own and laughed at the irony of it all. We had come all this way to have a party, yet it had been spoilt by events hundreds of miles away. I heard a voice nearby and looked up. In front of me were four people, one of whom was snarling at me. He had a moustache and a northern accent, was in his early twenties and was stockily built.

"What are you laughing at?"

"I'm laughing because I think it's funny."

"What's funny?"

"All of us standing here, being upstaged by a little country called Denmark."

I could see that he was going to hit me, and he had three other people with him. I decided to give it my best shot. I didn't realize it, but the big group of London fans had got together and were attacking and beating groups of northern fans. A couple of them had spotted the four picking on me. I didn't see them approach and the scowling face in front of me changed to one of shock and pain as a punch hit him on the side of the head. His eyes rolled around in their sockets and he staggered forward and dropped on to one knee just in front of me. His friends all ran as the Londoners went into them. The Cockneys, tired of the chase after ten yards, turned and walked back past me. They were laughing.

"Cheers, lads," I said.

"No problem, mate, any time," one replied, and continued walking.

One of the group, which consisted of Chelsea, West Ham and Millwall fans, walked over and kicked the kneeling fan in the ribs.

"Go on, mate, give him a dig. After all, he was gonna do you."

I looked at the poor fellow, who was on all fours but was trying to get up. I walked over and pulled him up by his lapels. "I'm still laughing, mate. How about you?"

With that I punched him in the stomach and let him go, leaving him to slump to his knees once more. I decided to go and stand near the London fans as it seemed safer, and I had a conversation with a couple of them. Then I went to the toilet, which was underneath the terraces. I walked down the concrete steps just behind a fan who, I noticed, had MUFC (which stands for Manchester United Football Club) tattooed on his hand. He went up to the urinal and as he stood there a Londoner, who must have followed us in, came up behind him and kicked his legs away. He hit the urine-covered floor with a sickening thud. Three guys then set about him with their boots, one hitting him in the side of the head and causing it to jerk violently back and strike the wall behind the urinal. I thought the kick had killed him, but he still had his wits and curled up against the wall plumbing. The three Londoners were in no rush, and stood back picking their spots to aim at. I just ignored the assault, as did two others who were in the toilet at the same time. But one other guy tried to leave. He was barely twenty years old and petrified. One Londoner confronted him.

"Where are you from?"

"Birmingham," he replied, the fear evident in his voice.

"Birmingham supporter are we? I fuckin' hate Birmingham."

"No, mate."

"Don't tell me: you don't go to watch any team regularly."

The Londoner knew the poor guy was frightened out of his mind, and was enjoying the sight of him shaking. The two other Cockneys had tired of kicking the prostrate and motionless Mancunian and walked over. One of them grabbed the young fan by the hair.

"Do you fuckin' want some?"

I turned and walked up to them. "Come on, just get the main faces. You know the people you're after."

The one who had hold of his hair looked at me. His face broke into a smile. "You struck lucky, pal?" he said, looking at the young and frightened fan. We walked up the steps and the guy from Birmingham thanked me. I don't know what happened to the Mancunian who had taken a bad kicking. I was just pleased to get out of that toilet.

All through the rest of the game it was the same: any non-London fans were going to get it. For the first time at a football match I felt really fearful of what might happen. The vicious kicking handed out to the Mancunian had shocked me. The final whistle went and everybody surged out of the ground. The riot police tried to keep everyone together, but splinter groups just broke away. I had never seen anything like it. Most people were determined to smash and destroy. The group I was following threw a road-works sign at a police motor cyclist, causing him to fall off. Within seconds he was being kicked, and one young fan tried to steal his gun. The riot police charged in to save him. Windows were being smashed with bricks, and the looters saw their chance.

A road sign went straight through the middle of the window and the rest of it was knocked out by a couple of others with big lumps of wood. Two people moved in with cardboard boxes and filled them with jumpers, best cashmere Giorgio Armani. These would be highly resaleable back in England. Chancers who were going past dived in and grabbed jumpers. It was all over in less than two minutes. People were waiting round the corner and the booty was put into holdall bags. Everyone dispersed and agreed to meet up later at the train station. The two bag-carriers went on their way – two mugs who had to do as they were told. They just liked the thrill of hanging round hard men and nutters.

It was then that the plan went wrong. The two bag-carriers walked into a street and a riot van came down it in the opposite direction. The carriers lost their nerve, dropped the bags and ran, leaving the riot police to retrieve the jumpers. I saw the same two on the corner of the main street by Club 42. They were frightened to go back to the meeting place because they had lost the gear. I left them looking very scared.

The Scousers, many of whom had left the ground during the match, were concentrating on the jewellers' shops and a good few were looted. People who were probably law-abiding citizens at any other time just went berserk. The faces of people as they went into a smashed shop and grabbed goods were amazing: all signs of reason had disappeared from their eyes. One guy came out of a shop with his eyes rolled up, his tongue hanging from an open mouth and breathing heavily. His trip into the shop had been positively a physical experience, and he was beginning to smile. He had dared and won. Others, of course, were not so lucky and were grabbed by riot police. Later they would all plead their innocence to the watching world. In a very short space of time the streets of Luxembourg had been transformed into a madhouse. Sirens blared out and police vans screeched around the cobbled streets.

Back on the open space in front of the station the police were searching bags to try to find out who had stolen goods. I think it was only a token display; they had shut the stable door after the horse had bolted. I decided to cross the border out of Luxembourg and wait elsewhere for a train. I ended up in a bar in Aarlon, in Belgium. About ten or so England fans were in there and we were approached by two Belgians who asked us if we wanted a laugh. Three of us went with them and ended up back in Luxembourg, being chased by the police through the city centre at three in the morning. One of the Belgians was a rally driver, and he made the police look silly. Unfortunately, he also frightened the pants off us. I was more frightened in his car than I had been earlier in the toilets at the ground.

The next morning I arrived in Brussels and decided to go for something to eat. I sat down in a restaurant and got chatting to some Scousers.

"What did you get last night?" they asked.

"Nothing. It's not my scene."

"Want to buy any gear? Watches, chains, good gold – 18-carat stuff?"

I laughed and declined the offer. I thought they might

have some trouble at British Customs, but they told me they would stash the gear at Ostend in the left luggage lockers and return in a week's time when the heat had died down. They were all in their early twenties and I doubt if they had ever had a chance of a proper job. To them stealing was a legitimate pastime and anywhere was fair game. I didn't agree with what they had done, but I could understand their point of view.

On the way back to England Keith and Sandra bumped into Kelly at Ostend; he had not lost his passport after all. His luggage arrived back in England five weeks later. Typically, on the jetfoil travelling home Kelly got stuck into the drink once again, and totally abused all the staff on board.

The aftermath of the trouble in Luxembourg was not as bad as first feared – at least England were not banned from Europe. But I do not think any English teams will ever be allowed to play in that country again. I had seen behaviour which I never thought I would see from English football fans. On returning to England I wrote to Ted Croker, the Secretary of the Football Association, telling him that he must find a way to stop people travelling who would cause trouble on that scale. But he made the usual sort of noncommittal noises. In all fairness, though, his hands are tied by the politicians. I vowed never again to follow England to an away match. However, my self-enforced ban was not to last very long, as once more the urge to travel was to take a grip.

France against England was always going to be a flashpoint.

Paris is too easy to get to and too full of nightlife for any hooligan to want to miss a match there. England played in Paris at the end of February 1984 and once more serious disturbances broke out. The fighting began on the ferries, between West Ham and Chelsea fans. West Ham, encouraged by the fact that they had the numbers, started taking liberties; serious disorder broke out, and knives were brandished.

Once in Paris the St Germain skinheads were waiting for the England fans and ambushed the Metro trains with CS gas. (When someone sprays that at you, you automatically reel backwards. When it is sprayed in a tube train you are done for. Football fans learn quickly, and CS gas is often used nowadays in a raid on rival fans' public houses.) The disorder continued in the ground and despite the firm hand of the French riot police, there were disturbances in the streets afterwards and cars were overturned. This was apart from the normal, almost ritual bad behaviour displayed by English fans in France.

The Football Association officials and players normally do not hear what goes on with the fans as they stay and travel away from them, but on one occasion it was forced home to them what morons some fans can be. It was the 1984 South American tour and England had won 2–0 in Rio de Janeiro. John Barnes, who is black, had scored one of the all-time great international goals. On the plane flying to Uruguay were the officials, players and press. Also on board was a group of Chelsea fans, every one a racist. To them black players' goals don't count, so England had won 1–0. It was an absurd attitude, but everyone could hear them being boorish and pathetic. Why some of the players didn't go down and say something I don't know, but it took the press to have words with them. It didn't make any difference, but after that incident the players ignored all the fans, which was hard on people who had paid a lot of money to follow England and had nothing to do with the racist cant.

Later in the year England were to play in Istanbul and I was determined to see them play at the meeting of Europe and Asia. I applied for one ticket for the match and received a letter from Ted Croker saying that I had to produce this letter at the Sheraton hotel in order to pick up my ticket. They had learnt a lesson from the Hungarian experience. I bought a cheap ticket from a bucket shop in Soho and decided to travel on the Monday and return Saturday night. I found out that Hickey had organized a four-day trip, so I phoned him and discovered that his group was on the same flight as me.

It was a chilly Monday morning at Heathrow. Once checked in I went through passport control. It was only eight in the morning but already people in Hickey's group were drinking beer. I sat down and had a good chat with Hickey. Everyone was waiting for Salford and Binman. These two are a dynamic, albeit loony, duo and they go to all England games. Every penny they earn is saved for their travelling expenses. They both hail from Manchester, and Binman works on the dust-carts – hence his nickname. Salford is a staunch Protestant and often turns up on away matches dressed in jeans, T-shirt, donkey jacket and carrying a William of Orange Battle of the Boyne flag. He brings nothing else, and he stinks by the end of the trip. It was the first time I had ever seen Salford but I had heard of him. Sure enough, he arrived with his flag, but no kit. I wouldn't like to have sat next to him on the return journey. Binman, again, is not renowned for his cleanliness, which is one reason why he and Salford make a good duo.

We were all due to travel on KLM, the Dutch national airline. The flight to Istanbul was pretty normal apart from the amount of beer being drunk. It was free, and when the beer stocks were exhausted the stewardesses dished out small screw-top bottles of wine. Everyone stocked up. Salford was singing his anti-papist songs and a good few people on the plane gave us funny looks. The Dutch are a gentle people and seem to find it difficult to understand English football fans. As we disembarked at Istanbul I jumped on the coach which was taking us to the hotel, I was not officially on Hickey's tour but he told me that if any room had a spare bed I could jump in free of charge. There was a varied assortment of different football fans on the coach including Bolton, Brighton and Arsenal supporters. This was also the first time I met Terence Last, or "Ginger Terry" as everyone called him. Terry asked me if I wanted to go to the under-21 game the next day in Bursa, which sounded like a good idea.

At the hotel I shared a room with two other Chelsea fans called Don and Steve. Steve was the stereotype of a football fan as portrayed in the press: five feet ten inches tall, well built and with a beer belly. He wore T-shirts which because of his belly didn't fit him properly. His trousers had to be worn under his stomach, and consequently the top of the cheeks of his bum were frequently on parade. I always find it very funny to watch these types trying to chase after other fans, bellies wobbling outrageously. Steve was also the type of fan who, no matter what the weather, will go to a football match wearing just a T-shirt, usually with something irrelevant written on it. It could be a freezing cold day in January when most people are wrapped up warm, but you will still see one of these half-wits in his T-shirt. It makes me shiver just to look at them.

That night everyone assembled in the bar while I went out to find the pudding shop, made famous by the film *Midnight Express*. Istanbul is a haven for travellers of the backpacking variety, and I spent an enjoyable evening talking to some of them. A couple of them didn't even know England were due to play there the coming Wednesday. Later in the evening, as I was sitting downstairs in the pudding shop with a couple of backpackers, I noticed three people standing near a couple of girls. West Ham fans, I thought. The people I was with couldn't understand how I knew, but I could tell by their general demeanour. I decided to leave and drank up.

Istanbul at night is a strange place, for there are no women around. During the day you see plenty of very attractive women, but at night they disappear. The bars are full of men, and it brought back memories of the crazy Turk at Liverpool, and also things I had read about the way the Turks fought in the First World War. I decided I wouldn't be getting into any fights in Istanbul. There was also the unnerving sight of the army on the streets with machine guns. The all-pervading presence of the army reminded me that military rule was in force.

One dynamic duo that came to the fore in Istanbul consisted of "Doddy" and "Crazy Bob".

Doddy was mental – not a nutter like Smiler, but crazy. It was always inevitable that Doddy would team up with someone, and sure enough a dynamic duo was formed when he met Crazy Bob from Leeds. If ever two people were destined to upset the Turks, then these two fitted the bill perfectly. Doddy had flown over on a seven-day excursion package with the Turkish national airline, and had met Crazy Bob on that flight. For their first night in Istanbul they decided that a night of abuse of the locals was on the agenda, which would go something like this.

They would walk into a bar and order a drink. "Oi, Turkface, give us a beer."

While they drank they would abuse people who spoke no English.

"Is it true all Turks are faggots?"

"Are you a bummer?"

"You look like a bummer."

The conversation would go on like this all night if trouble didn't break out. The first night they entered a bar and after twenty minutes of non-stop abuse the whole bar erupted and turned on them and they only just made it out of the door. Doddy made me nervous. Crazy Bob petrified me.

The coach for the under-21 match turned up at the hotel and apart from the Chelsea fans a group of other people had turned up. Lenny and Neale were two Arsenal fans whom I had played football against and I tagged along with them for the coach journey to Bursa, which would take about six hours. On the journey Ginger Terry found out I was a keen chess player and challenged me to a game. We crossed the Bosphorus and entered Asia, arriving in Bursa about an hour before kick-off. We bought tickets from the box office, where the Turks gathered round us, chattering noisily and excitedly. A few of us bought Turkish hats and put them on, and this upset a couple of the Chelsea fans.

"Take off those hats. We're England fans," shouted one. This really annoyed me because at six feet three inches tall and with ginger hair I don't need to walk around with a flag draped around myself to be recognized as English. I hate dawdling, and as everyone was just hanging around I decided to go on to the terraces on my own. As soon as I entered the ground the Turks spotted me and a small group of them called me over. One of them scurried off and fetched a sheet of cardboard for me to sit on. I was being made guest of honour. The Turks are fanatical about football, but they obviously respected this Englishman coming to their country and sitting on the terrace alongside them.

The ground was small and most of it was terraced. The steps on the terrace were about two feet high, so as the crowd was small everyone was sitting down. Just as the teams came out I saw Hickey and his group enter the seated section above the tunnel where the players enter and leave the field. The army had seen them and taken them into the seats. I felt a bit sick that I was sitting on my own on the terraces. When the Turks noticed the Union Jack with Chelsea written on it, they jeered loudly.

The game was very boring and ultimately finished with no score. But one pathetic incident brought attention to the Chelsea fans: those same racists who had caused such scenes on the South American tour were up to their tricks again. At half- and full-time they made monkey noises and threw bananas at the black players representing England.

There was also the amusing spectacle of young Turks trying to get into the ground without getting caught. One lone security guard had the job of stopping these young urchins from slipping in. The procedure was that if he caught one on the fence in the process of clambering down he ejected them, but if they managed to get on to the terraces he left them alone. The irony of it was that once he caught one and took him to the gate, another ten would slip in.

After the game the Turks shook my hand warmly and wished me well. Young fans were lighting fires all over the terraces. I decided to make my way round to the seated area where Hickey's group was sitting. The seats were segregated by a big fence so I decided to cut across the pitch which, although it was surrounded by big fences, had gates at the corners, and as most of the crowd had dispersed the groundsman had opened one. I walked down and the head groundsman spotted me and called me over. He was honoured that an Englishman wanted to look at his pitch. I didn't want to, but neither did I want to insult this amiable Turk. The pitch was in fact extremely bumpy, and the grass very patchy. After going through almost every shot the Turks had played throughout the whole match, the groundsman took me through the players' tunnel and I emerged into the daylight. In front of me was the players' coach, and a policeman, thinking I was an England player, herded me on to the coach where all the under-21 players were sitting like robots in their tracksuits waiting for the manager and officials to get on the coach.

"All right, lads?" I said.

No reply. Everyone just looked at me. I was really annoyed.

I had travelled thousands of miles to see this mob play and they couldn't be bothered to say hello to me.

"What's up with you lot, can't you talk?" I sneered at them. I jumped back off the coach extremely indignant that the players hadn't had the decency to speak to me. But in fairness, I didn't know then about the racial chanting and banana throwing that had gone on earlier.

I spotted Hickey's coach and climbed aboard. As we journeyed away from the ground a few young Turks threw stones at the windows, but nothing serious. On the trip back to Istanbul the coach had a refreshment and toilet stop in a small town. I got off and went to get something to eat. When I returned to the coach Lenny, Neale and a group of three others were standing about ten yards away from it. They called me over.

"What do you think about the racist chanting?" one of them asked me.

"What do you mean?" I replied.

He explained to me what had happened at half- and full-time, and I suddenly realized why the England players had ignored me.

"I don't reckon it."

"It spoils it for everyone. I think someone should have a word with them," said Lenny.

Back on the coach Lenny and I approached a couple of them. The conversation went something like this. "Why do you chant at black players?"

"'Cos they're niggers, ain't they?"

"But surely they are representing England?"

"Black players don't count, do they."

"You must cheer when one scores?" (For Chelsea.)

"Nope. I just sit there."

"What about Paul Cannonville?" (A black Chelsea player.)

"Don't cheer if he scores."

I found the conversation quite hilarious. We all devised situations where the racists would cheer if a black Chelsea player scored. "Chelsea are drawing 0-0 in the FA Cup Final against Spurs [Chelsea's greatest rivals], and Paul Cannonville scores. What would you do?"

"I would just sit there, wouldn't I."

We all roared with laughter. The more blatant the racist remarks they came out with, the more we laughed and the more outrageous became our situations. I hoped that in the next day's full international a black player would score so that I could observe their reactions.

Racism at football does exist, but apart from the small number of hardcore racists who have attached themselves to certain football clubs, real racism is not as widespread as is often thought. Though some white fans may say "I hate niggers," almost all will cheer like mad when a black player scores a goal or proves he is a good player. On the terraces, for the most part, everyone is the same colour – that of the team. There is some polarization: Arsenal, for instance, have black gangs. But I have never seen or heard of racial clashes at football matches. In adversity or triumph, black, white, yellow and brown come together under the club colours to fight or to celebrate. The media are over-sensitive and have considerably exaggerated football racism; and it is significant that the National Front have had very little success recruiting at football.

Once back in Istanbul I decided to catch a taxi down to the ground with Lenny and two others who didn't have tickets, to try to buy some. We pulled up near the ground and as we went to get out a huge gang of young Turks spotted us and ran towards us. I don't think they wanted our autographs, so we all jumped back in and shouted at the driver, "Drive on."

He just sat there.

"Drive on," I screamed.

We were all shouting, gesticulating and even praying for him to drive, but he didn't move until the first youngster banged on his car. He stuck it into gear and revved through them all like a raving madman, scattering young Turks everywhere. As we drove down the road we all breathed a sigh of relief. I looked behind and saw the gang shaking their fists.

We pulled up near the hotel and spotted a restaurant below the level of the pavement. It was our lucky night, for not only was the food superb and cheap but it was opposite the international university and was full of pretty girls. We sat in there all night, talking, drinking and laughing. When I got back to my hotel I saw a group of Chelsea fans sitting at the bar.

"All right, Ginger. Where you been?"

"A little restaurant up the road."

"I bet the food was shit. Everything's shit in this city."

"Yeah, something like that," I replied.

I retired to my room. It would have been pointless trying to put them right, because they would only have abused the place.

The next day I had breakfast in the hotel restaurant and then went into the bar. The match was not until later in the afternoon so a spot of sightseeing was on the cards. A group of four guys were going to the covered bazaar; one of them, Willie Jones, had a stolen Visa card, and he invited me along. The bazaar in Istanbul is quite a sight, and anything can be bought there. Nothing has a price on it so everything has to be bartered for. Willie's eyes lit up when he got to the bazaar.

Everywhere accepted Visa cards, and there wasn't a telephone in the place. He went berserk, and he didn't even want to go to the match later in the day. If he had stayed a week he would have owned half of Istanbul!

I was very nervous and kept out of the way, but I had to marvel at his cheek. He was buying gear for everyone and charging nominal fees for the goods: gold, silver, onyx, a replica medieval ball and chain, and leather coats for everyone. In one shop he bought another member of the party a leather coat, and when the Turkish shopkeeper asked him how he would like to pay he replied, "Visa card, of course. I like to travel with plastic money because there are so many criminals about nowadays."

We left the bazaar and headed back to the hotel. Willie turned to me.

"Oi, Ginger, you're the only guy who didn't ask for anything in the bazaar. Why's that?"

"Didn't have what I wanted in there."

"What you after?"

"Rolex Oyster Perpetual."

"No problem, Ginger, I'll get one up the Sheraton. You pay me 20 per cent of the asking price."

"You've got a deal," I said.

Willie walked up the road moaning about how little time he had left in Istanbul and how he could make a fortune in this city. He even thought about flying back a couple of days later and buying up all the gold, but I don't think he had the nerve to smuggle it back on his own. It was noticeable that a big plank of a guy called Al was carrying his gear. Especially heavy was an onyx chess set for Ginger Terry.

The Sheraton Hotel in Istanbul is on top of a hill and overlooks the ground where England were due to play. The England team were staying in the hotel and it was here that

I had to pick up my tickets. I made my way up to the hotel about two hours before kick-off with Willie and two other Chelsea fans who were ticketless. Willie went off to buy the Rolex but it fell through because they wanted to check the card, although he did manage to wangle his way out without losing the card. A few England fans were hanging around in the foyer looking for tickets but not having any luck. A desk had been set up and I went and collected my tickets. Ted Croker came into the foyer and a couple of fans approached him for tickets. I heard his reply: "The match is sold out. There are no spare tickets and the FA will not attempt to get any for you. You've all wasted your journey and it serves you right."

He looked and sounded so smug, but he didn't realize that getting a ticket abroad is not really a problem. Foreigners don't have the same "do it right" attitude the British have, and anyway an English five-pound note would be enough to bribe most Turkish gatemen. Two Southampton fans spotted Mark Wright, Southampton's centre-half, and went up to him. Southampton is a small, homely club and after a friendly conversation he disappeared and turned up about ten minutes later with a couple of complimentary tickets. These were red- and gold-edged embossed cards which looked really elegant. I was jealous as hell: what a souvenir to take back to England! They were overjoyed, and we all went back to the bar to celebrate. I spotted Ron Greenwood, the ex-England manager, and walked over to him.

"Hello, Ron," I said.

He totally ignored me and hurried off looking petrified.

I found his attitude and that of the other England officials strange. We were not wanted. But I didn't really care, and just before we left the bar to travel the short distance down the hill to the ground Brian Moore, the TV commentator, spoke to us in the bar.

"How's it going, lads?"

"All right, Brian."

"Being treated fairly by the Turks?"

"No problem from the Turks, it's the pompous FA twits we have to worry about."

He laughed and we shrugged and left. The trip down the hill took about three minutes and as we got to the ground I noticed the army out in force. We were recognized as English and pushed towards an entrance. We had to walk past a steep wall which formed the back of the terrace containing the Turkish fans. About fifty Turks were screaming things at us, but I don't think it was malicious; they just get so worked up about football. Suddenly a stone was thrown, but no problem because we were soon under cover and out of harm's way. We were being herded by the army through a small turnstile. The officers weren't interested in whether or not we had tickets, they just wanted all the England fans in the same section.

"Look at this, boys," shouted a voice.

I turned round and saw the England under-21 players coming towards our entrance, and the look on their faces was one of anxiety. Dave Sexton, the team's manager, led the way and walked straight through the crowd. The Chelsea fans made a gangway and shook his hand, for he used to manage Chelsea. He went through, but then as the players followed him the ranks closed. A Chelsea fan turned to them. "Listen boys, down here on the streets you are the kiddies and we are the guv'nors, so you wait until we have all gone in. If you lot are so ignorant you won't talk to us, then we won't be polite to you." Not one of the under-21 players made a move; they just stood there and waited in line. The Turkish army did not seem bothered – as far as they were concerned we were all Englishmen together.

Once inside the ground all the English were being

searched, and Dave Sexton was standing by the gate to smooth the passage of the under-21 players. I got to the gate and said, "Hello Dave, how's it going, mate?"

Dave turned and said to me, "Where are all the players?"

"Outside, queuing up like polite Englishmen," I replied. He looked bemused, and I went on up the steps. Dave is a kindly-looking man, but his attitude, like that of all FA officials, is one of strained toleration towards the supporters.

At the top of the steps I looked out on the ground, which was compact and mostly terraced. The pitch was surrounded by a running track, and we were in the main stand. There were not many England fans present, but they had put us in a small section together. A large contingent of Turkish army senior NCOs sat in the stand on the left. This was obviously the place to sit, and they were not going to be moved by anyone. They all had three stars on the front of their flat-topped peaked caps. Hickey, who was wearing a ridiculous First World War flying cap and goggles, made his way forward with his Chelsea Union Jack and draped it over the front of the stand for the benefit of the TV cameras around the world. He looked back and shouted out, "I'm in with the three-star generals."

Most of the seats were taken, but everyone squashed in and I sat on the concrete steps on my newspaper. Ken Bailey was sitting near the front. Ken is an old-age pensioner who travels round the world watching England play sport, and he always dresses up in Union Jack clothes. He is a harmless old man who is living out his last days doing something he enjoys. You get the impression, though, that the FA officials do not like him – possibly because he is more famous than they are.

After taking a few photographs of the crowd, I came back to my spot and struck up a conversation with one of the under-21 players who, I think, was Bradford City's goalkeeper. I asked him if any of the players had been sightseeing in the city, but he told me that they had just stayed in the Sheraton all the time. I found it quite amusing that most of the under-21 players expected us to give up our seats for them simply because they were footballers. The most arrogant player among them was Barry Venison, but Hickey made him look silly at half-time. Hickey walked up the steps and Barry, who had stood the whole time on the steps, barred his way.

"Excuse me," said Hickey.

"Why, mate, have I got your seat?" enquired Barry.

"No, you plum, we've got your seats. Now get out of the way or else you'll get another terrace lesson." Barry moved to one side, very red-faced.

England came out and slaughtered the Turks on the football pitch, winning 8–0. It was a momentous victory, and when John Barnes scored I immediately looked towards the Chelsea racists. Sure enough, they never moved an inch. I meant to ask them their idea of the score of the match later in the hotel, but it slipped my mind. I wished black players had scored all the goals, because that would really have spoilt their day.

In the second half I looked across to the next section and I saw Clive Allen and Remi Moses sitting on the concrete steps looking very glum. The million-pound footballers were having to slum it, and they didn't like it one bit. One of the Chelsea fans shouted over, "Oi, Clive, want a bit of newspaper to sit on? I would hate the thought of you having to buy a new suit." The footballers definitely showed themselves up for what they were. Players would do well to remember where they came from.

At the final whistle Salford and Binman both appeared behind us, having previously been spotted at the Turkish end waving the William of Orange flag to screams of abuse by the Turks. We all left together and walked up the hill towards the Sheraton with a large contingent of army surrounding us. On our left was a huge grassy bank which was quite steep. On the top of the hill was a large group of young Turks who were throwing rocks and bottles at us. This continued until the army charged at them and they scattered. Salford was at the front and charged forward at the Turks who stood in the road in front of us. The Turks ran everywhere, but the army were not happy and one Turkish captain said loudly in English: "Do not misbehave in Turkey." I had seen enough of the Turkish army to know that he meant what he said, but there were no more incidents and everyone filed into the Sheraton.

The Istanbul Sheraton is very plush and has a little pond and waterfall in the foyer. It is all marble, and the beer is quite expensive, but everyone just sat around talking and drinking beer. Later, in the early evening, Ray Wilkins the footballer went to sit with the Blackburn group and bought a monster round of drinks. He lives and plays football in Italy, and was pleased to talk to English people while he waited for his plane back there, the rest of the England party having flown back home straight after the game. Unlike most footballers, I found him quite intelligent and articulate.

There were quite a few people sitting about, and when a small group of Turks appeared outside the glass doors, all hell broke loose. Everyone charged up to the doors; but no one had the bottle to run out and charge into the Turks, and the Turks didn't have the courage to come in. The hotel workers were saying, "No, no". A glass was thrown and shattered everywhere on the hotel frontage. One guy snatched open the door and shouted to me, "I'll hold the door, you go and get them."

"I'll hold the door, you go and get them," I replied.

The Turks ran when two burly barmen charged out and whacked a couple of them. I thought it was quite amusing, but the chap who had held the door didn't see it in the same light.

"They're all wankers," he said.

"How's that?" I asked.

"Well, if two or three more West Ham had been here then we would have gone out and into them."

"You had your chance to go out the door and flunked it," I said.

I found out that this particular guy was called BJ and was reckoned to be a face in a gang called the Under-5s, a group that follows West Ham. He was tall, had dark hair and wore a Burberry anorak. I found him obnoxious, like most West Ham fans. He didn't like me because he realized that I had seen him show fear. He did have another chap with him who seemed quite a reasonable person. Later in the evening the rest of the West Ham fans turned up and after a little sneer at everyone they all left together.

I went upstairs to have a drink in the top-floor bar with a wondrous view of Istanbul, which at night looks quite spectacular. On coming downstairs I bumped into Lenny and Bruce and we had a quick drink in the downstairs bar where we met Brian Glanville, the *Sunday Times* journalist. Usually I haven't much time for newspapermen but I found Brian an exception. He had a passion for Italy and Italian football, and he was certainly very interesting to listen to. I have very strong views on football and I love debating. Brian Glanville is a worthy adversary.

Back at the hotel, Hickey was disappointed that he had missed the one and only row of the trip. We sat in the bar all night talking and telling stories. I listened to some fantastic tales about Salford and Binman. Apparently Binman had lost his trousers in the surf in Rio de Janeiro, and from the stories I heard I felt a little regretful that I had not gone to South America. I turned in at about two in the morning, and on arising at nine I surveyed the carnage in the bar. Some of the guys had been drinking all night and were in a right mess. They were all due to go home that morning and I laughed as they staggered on to the coach.

When they boarded the aeroplane at Istanbul the other people on the plane gave them some very strange looks. It was a KLM plane flying to Amsterdam, and had flown in from Cairo. One of the England fans knew one of the stewardesses on the plane and she told him that before boarding had begun at Istanbul the captain had made a special announcement: "There is a small contingent of English football hooligans getting on board. Please do not be alarmed by their behaviour or appearance." No wonder everyone had looked at them like circus animals when they boarded the plane. The irony of it was that no one drank a drop on the trip home, and most of them spent the entire journey in the toilets causing huge queues for the economy-class passengers.

I went and found myself a hotel next to the pudding shop and spent an enjoyable day sightseeing. A lot of England fans had booked weekly flights and that Thursday night a lot of us gathered in the pudding shop for a drink. Thankfully the West Ham fans had gone to Anatalia for a few days, so it was just good fun. I met some very interesting people, especially a Leyton Orient fan who dressed like an ageing hippie. One guy from Birmingham warned us about walking down by the docks at night, as the first night he had been in Istanbul he had almost had his throat cut. He had been walking along when he had been dragged into an alleyway, had a ten-inch carving knife put next to his throat, and been told, "Give me your money." He had had £60 on him and had lost the lot. Later in the evening BJ and his friend came in and I went over to them.

"Want to join us?" I asked.

"No thanks," replied BJ.

"Why not?"

"Well, I can't be your friend, can I – I might have to give you a kicking when we play Arsenal."

"That makes you the loser then, because you've got to sit here and stew while we have a good time."

I could see his friend wanted to join us, but they drank for another thirty minutes and left. The beer flowed that night. But the pudding shop was nothing like the place portrayed in *Midnight Express*. In the film it looked atmospheric and romantic, but in reality it was like a transport café with plastic chairs and white and brown formica-topped tables. Being a football fan, though, this doesn't matter, for roughing it on your travels is part of the fun. Watching football and the excitement generated at venues all around the world is great, though it really cheeses you off when you travel half-way across the globe and England players and officials just turn their backs on you. After all, a few polite words and a smile cost nothing. We spoke at length about this in the pudding shop that night.

Friday came and a boat excursion was planned across the Bosphorus. As we cruised over to Asia I looked back on the walled city and imagined what it must have looked like hundreds of years ago. I felt sorry that the England players had not had the chance to see such a wonderful sight. In today's climate the win-at-all-costs mentality has deprived footballers of the chance to savour the delights of foreign travel. Most of them are young men with little or no experience of life, and for some of the under-21 players who will not make the grade, the chance to see Istanbul may have been lost for ever. To travel all the way to Turkey and remain in the Sheraton seems an appalling waste of opportunity.

Friday night saw us create a huge party in the Sultan

pub, which was just like a British public house complete with a stereo system on which the owner played English music. We got all the Turks singing and dancing. The army waited outside, and huge crowds peered in through the windows. Doddy nearly started a riot by upsetting the Turks with Crazy Bob, but it was soon smoothed over. A few Sudanese guest workers were in the bar and they thought it was great fun to join in the dancing. As celebrations go I think this was the best I have ever participated in.

After Friday, then, Saturday night was bound to be an anti-climax, but when I saw the group of West Ham fans at about seven o'clock I knew that trouble would ensue. I got into the Sultan at about 7.30, and everyone was in there. The owner welcomed me and wanted to know what time the dancing would start. The West Ham fans, about seven of them including BJ, sat at the far end next to the exit to the toilets. They were abusing everyone, especially the Leyton Orient fan who after ten minutes got up and left. I went round a few people to see if anyone was prepared to fight them, but no one had the courage. One of them, called Danny, had some eggs which he threw at me. I went over and told him to pack it in, but they just laughed. It was embarrassing, especially as the happy atmosphere of the pub changed to one of trepidation. The two Sudanese guys who had been in the pub the night before were dancing around and shaking everyone's hand. But they made the mistake of trying to shake the ginger-haired West Ham fan's hand.

"Piss off, nigger," he said.

The Sudanese guy was stopped in his tracks, but tried again to be friendly.

"Piss off, nigger," said Danny.

One of the others punched him quite hard and cut his lip. The owner of the bar came over and quickly restored calm. The Turks are not too keen on the Sudanese, but the owner didn't want any trouble and he had seen the egg throwing. He spoke to me.

"Sort out your friends."

"They are no friends of mine."

"They are English, aren't they?"

"Well, yes, but they're the scumbags of England."

The ginger-haired guy overheard my conversation and walked over. "What's your game?" he asked.

"What do you mean?" I replied.

"Talking about English people like that."

I grabbed hold of his lapels and he went berserk, yelling "Let go of my coat." I held on, but he went crazy. "Get your hands off me," he shouted.

He didn't frighten me, and despite the fact that I could only have improved his looks by thumping him I was wary of his mates, so I let go. But I was determined to give him a piece of my mind.

"Now listen here, we have been well liked and respected by everyone in this bar but you lot of slags have spoilt it by your pathetic behaviour. You should be ashamed of yourselves."

He had no answer and simply told me, with great originality, to "fuck off", then walked away. I went and sat down with a few other people whom I had met the previous night. The thing that annoyed me the most was the fact that they would not have done a thing if the Chelsea fans had been in the bar. But now Doddy and Crazy Bob were drinking with them, and the dynamic duo were taking great delight in abusing the Sudanese.

Their final act of moronic behaviour was reserved for two young English girls who had run out of money and were travelling back to England. There was a lorry park just outside Istanbul and they needed money to get out there and back each day to try to hitch a lift back to Munich. I saw the way Turkish men looked at English women and realized why they needed to be able to refuse lifts if they felt the driver was a bit dodgy. One of the girls was selling her camera and other gear. A whip-round was organized for the girls and a reasonable sum of money was raised. One of the West Ham fans came over with a small sum of Turkish money. "This is for you if you do me a blow job, luv," he said to one of the girls. It was disgusting and I felt ashamed. The girl told him to clear off, but his friends thought it was great.

This, unfortunately, is the mentality of many English football fans abroad. They left shortly afterwards and got involved in a punch-up outside the pudding shop. Saturday night in Istanbul is not the place to have a punch-up, and they soon found about fifty Turks coming at them. The West Ham fans and Doddy ran for dear life, leaving Crazy Bob to take a fearful beating. He came back into the Sultan well battered and bruised, but luckily nothing was broken. Bob and I decided to take a taxi back to Doddy's hotel, and we shook hands with the owner. I gave him my England hat to put above the bar and we went to the door. Unfortunately, the Turks who had beaten up Crazy Bob were waiting outside. We decided to make a dash for the taxi rank and shout "Airport!" once inside a taxi. The door opened and out we shot – a quick sprint across the road and into a taxi. "Airport, pronto," I shouted. He sped off, but 200 yards up the road and with the danger passed we gave him the card of the hotel and, looking slightly bemused, he drove there.

Doddy was sitting in the bar of the hotel still shaking from the punch-up, even though he had neither thrown a punch nor received one. Within half an hour, though, he was back to normal and was abusing the hotel waiter. We shared a taxi back to the airport but I wished I hadn't when Doddy, sitting in the front seat, kept grabbing the steering wheel causing the taxi to swerve, and Crazy Bob kept sticking his smelly feet right under the taxi driver's nose. As we were sorting out the fare at the airport Doddy and Bob started abusing the poor taxi driver and disputing the fare. Another Turk who intervened to try to help and reason with Bob ended up with a bloody nose, courtesy of a Crazy Bob head-butt. "Now butt out, Turk face," shouted Bob, then paid the fare in full and even gave a tip.

We walked into the airport. I had three hours to wait for my plane; Bob and Doddy had seven. We went into the buffet and there met a real character. Frankie was sitting in the buffet drinking beer, but was not drunk. He was alone, and his first words were: "What do you think of Istanbul whores?" We explained that none of us had tried them. He was absolutely appalled. "It is the duty of every Englishman to sample the whores in every city where England plays football."

I found him very amusing and good value for a three-hour waiting period at an airport, pretty boring at the best of times. Frankie came from Luton and had just flown back from Ankara where, it seemed, he had found the whores far superior to those in Istanbul. We sat around a table talking for two hours about the relative merits of prostitutes the world over although we didn't talk so much as listen to Frankie. He was very proud of his passport stamps because each had its own particular story. He was enthusiastic about Copenhagen and ecstatic about Rio de Janeiro. I wondered where he got his money, and he told me he had inherited a large sum at the age of twenty-one. I couldn't fault the guy. This was his hobby, however bizarre it might seem to you and me. His final words to me as I left the buffet to go to the gate for my plane were: "I have got standards, you know. I always give the girls a tip when England win!"

I didn't stop laughing to myself all the way back to

England. Turkey had been great fun, but the old cliché had been proven: it takes only a few people to spoil all the good done by the majority.

The only other away game I fancied in our group was in Northern Ireland. I knew that the Northern Irish fans liked a punch-up, because at their previous meeting Hickey and a few others had been set upon and Hickey had taken quite a beating. I phoned him a couple of weeks before the match and he told me he had a coach leaving on the Tuesday night and returning to London Thursday evening. We would be in Belfast for Wednesday at 11 a.m. and would only have to miss two working days. Everybody met up in the Black Bull at about six Tuesday evening. Doddy was in the pub and he greeted me like a long-lost friend. He promised me faithfully he wouldn't abuse any Paddies, but I didn't believe a word of it.

Hickey's coach was not full and it was a pretty old-looking thing. The driver was covered in grease and oil and he looked as if he had been repairing it to get it on the road. The route we were due to take was via Holyhead and Dublin. The coach party consisted mostly of Chelsea fans but, as on the Turkey trip, a large cross-section of other fans was also on board. The coach had to stop in Kilburn, north London to pick up Salford. To him the trip to Northern Ireland was a religious exercise. He was looking forward to a trip up the Shankhill Road, the stronghold of the Protestants in Belfast. A couple of younger guys at the back of the coach had a lot of National Front literature which I read, but they expressed dismay that I didn't support the Front or its views on repatriation. A large Union Jack which had Chelsea written in white letters across the centre was hung at the back of the coach. A couple more Union Jacks were hung across the windows, just to let everyone know who we were.

A beer stop was made at an off-licence in north London, where Hickey informed everyone that if they must steal beer then they should be discreet because we had a ferry connection at Holyhead and had no time to spare. The coach also stopped on a motorway somewhere to pick up a man called Mark, who came from Nottingham. He boarded the coach with a carrier bag full of National Front literature. He wanted to show his loyalist brothers in Northern Ireland that certain political parties would not give in to the cowardly IRA – or at least, that's how he put it.

There wasn't much beer drunk. It was like a day trip to the seaside with lots of sixties Beatles songs being sung. Hickey sat at the front of the coach like a schoolmaster, taking requests for the video screen. One of the guys had put together a video of all the news clips he had seen on football violence. It made for interesting viewing, and the clip of trouble in Copenhagen was made even more appropriate by one of the coach party recognizing himself getting a punch in the mouth from a policeman.

The only incident occurred at Holyhead, when two brothers who were having a family feud decided to have a punch-up and a seat got broken. The woman in the cafeteria made such a fuss that you'd have thought it was World War Three, but there was no real damage so off we went, with the brothers still arguing.

The next morning we docked in Dublin, where we drove out and through customs without getting stopped at all. About an hour out of Dublin the coach broke down. The driver had come prepared and unloaded a tool box and set to work on the engine. All we could do was sit and watch, but a couple of guys took the opportunity to clean the back window so that everybody could see that we were Chelsea fans. After about forty minutes the driver got back in and started up the coach. A huge cheer went up and we were on our way again. On the drive to Belfast, and even at the border crossing, the army presence was minimal. The countryside was lovely, hard to equate with the images one has of Northern Ireland from the TV news.

Upon arrival in Belfast the coach dropped us outside the Europa hotel, which is done up like a fortress because it has been bombed so many times. Some of the people on the coach explained that on the previous trip the army had manned checkpoints into the town centre, but now the security situation had eased and although the checkpoints were still there they were unmanned. A pub opposite the Europa called Robinsons was named as the meeting place where the coach would pick us up at midnight after the match.

Within half an hour of us arriving in Belfast, Mark, the National Front guy, had been pulled in by the Royal Ulster Constabulary for distributing his literature. The RUC confiscated all his material and told everyone that the wearing of NF badges would not be allowed in pubs in this part of town. Salford, who had travelled to this game without Binman, who had come by train on the Stranraer–Larne route, made his way up to the Orange Cross Club, a strong Protestant club which made no bones about what it stood for. When you walked in it had military decorations and pictures of the Queen everywhere. Pride of place went to a Victoria Cross won by a member of the club in the First World War.

One of the guys on the trip told me that although all the people at the match supporting Northern Ireland would be staunch loyalists, this would not prevent them from giving you a punch in the mouth after the game. The previous time England had played in Belfast the police had simply left the England fans to make their own way back to the station, and all the Paddies had come out of the pubs for a good punch-up. This didn't bother me as much as the fact that nobody on our coach had match tickets and the match

had been sold out for two weeks. The newspapers were
saying that nobody would gain entry without a ticket and
not even to bother turning up as it was a pointless exercise.
I felt confident because most of the other people on our
coach didn't seem worried about getting tickets. We had all
heard the "sold out, won't gain entry" business bandied
about before.

I went for a drink in the Orange Cross Club, which from
the outside looked pretty drab. It had an Orange Cross
hanging on a flagpole, representing the Battle of the Boyne.
Nobody was inside and I found out that everyone was
drinking further up the road. I finally found most of the
guys and even managed to have a sensible drink with
Doddy, which must go down in history. The Irish were very
friendly, especially as they saw our coming as a vindication
of the strength of the Unionists. I was determined to go
down the Falls Road, the staunchly Catholic area of Belfast,
and asked what my chances were of walking down there. I
was warned off that, but as no buses went there I decided to
take a taxi as far as the army barracks. I found another
England fan who wanted to see a bit more than just the
inside of a Protestant club, so off we went. An old Protestant
told us: "I wouldn't give the Fenian bastard taxi drivers one
penny to take me down the Falls."

We had been told that it would be difficult to get a taxi
down the Falls, but the first taxi driver we came across was
only too willing. The other England fan who accompanied
me was named Raymond and was just twenty-one years
old. All he had with him was a carrier bag with his Union
Jack in. I hoped the taxi wouldn't break down because I
didn't fancy a walk back up the Falls with a Union Jack.

The journey was quite interesting. Belfast seemed just
like any other city, apart from the paintings on the walls.
There was one which showed the sign representing the

female species, and in the centre was a picture of an Arab female, an African female and an Irish female. It was a huge picture in black and white and took up the whole side of a house. Next to it were the words "Cowardly Loyalist Backout". The murals were very impressive, and almost all depicted the struggle for freedom. It was a total contrast to the loyalist paintings on the sides of the houses on the Shankhill estates, which depicted solidarity with the mainland. The army barracks at the bottom of the Falls was an incredible sight. It had huge smooth walls which pointed outwards at the top – to stop mortar attacks, I think. It must be horrible being inside, rather like being in prison.

We cruised back to Robinsons bar feeling rather pleased with ourselves. Once inside I spotted my old friends the West Ham fans. They were all there – BJ, Danny and Taffy to name but a few. My old ginger mate from Istanbul was there, but he ignored me. Danny said an arrogant "Hello" in a voice which informed that he was in charge. Thankfully they left shortly afterwards. We settled in for the afternoon drink and most England fans were congregating down there. At about 4.30 in the afternoon a group from our coach decided to go for a walk up the Falls Road, but they didn't get very far before the army and RUC turned them back.

The Irish seemed quite friendly. I spoke to a few and they all had tickets but seemed very sure we wouldn't be able to get any. I decided, along with a few friends, to make my way down to the ground at about 6.30. When I got to the bar I saw that a large contingent of RUC had gathered outside to pre-empt any trouble that might break out. They all carried big truncheons and had sten guns. The walk to the ground took about twenty-five minutes, and once outside we all stood asking people for any spare tickets. One young Irishman came over and I asked him if he had a ticket. He replied, "I would rather burn it than give it to an Englishman."

At that point the West Ham fans turned up and started a huge punch-up with some Paddies. The Paddies were well game and it became a stand-off situation. Just as I was hopeful of getting a ticket, the RUC moved me on. An Irishman came up and told me that tickets were being sold in the street over the bridge behind the ground. I was getting pretty desperate by now. I went over the bridge, but all the England fans I met told me that they were having no luck. I was standing in a big car park asking everyone, and all of a sudden an Irishman approached me. "Looking for a ticket?" he asked.

"Yeah. How much?"

"Face value, I don't want to make a profit," he replied. I laughed at all the English press who had quoted official sources as saying, "Don't bother turning up without a ticket." I never saw anybody fail to get a ticket that night, although some did bribe the gatemen instead. Even the West Ham fans got in. Once inside I stood to the left rather than behind the goal with the rest of the England fans.

The match was won by England 1–0 and at the end the Irish filed out while the RUC stood in a line to stop any England fans leaving. They decided to give them an escort back to the station. The young Irish fans were walking right up to the lines to try to have a swing at the English, and the RUC practically had to punch them to get them to back off. There were about five of us standing alone on the terraces. I decided to walk outside to have a look at the car park, but as I got to the exit I saw a huge mob of Irish waiting for us. I came back in and saw Ginger Terry. I told him what I had seen but he just shrugged his shoulders. "I expect it'll be a big punch-up, like last time," he said.

After about ten minutes the stadium was cleared and Ginger Terry was talking to an Irishman who had lived a long time in Kilburn. Another big Irishman walked into the stadium and spoke to him: "Are we going to have a go at the English or not?"

"I'm not," he replied. "But they're all there, so if you want to, feel free."

The big Irishman scowled and walked out of the ground and back into the car park. Five minutes later the RUC began to beckon the English fans forward. The West Ham fans took pole position. I took up residence in the middle, trying to spot any of the group I had travelled with. The walk back to our pick-up point took us through a labyrinth of dark back streets with terraced houses on each side. The Irish had no fear of us, and they had no fear of arrest. They stood around the streets just waiting for the punch-up. The West Ham fans at the front were fighting all and sundry, along with Hickey and his group.

Suddenly I saw the huge Irishman whom I had seen enter the ground earlier standing on the pavement. He was wearing a Linfield FC jumper. "I'll fight the best Englishman among you," he said. I hit him with an absolute beauty which rocked him on his heels. I hit him again and again. He reeled back and I kicked him once. The next thing I knew I was being dragged backwards with a truncheon across my throat by three RUC officers. They threw me up against the armoured Land Rover. One of the officers hit me across the back with his truncheon, and it hurt. The sergeant gripped me round the throat. "If I see you blink, I will lock you up for the night." He pushed me away from the Land Rover and I walked back to the pavement. I was pleased to get away with that one, for I didn't fancy missing Hickey's coach back to Dublin.

As soon as I got round the corner I received a punch in the mouth from another Paddy. I didn't hit him back as I didn't want to get arrested. The RUC were all around and told us to stop where we were on a bridge. The Irish stood on the other side of the road. A group of Geordies, who had been involved in the fight alongside the West Ham and had seen me get pulled up by the RUC, struck up a conversation with me.

"What did the RUC say?" one asked me.

"Just threatened me with arrest," I replied.

"Are you West Ham?"

"No, I'm Arsenal."

"Those West Ham are well game."

Our conversation was interrupted by a group of Irish across the road taunting us.

"If it wasn't for the coppers, you'd be mincemeat."

"I think you live in dreamland, Paddy," replied one of the Geordies.

The RUC tried to move the Irish on, but they just ignored them. I presume that arrests are kept to the minimum because they haven't time to go to court for such trivial matters. We stood on the bridge for no apparent reason, but in the distance we heard a bang. A bomb had exploded. The sound chilled our bones. We moved off, with the Irish following us at a discreet distance. I felt good now with the Geordies, because I knew they could handle themselves. A group of three British Army armoured cars sped past and a loud cheer went up from the English football fans.

At a fork in the road with a large pub on the right the bulk of the fans went off with the escort towards the station. The Geordies went with them, while our group walked back down the road to the Europa hotel. We had only about four RUC men with us and one armoured Land Rover. A group of Irish fans was standing outside the pub, shouting, "Come back, you English cowards, and fight like men." The sound rang in our ears as we walked down the road. Three Irishmen were following just behind, taunting us and casting doubt on the legitimacy of our birth.

Just as we got to Robinson's bar the West Ham fans

spotted them and ran for them, but the RUC intervened. I walked across the road with Big Ralph, a giant of a guy, who was on Hickey's coach. We waited on the corner expecting the Irish to walk away, but to our surprise they walked over and called us cowards. The punches rained on them thick and fast, and I particularly enjoyed punching the big-mouth. Ralph was incensed, and also punched the big-mouth as he tried to run away. Unfortunately Ralph was still thumping him when the RUC turned up, and he got himself arrested and thrown into the back of a Land Rover. The West Ham fans were ignored although they were still knocking the hell out of the other Irishmen. I bet that was the last time those Paddies called a group of Englishmen cowards.

The RUC wanted us off the streets, but it was only 10.15 and our coach wasn't due until midnight. The senior RUC man negotiated with the Europa hotel to let us in for a drink, but people began to drift up the road. A couple of guys got Ralph released from the Land Rover, and we walked back up the road towards the pub where we had been called English cowards. However, we didn't get that far as another bar was spotted down a side street. We all filed in and played pool and drank beer until closing time. People were filing in, and one guy appeared with a juicy back eye. He had no scarf on, but he had fallen for the classic ruse.

"What's the time, mate?" the Paddy had asked him.

He hadn't replied but had got a punch in the face for his trouble.

It was an enjoyable evening out, but I was glad when we got on our coach. The Paddies are a tough crowd, and they take no prisoners. The coach journey home was pretty uneventful except for the two young National Front guys sniffing amyl nitrate and offering me some. What it did for them I do not know. I think I'll stick to Vitamin C. To cap it all the coach broke down on the M1 just outside London and everyone got off and left the coach driver to it. So that was it. Another eventful away trip with Hickey was over.

England matches away are much more fun than home games, mostly because of the camaraderie among the people who travel. Sometimes, though, it is upsetting to see the hooligans besmirching the name of England. It is interesting to note the way other countries' young fans have copied the English hooligans, and now every major city boasts its own "crew" or "firm" who follow their team, which can make it very awkward for England fans abroad. With everyone fired up on a heady cocktail of jingoism and booze, it is hard to see how the fighting between home countries' hooligans and our own can be prevented. After all, a country that has as its best-selling newspaper one that glories in the death of three hundred sailors with the heading "GOTCHA" has only itself to blame if it is breeding a nation of delinquents.

12

The Police

Dougie Brimson

Football is played between two teams and football violence usually takes the form of clashes between the two rival sets of supporters. However, there is usually a third group present, be it the match officials on the pitch or the police in the stands. Just as the referees and linesmen are supposed to enforce the rules of the field, the police are supposed to control the fans on the terraces. And just like referees, the police do this with varying degrees of success.

In his book *Kicking Off*, Dougie Brimson looks at the police's involvement in football violence and asks: are they really just another casual firm?

In recent years, hooliganism has been written about from all kinds of angles. Those who were once at it, those who are still at it, those who love it, those who hate it – they've almost all had their turn at one point or another. Yet there is one area that has thus far received little or no attention from within the world of hoolie lit and quite why this is so remains a mystery to me, because in many ways it is the most secretive and misunderstood element of this fascinating issue and it would certainly be more worthy (and certainly more controversial) than yet another "we did this, they did that"-type exposé of the scene. I am, of course, talking about the people who have come to be widely regarded by those "in the know" as British football's biggest and most organized mob. I am talking about the police.

What would make this so intriguing to me is not so much the operational aspect, but more the personal side. I have spoken to enough coppers over the years to know that many veterans of football have some quite amazing stories to tell. Indeed, some have featured in previous books. For example, a good number of the officers who were in the front line during the riot after the Millwall versus Birmingham play-off game in 2002 regard it as one of the most terrifying experiences of their careers, while the exploits of some of those football intelligence officers who have sailed a bit close to the wind with the lads they are supposed to be keeping an eye on would make for great reading.

Sadly, as yet there is no sign of such a book and I suspect one of the main reasons for that is because, unless it is in relation to specific high-profile cases, most policemen seem to be quite wary of committing anything to print for fear it will reflect badly on the force. Similarly, I can state from experience that the upper echelons of the police are far from accommodating when questioned on the hooligan issue, so I'm guessing they wouldn't be overly supportive of the idea either. In fact, I know they're not because I've asked them.

That is a great shame. Like many people who follow football I would like to read more about how hooliganism as a culture is perceived by those charged with the responsibility of dealing with it. After all, it is clearly a very difficult and occasionally extremely dangerous job. Furthermore, if we are ever to fully understand the nature of the hooligan menace then it is vital that the experiences of all those involved are taken into account. Obviously that must include those who uphold the law.

However, the fact that they are seemingly so reluctant to talk about their personal experiences illustrates perfectly one of the fundamental problems that has traditionally affected the relationship between football fans and the police and that is the existence of an "us and them" situation. It is a sad fact that over the years many football fans have come to regard the representatives of law and order as something akin to an enemy. While that in itself is bad enough, the real tragedy is that this isn't simply limited to the Saturday lads. Oh no, it extends right across the board.

At this point I should make it clear that on a personal level I am no fan of the boys in blue and I have never made any secret of that. Oh for sure they're the first people I'd call on if my family needed protection or assistance and I feel nothing but admiration and respect for the men and women who routinely place themselves in the front line of the fight against terrorism and organized crime. In that sense, the British police are the finest in the world. No doubt. But when it comes to football, things are different – very different.

However, before we get into all that, in the absence of any contribution from the police, we need to briefly examine how the police have dealt with the problem of hooliganism in the past, for they are obviously central to the future of this most complex of issues, given that they have played such an important part in its history.

It is fairly well accepted that of all the nations where the great game is played, England has had by far and away the biggest problem with hooliganism. This is not something we should be proud of really, but it's hardly surprising given that we have more clubs and a higher percentage of travelling fans than any other country on earth.

The fact that this situation has existed for more than a few decades now is nothing less than a disgrace and, while

I frequently blame all and sundry for that, I know as well as anyone that the real culprits are the Saturday lads themselves. If they hadn't driven the culture of violence on to the terraces of England back in the seventies and kept it rolling through the eighties and nineties, right up to the present day, then you would not be reading this book. It really is as simple as that.

But they did, and one of the consequences has been that the police in this country have become universally regarded as the best anti-hooligan force there is. Again, it's not something we should be proud of, because it clearly illustrates an abject and long-term failure to bring the problem to any kind of a resolution. However, as I have stated on many occasions, I do not believe that the police should be responsible for that resolution, because that's the job of the game and the Government. The police's role is to uphold the law of the land and react to things on the ground, as and where necessary. To this end, over the years they have developed all kinds of methods and tactics to try and carry out this duty and contain the hooligans' activities. Many of these approaches have been aided by the development and use of increasingly sophisticated technology, while others involve good old basic policing.

In the seventies and eighties the most visible example of this was the use of escorts. At a time when the bulk of the travelling support at many clubs comprised active lads, the police would simply surround them with bodies, dogs and even horses and literally drive them from the railway station or coach park to the ground. Then, afterwards, they would simply herd them right back and away.

It was incredibly confrontational, but for those of us who followed our clubs away, extremely exciting. Being marched through the streets like some kind of invading army, especially at somewhere like Stoke or Derby where the locals were often hostile, was a real buzz, especially when the police were busily winding everyone up or things kicked off as they frequently did. More often than not, this would involve some kind of ambush at a particular spot en route or local lads infiltrating the escort and giving it large – something that took incredible nerve given that they often came unstuck.

Inside the grounds things were often equally exciting (or terrifying, depending on who you followed and where you were). In the days before clubs really got their act together, mobs would sometimes be separated by nothing more than a single line of policemen – with inevitable results. At a time when the taking of ends was the standard aim for all visiting mobs, it was certainly not uncommon for fights to spill over on to the playing surface.

By the end of the seventies just about every club in the land had erected fences around the pitch and pens to keep the fans apart, and the amount of trouble inside grounds began to decline. As a result, if things did kick off inside the pens the police, sure in the knowledge that the trouble would be contained in a relatively small area, would often let it continue for a while before going in to deal with those involved.

Or at least some police forces would, for one of the criticisms often levelled at the police back then was that their approach to hooliganism varied from force to force and even from matchday commander to matchday commander. It is certainly fair to say that some constabularies would allow lads to get away with things that would result in arrest in another part of the country.

Thankfully, those days have long-since been consigned to history, as has the use of escorts. These days, officers are posted at various points around the ground with the odd beat officer or van shadowing any suspicious group. Similarly, inside grounds the move towards police-free matches continues apace, with stewards increasingly employed to deal with security issues, albeit under the watchful eyes of the boys in blue. Not as much fun, but just as effective.

Another tactic the police began to employ early on was the use of plain-clothes officers to gather information and infiltrate hooligan groups. This actually first began at the request of the FA back in the mid-sixties, when it was becoming increasingly concerned at the growing number of incidents involving travelling fans. By the eighties this had become one of the most important weapons in the fight against the hooligans, largely because the police had somehow convinced both themselves and the media that the organized groups were becoming so structured that sooner or later a move towards more recognized criminal activities was inevitable. Hence, in an effort to smash the organized firms once and for all, they handed numerous officers new identities and tasked them with "living the life" to get as far inside the mobs as they possibly could. In 1986, a year after Heysel and the Millwall riot at L*t*n, they finally struck. And they did so in the full glare of the media spotlight.

One of the first to hear the "six o'clock knock" was Chelsea. On 26 March 1986 Operation Own Goal (a title that was to prove strangely prophetic) saw seven men, alleged to be the ringleaders of the so-called Headhunters, dragged from their beds and hauled into court. Over the next four years clubs including Leeds United, West Ham, Millwall, Wolves, Manchester United and Birmingham City were targeted in this way, with the majority of men arrested charged with conspiracy to commit affray or conspiracy to commit violence. For those who pleaded guilty, justice was swift and heavy, with sentences ranging from long periods of community service right through to ten years' imprisonment.

However, it quickly transpired that not all the convictions were safe. In some cases evidence, which ranged from possession of calling-cards to ownership of weapons, was allegedly tampered with or even falsified and the behaviour of the undercover officers was frequently called to account. As a consequence, within four years a number of operations, including Own Goal (Chelsea), Full-time (West Ham and Millwall), White Horse (West Ham), Back Yard (Crystal Palace) and Spoonbill (L*t*n), had collapsed with all charges dropped. Despite these very high-profile and very expensive failures, the use of infiltration as a source of intelligence-gathering continues to this day. However, with the organized groups becoming ever more cautious of both the police and the media, outsiders are increasingly regarded with suspicion.

Another intelligence-gathering technique universally employed in this country is the use of dedicated football intelligence officers (FIOs). First pioneered at Euro '88 and now widely copied across Europe, FIOs work closely with the clubs to which they are attached to identify local hooligans and pass on details of their movements during away trips. This has proven to be extremely effective over the years and has certainly worked well during international tournaments. However, as a weapon it has had a number of downsides. Not only does the sight of an FIO invariably raise the hackles of the Saturday lads, but over the years certain FIOs have forged relationships bordering on friendships with some of the people they are supposed to be keeping an eye on. It has even been alleged that in some instances they have actually passed on information to facilitate incidents or help their own lads avoid arrest. This was certainly widely reported during Euro 2000, when the Belgian police were busily running amok and attacking anybody English.

The other downside is that supporters are occasionally placed in situations where they look to their own FIO for help and when that isn't forthcoming problems inevitably ensue in the aftermath. The most high-profile example of this was in April 2000, when the two Leeds United fans were murdered by Galatasaray supporters in Istanbul. Many of the Leeds lads involved in that incident claim that shortly before the attack took place their FIO had told them he was perfectly happy with the situation and was going for a meal. This was totally at odds with the officer's version of events, for he claimed that he had witnessed the entire incident, but had been unable to intervene because he had not been in uniform. Not surprisingly, this disparity was the cause of much anger after the event, with many Leeds fans inevitably levelling a degree of blame in his direction.

In the main, however, most FIOs manage to strike exactly the right balance between the requirements of their role and the need to forge a working relationship with supporters who potentially could be a problem to them. As a deterrent, they can be mightily effective.

Of course, aside from standard policing the other weapon employed to combat the threat of violence is technology. Indeed, we have seen some quite astonishing developments in this area in recent years. The most high-profile of these has been in the use of CCTV. First used in the mid-seventies, CCTV has now become one of the most vital tools in the battle not just to police the hooligans inside grounds, but to track them in the streets outside and supply the evidence to convict should things end up in a court of law.

These days, the cameras trained on crowds and monitored from state-of-the-art control rooms, many of which overlook the playing surface, have been supplemented by the increasing use of handheld cameras, to film crowds as they head to and from grounds, and the hooligans, which provides not only additional cameras, but can also serve as a mobile control centre. The idea – and excuse – is to both deter hooligans and provide additional intelligence where possible.

The game has also witnessed the development of the photophone. This quite amazing system was used to incredible effect during Euro '96 (as I know to my cost, as I was stopped and photographed fifteen times over a period of three days), as it allows the instant exchange of information between the control centre and the officers on the ground, via an electronic mail network known as EPI. Aside from that, football has also been used to trial cameras in policemen's helmets, cameras fixed to dogs and horses and even listening devices placed under seats. The area around Millwall was also used to test a face-recognition computer system known as Mandrake.

These technological developments have been more than matched by the advancement in information and intelligence management. The original football unit was formed in 1989 to try and combat the growing problems associated with England fans abroad. This was absorbed into NCIS in 1990 and comprised six full-time officers led by a superintendent. Although initially established in 1992 to combat serious and organized crime, the football section of NCIS not only provided a central coordinating point for the various FIOs around the country, but provided planning and intelligence for all overseas trips involving both England and club sides.

Key to the agency's success was its database. Astonishingly, by 1992 the unit had the details and photographs of over 6,000 known or suspected hooligans on file and this grew with almost every single incident. Anyone involved or suspected of being involved in trouble was added, as was each and every individual arrested for a football-related offence abroad. Once on the system, people would be allocated a specific category, depending on the severity of the offence: category A (peaceful supporter), category B (possible risk of involvement in disorder) or category C (violent supporter or organizer of violence).

This information would be routinely exchanged with foreign police forces in accordance with a number of established bilateral agreements. As a result, NCIS had the option of applying for a domestic and international banning order for anyone either causing or becoming involved in trouble in those European states where agreements existed. Furthermore, NCIS was responsible for upholding certain European directives on spectator-related violence and the conviction of anyone charged with a football-related offence in England.

Although it has been widely known about in hooligan circles from day one, what really brought NCIS to the public's attention was Euro '96 and the huge operation to stop violence surrounding the first major tournament to be held in England since the 1966 World Cup. But it wasn't so much the success or even the size of the operation that caught the public eye, it was the cost. Initial rumours put the cost in the region of £10 million, but the true price was actually nearer £25 million, although 75 per cent of that was funded by the Football Trust.

For the first time people began to look seriously at what policing the game was costing. It was often quite a shock – Premier League clubs alone paid out £2.9 million to police the 1996–97 season – and that perception wasn't helped by some bizarre and very public admissions of failure. Three of the most high-profile of these were the riot in Dublin in 1995 when English supporters forced the abandonment of a friendly against the Republic of Ireland; the 1998 World Cup in France when the fans rioted in Marseille; and Euro 2000 and the disturbance at Charleroi.

Prior to all three occasions NCIS had stressed that it was way ahead of the game, which clearly wasn't the case. Indeed, on the morning after the riot in the South of France it publicly stated that hardly any of the large number of hooligans involved were known to them, although, to be fair, this riot was more a reaction to the way the locals were behaving than simple, bog-standard hooliganism. Similarly, in spite of a massive police operation to prevent trouble at the tournament, of 965 England fans arrested only one was subject to a football banning order and only thirty-five were known to NCIS as prominent football hooligans at all. While NCIS claimed that this was proof its operation to stop known hooligans from travelling was working, it couldn't hide the fact that this was a major embarrassment for the English police.

In spite of this, NCIS continued to forge ahead with its work and, to be fair, has enjoyed a huge amount of success, particularly in relation to the travelling England fans and the training of both foreign police and domestic stewards. It even took on the running of the Football Banning Orders Authority for England and Wales (FBOA) on behalf of the Home Office. In fact, so solid was its reputation that the agency has served as a model for the creation of similar anti-hooligan organizations in various countries across Europe. However, on 1 January 2006 NCIS was absorbed into the larger Serious Organised Crime Agency (SOCA) and prior to that happening it was decided that the football department would be better suited outside. As a result, both the national football intelligence function and FBOA were merged into a single dedicated unit, the UK Football Policing Unit (UK FPU).

This was charged with responsibility for all matters relating to policy and operational delivery, including the coordination of ports policing operations when required, and the management of all funding for anti-hooligan operations, all of which had previously been carried out by the Association of Chief Police Officers. It also took over the existing football intelligence role, as well as those duties previously undertaken by the FBOA.

Not surprisingly, with the World Cup on the horizon, the UK FPU was launched in a blaze of publicity. However, just to enhance its chances of success, prior to the 2005–06 season the Government tightened up the legislation relating to banning orders, thus ensuring that the figures went through the roof. Time will tell how effective the UK FPU will be, but having spoken to some of its senior staff, they are confident of success at least on the international stage. Indeed, both FIFA and UEFA have recently acknowledged the good work being done here on the anti-hooligan front.

Yet no matter how dedicated or efficient the police might be, they are only as effective as the legislation they have to work within. Luckily, of all the areas that have seen major changes in recent decades, the legal framework set in place to help the police deal with anyone who commits an offence at football is by far and away the most significant. It is also one of the most contentious.

In the early days, hooliganism was dealt with under normal bog-standard law in place to prosecute anyone causing bodily harm to another individual or criminal damage to property. However, the nightmare events that took place during 1985, and in particular the Bradford fire and the riot at St Andrews, finally forced the government into action.

The Justice Popplewell report into the fire was released in 1986 and focused on the issue of supporter safety inside grounds. It also formed the basis of the 1989 Football Supporters Act, which handed the courts the power to award legally enforceable restriction orders to any fan convicted of a football-related offence. This not only stopped them attending games at home, but abroad as well, and was seen as a major victory for the police.

However, the other key recommendation in the act, the setting up of a compulsory national identity card scheme for supporters, was more problematic. Even before the act came to pass the Football League had agreed to set up such a scheme at all its professional clubs, but in the event only thirteen of the ninety-two actually bothered. Thankfully, despite strenuous backing from the then prime minister Margaret Thatcher, the entire thing was dropped in the wake of the Hillsborough disaster as being both unworkable and unwanted. In fact, the Lord Justice Taylor report into the tragedy equated the idea with "using a sledgehammer to crack a nut".

While a very positive and long overdue step in the right direction, just two years later the act was supplemented by the Football Offences Act 1991. This strengthened the law with regard to three specific areas: throwing missiles, invading the pitch and taking part in racist or indecent chanting.

A revised Football (Disorder) Act was issued in 2000 which, among other things, made it clear that from that point forward the courts were actually required, not merely allowed, to make an international football banning order if the nature of the charges met certain criteria. Any fans handed a ban were also required to hand over their passports at a police station and report there at a specific time and date.

Also included in the act was the recommendation that anyone arrested for involvement in a football-related offence overseas should be charged and serve any subsequent sentence in the country where the offence took place. The problem was that despite this being an obligation of the European Convention on Spectator Violence and Misbehaviour at Sports, the vast majority of signatory countries merely rounded up and shipped out anyone who stepped out of line, much to the chagrin of NCIS.

In response to the trouble at Euro 2000, the act was amended again to combine both domestic and international banning orders. But, more importantly and controversially, it gave the courts the power to apply a banning order to an individual if the police lodged sufficient evidence with them to suggest that they had been involved in violence in the UK or elsewhere in the past and that there were "reasonable" grounds to believe that a banning order would help prevent acts of hooliganism in the future.

With bans lasting anywhere from two to ten years, depending on the nature of the offence or complaint, so effective a weapon have they become (almost a thousand were issued in 2005 alone, bringing the total to almost 3,500) that the police and the CPS strengthened the entire system even further at the beginning of the 2005–06 season by announcing that cooperation between the two groups would now become standard practice for all football-related cases. Furthermore, any case which passed a basic evidential test would almost certainly be pushed forward for prosecution rather than dropped. As a statement of intent, it was as good and public as they come, implying, as it did, that if the battle to defeat the hooligans hadn't been won, the end was certainly in sight – except it was all a distortion of the very unpalatable truth that, far from being over, domestically the war is still raging, while victory on the international stage might be in sight, but only largely thanks to the sterling work being done by the fans themselves to change our image abroad.

However, worse than that, the continuing drive to instil confidence in the performance of the police at football disguises some very unsavoury facts, many of which involve either misleading the public or simply abusing the power the police already have at their disposal. And while some might argue that this is nothing more than another case of "well, he would say that", the reality is that the evidence to support this thinking isn't too hard to find if you know where to look and what crimes could be legitimately tagged as being hooligan-related violence. These are public disorder (1,428) and violent disorder (428). That makes 1,856, in addition to which a further 314 individuals were arrested for offences which could be termed as being hooligan-related: possession of an offensive weapon (36), missile-throwing (76), breach of the peace (140) or breach of a banning order (62).

That's a total of 2,170, which to me is the true arrest figure, as the remaining 1,458 were charged with offences which have little or nothing to do with hooliganism at all. These included racist chanting (51), ticket-touting (146) and even 976 people arrested for offences relating to alcohol. Quite why they even appear in this evidence escapes me.

Things become even cloudier when you look at it from another angle, for of that 3,628, 1,491 were arrested actually inside a ground, which almost certainly rules out the vast majority of those 2,170 people who were detained for anything to do with hooliganism and certainly those nicked for ticket-touting.

When one considers that in the 2004–05 season over thirty-seven million people walked through a turnstile into an English football ground it seems to me that, given those figures, our stadia appear to be fairly safe places to visit. With an average of 1.21 arrests per game, even outside looks to be far safer than my local town centre on a Saturday night.

This begs two questions, and which one you ask depends on what you know about the game and the issue of hooliganism.

If you know very little and take the figures as read and in simple black and white, the fact that they are so low seems to indicate that hooliganism isn't anything like the major problem the police say it is. So in that case the question has to be asked, why the big fuss? After all, just over 2,000 arrests per year is hardly value for money given the millions it costs to police the game.

However, if you know a bit more about football and attend matches on a regular basis, then the question you would have to ask is how come those figures don't seem to equate to what I see on a weekly basis? Because in all honesty, they don't. What they do, however, is disguise a simple truth, for while they might suggest to Mr and Mrs Average that things are improving, the only thing they really seem to prove is that the police don't arrest anyone any more. At least not there and then. After all, anyone who has attended a major local derby or cup tie recently will know only too well that the threat of hooliganism continues to be a very real one and the police operations to combat that threat are often huge. For example, 300 officers were on duty for the Sheffield derby in February 2006, a game at which a number of policemen were injured during clashes between fans from both clubs.

Even small games at a relatively hooligan-free ground such as Watford's Vicarage Road are being overseen by numerous police patrolling in vans, on foot and even, occasionally, on horseback, yet no matter how many police they have on duty, they will invariably be guided by someone in a control room with access to CCTV. And therein lies the problem, because the police increasingly rely on the use of cameras to help contain events on the ground, while using them to gather evidence to make any required arrests at a later date.

By approaching the problem in this incredibly time-consuming and expensive way, it is surely obvious that the number of arrests for actual acts of violence or aggression will be lower and even the police must realize that the lower they are, the fewer resources they will be able to demand. Could this, in part, explain why the figures for hooliganism are clearly padded out with the addition of 976 drunks?

Or is it, as some people argue, because they know that by keeping hooliganism out of the public eye on match-days and in it through the use of high-profile early morning raids and court cases, they can continue to fuel the ongoing demonization of the football hooligan? And by doing so, can exploit their existence to develop measures of control that might prove useful when dealing with other potentially more dangerous and volatile public order situations in the future?

That might seem a slightly fanciful notion, but given the attention the problem attracts, as well as the severity of the sentences handed out to anyone found guilty of a football-related offence – sentences which are wholly disproportionate to the nature and severity of the crime – then it makes a degree of sense. Even more so when one remembers that of all the areas of British society covered by the law of our land, football is just about the only one where the civil liberties groups refuse to tread. There are plenty of lads who have ended up in cells both here and abroad who will willingly testify to that.

The reason for this is fairly obvious in that, by its very nature, hooliganism is an illegal activity and, as such, is not only frowned upon by just about everyone, but is also one of those activities where people have been conditioned to feel that anyone caught and convicted deserves whatever comes their way. As a consequence, anyone wrongly arrested at football is, not to put too fine a point on it, up shit creek.

At the beginning of this chapter I highlighted the fact that to many lads the police are British football's biggest and most organized mob, but an addition to that is that they can never lose. After all, they have the law on their side, so how can they? What that means in real terms is that no matter what the circumstances, if the police say you are guilty, chances are that no one with any degree of power or influence is going to take up your case for fear of it backfiring and making them look stupid. Hence, it's your word against theirs and in 99 per cent of cases that means you lose.

Similarly, given that the police are so active in this area, even fewer in authority seem willing to question the tactics they choose to employ in the seemingly never-ending battle to defeat what has come to be accepted as one of society's great ills. This, in part, is how they have been able to blanket the nation with CCTV and place some of the most draconian and frightening restrictions on individual freedom ever seen in a civilized country on to the statute book without attracting more than a whimper of complaint. Then again, at a time when most people equate the term "Big Brother" with a Channel 4 reality TV show as opposed to the George Orwellian vision of the future, that shouldn't really be a surprise. After all, Orwell's future is already here in all but name and no one seems to care, if indeed they actually realize.

In respect of football, banning orders provide the best example of the kind of thing that is going on. For although they have proven to be incredibly effective, parts of the legislation governing their use border on scandalous. Don't get me wrong. If someone steps out of line, breaks the law and is convicted in a court of law for a football-related offence, then I am all for seeing them banned from games for a period of time. To me, that is both a sensible and just punishment. After all, no one has a divine right to walk into a football ground just because they are a football fan. I even accept and support the idea of stopping people subjected to legitimate banning orders from travelling abroad for inter-national games. Why should the majority have to suffer from the presence of someone who may or may not become a problem at some point?

However, I have a major problem with the idea of those same "sentences", for that is what they are, being imposed on people who have not been convicted of anything. Indeed, I find the idea that someone can have their passport taken off them and be banned from a certain area of their own homeland simply because the police "think" they might be a problem absolutely abhorrent and so should every right-thinking person in this land. This is, after all, a democratic country not a third-world dictatorship. Or at least it was the last time I looked.

The fact that the police can make these assumptions based on so-called evidence dating back up to ten years is bad enough, but when one considers that even unwitting association with known hooligans could theoretically be enough to put someone before a court and potentially remove one of the most basic of human rights – the right to travel across borders – then that is simply frightening, and even more so when one considers that the chances of winning any appeal are almost certainly zero.

However, what really galls me about this is that I simply cannot understand why the police even need this legislation at all. Surely, given the resources, manpower and time they have at their disposal, if they suspect that someone is involved in what is after all a crime, they should be able to prove it? But now, of course, they don't have to, and now those laws are on the books not only will we as a society never be rid of them, but it is only a matter of time before their use spreads into other areas of both criminal and not-so-criminal activity to provide what amounts to state control over the individual. That, if anything, shows a major miscalculation by the various civil liberties groups, which only voiced half-hearted criticism when those laws were first mooted.

Sadly, the banning order system is not the only area of the law relating to football to cause concern, not just to me, but to fans the length and breadth of the country, because the behaviour of some of the officers who police our game is occasionally less than acceptable.

It is important to remember, however, that even the most active of hooligans has always accepted that the authorities are duty-bound to uphold the rule of law. The problem, in part, lies in how they apply that law, because often that isn't so clear cut and in too many instances certainly isn't fair. Anyone who has spent years following their club knows only too well that certain police forces are more tolerant than others, while some aren't tolerant at all.

To be fair, this is understandable to a degree. Policing games must be an incredibly daunting experience on occasions and I have spoken to enough coppers over the years to know that a good number of them are quite anti football fans, particularly lads, but there are also plenty more who get a huge buzz out of the thrill of the chase and the ongoing competition with the football mobs. After all, if you look at it objectively they get pretty much the same experiences in terms of excitement and they get paid for the privilege. That said, on occasions it must also be incredibly boring and so it's little wonder that, once in a while, some of them like to poke a stick into the hornets' nest to see what happens.

So just what do the police get up to in their ongoing battle with the Saturday lads? Well, it is fair to say that were the desire there I could easily fill another book with instances of abuses of power, simple assaults and even basic rudeness aimed at football fans in general, let alone active hooligans, but the bottom line is that in their desire to control, contain and occasionally antagonize the violent minority, the police are not afraid to adopt some very unorthodox spoiling tactics.

In the main, these will be designed to achieve a variety of things, from keeping one group apart from another, through to restricting the numbers who actually travel. However, most will be used simply to let lads know that Old Bill is on their case and show them that if they step out of line, they'll get hammered.

Possibly the most frequently used is Section 60, a part of the 1994 Criminal Justice and Public Order Act which permits the stopping and searching of anyone believed to have either been, or to be likely to become, involved with acts of violence – although the rules to authorize this depend on the mood of the local police, and that can be incredibly frustrating. But to be fair, the British Transport Police often have good reason to deal harshly with football fans. For example, the network saw a massive rise in incidents during the 2004–05 season, with over 332 taking place, of which sixty-two were deemed serious. There were also 292 arrests.

Even when you arrive at a ground, policing can sometimes be extremely oppressive and I've seen far too many examples of coppers herding fans along as if they were cattle and closing pubs after games simply because they want people out of their town or city.

Air travellers are also targets for attention, especially when attempting to travel to international games. Here, the search for anyone trying to avoid the restriction of a banning order is aided by the existence of the Football (Disorder) Act, which allows police to detain anyone they suspect could be travelling to cause trouble for up to six hours at the airport while they check into their background. This means supporters can often be seen being dragged out of queues and ritually embarrassed in front of everyone else in the terminal.

Interestingly, the police also have the power to issue a temporary order banning individuals from travelling if they have firm reasons for suspecting they are potential hooligans. This could lead to a formal court ban if it ends up in court.

I have also heard of numerous cases where lads have been held up so they miss their flights and even instances where supporters have been questioned and released, only to find that when they get to the check-in, the airlines refuse to carry them having been given the nod that they are suspected football hooligans.

I could go on here, but I'm sure you get the point that the police aren't above bending the law to get the job done. To be fair, most lads accept that as being par for the course and when problems do occur, it is usually because "normal" fans get caught up in things and take exception to the way they have been treated.

Of course that is when they, just like everyone else, realize that as a football fan, especially a travelling football fan, you have no right of either complaint or redress. As a visiting supporter no local copper is ever going to be interested in anything you have to say about a fellow officer policing a game and that assumes that you would be prepared to hang around long enough to even try and find one. Equally, a complaint made at your local station would soon be lost under a mountain of paperwork and confusion. So, with no organization to call them to account and no real body willing to deal with complaints relating to football matters, the police have been handed pretty much carte blanche to do whatever they like – within reason of course.

While understandable to an extent, one has to wonder why this situation has been allowed not only to develop, but also to continue, especially since it has an obvious knock-on and negative effect in terms of the public's perception of the police. Continue it does, though, and quite for how long goodness only knows. Indeed, just what the future holds for the policing of the game is unclear. I cannot for the life of me believe that the Old Bill will ask for any more legislation, especially since on 1 January 2006 they were handed the power to arrest anyone committing any offence on the spot! (Previously, they were only able to do that for offences which carried a sentence of at least five years in prison.)

However, it is clear that, like much of what has already gone on, new developments will be driven by technology. Already, during the build-up to the 2006 World Cup, we have seen the Dutch police send 17,000 text messages to the mobile phones of fans who attended the 2004–05 match between local rivals Feyenoord and Ajax asking for information about the ringleaders of the serious trouble which took place at the game. As a direct result, five people eventually handed themselves in.

Furthermore, the German Government intends to use biometric face recognition systems to identify known trouble-makers at the tournament and it will also employ a new mobile optical fingerprint system for fast identification based on data for people with a criminal record. There are even plans for the Germans to utilise AWAC early warning aircraft to track the movements of hooligans travelling across the borders and around the country. I'm not sure we'll go as far as to have military aircraft flying over grounds here, but certainly the electronic and remote identification of individuals is something the police in this country are keen to develop further. But whatever happens, it is clear to me that something has to be done to try and strike a balance between the need to deal with the hooligan threat and the wishes of the general public, because, on too many occasions, that balance is not being struck.

I opened this chapter by discussing the reasons why it

would be useful to see a book examining the hooliganism issue from a police perspective and mentioned a couple of reasons why we may never see it. But another reason is that, increasingly, like many people who commentate on this issue, I have come to believe that, over the years, the existence of hooliganism as a problem has been of huge benefit to the police. This is primarily because the continued lack of understanding about the root causes of it have allowed them to exploit the sport I love for their own ends, often at the expense of law-abiding fans who not only deserve but demand better. So why would they want to talk openly about that?

This is not an opinion I am proud of, nor is it one I am glad to hold. It is nevertheless a product of years of negative experiences, some of which were outlined in *Barmy Army,* along with a few more that were provided by people who, like me, have witnessed abuses of position and power that go way beyond anything one should ever expect from someone charged with upholding the law of the land. Unfortunately, nothing I have seen or heard in the five years since *Barmy Army* was first published has caused me to change that opinion. Indeed, if anything, I have become even more jaundiced. The reason, quite simply, is the police's attitude, not just to football lads, but to football in general. To be blunt, I think it sucks.

The fact that in most instances the police are never held to account is bad enough, but what really causes me problems is that after decades of policing football, they are seemingly always chasing more – be it money, resources, technology or even legislation – and, invariably, they are given it, usually without question.

Equally importantly, while the majority of fans welcome the success they are having at the moment in terms of reducing trouble overseas, the fact remains that this success is totally false. It is, after all, based not on conviction rates but on legislation which is quite simply disgraceful. Furthermore, in terms of solving the problem domestically, while I do not accept that this is wholly a police responsibility, there can be little doubt that all anyone is achieving at the moment is keeping a lid on things. The reality is that any kind of solution is as far away as it has ever been. Given the millions of pounds and hours spent on this problem over the years, that is simply not good enough. Football, and most importantly, those who follow and fund the game, deserve better. Much better.

The Clubs and Their Firms

Aldershot: East Bank Boot Boys
Arsenal: Gooners
Aston Villa: Steamers; Villa Youth
Barnsley: Five-O, Inner City Tykes
Birmingham City: Zulu Army
Blackburn Rovers: Blackburn Youth
Blackpool: BRS (Bison Riot Squad); BTS (Blackpool Tangerine Service); The Mob; Seaside Mafia
Bolton Wanderers: Billy Whizz Fan Club; Mongoose Cuckoo Boys; The Omega; Tonge Moor Slashers
Bradford City: The Ointment
Brighton & Hove Albion: Headhunters; NLF (North Lancing Firm); West Streeters
Bristol City: East End; Inner City Robins
Bristol Rovers: The Gas; The Pirates; The Tote
Burnley: SS (Suicide Squad)
Bury: The Interchange Squad
Cambridge United: Cambridge Casuals; Pringle Boys
Cardiff City: B Troop; D Firm; Dirty Thirty; The Motley Crew; PVM (Pure Violence Mob); Soul Crew; Valley Commandos; The Young Boys
Carlisle United: BCF (Border City Firm); BSC (Benders Service Crew)

Charlton Athletic: B Mob

Chelsea: APF (Anti Personnel Firm); Headhunters; North Stand Boys; Pringle Boys; Shed End Boys

Chesterfield: CBS (Chesterfield Bastard Squad)

Colchester United: The Barsiders

Coventry City: The Coventry Casuals; The Legion

Crewe Alexandra: RTF (Rail Town Firm)

Crystal Palace: Naughty Forty; Nifty Fifty; Whitehorse Boys

Darlington: Bank Top 200; Darlington Casuals; The Gaffa; The Townies; Under Fives

Derby County: BBLA (Bob Bank Lunatic Army); C Seats; C Stand; DLF (Derby Lunatic Fringe)

Doncaster Rovers: DDR (Doncaster Defence Regiment)

Everton: Scallies

Exeter City: City Hit Squad; Sly Crew

Fulham: TVT (Thames Valley Travellers)

Gloucester City: CDB (City Disorder Boys)

Grimsby Town: CBP (Cleethorpes Beach Patrol)

Halifax Town: The Casuals

Hartlepool United: Blue Order; Hartlepool ITA (In The Area); PTID (Pooly Till I Die)

Hereford United: ICF (Inter City Firm)

Huddersfield Town: HYC (Huddersfield Young Casuals)

Hull City: City Casuals; City Psychos; The Minority; Silver Cod Squad

Ipswich Town: IPS (Ipswich Protection Squad)

Leeds United: Service Crew; YRA (Yorkshire Republican Army)

Leicester City: Baby Squad; BIF (Braunstone Inter City Firm); ICHF (Inter City Harry Firm); MMA (Matthew & Marks Alliance); TRA (Thurnby Republican Army); The Wise Men

Leyton Orient: Doughnuts; Iced Buns; Orient Terrace Firm

Lincoln City: LTE (Lincoln Transit Elite)

Liverpool: Huyton Baddies; The Scallies

Luton Town: BPYP (Bury Park Youth Posse); MIGs (Men In Gear)

Manchester City: The Borg Elite; Guv'nors; Maine Line Service Crew; Moston Cool Cats; Motorway Crew

Manchester United: Cockney Reds; Inter City Jibbers; Perry Boys; Red Army

Mansfield Town: The Carrot Crew; MSE (Mansfield Shaddy Express)

Middlesbrough: Frontline

Millwall: Bushwhackers/Whackers; CBL (Cold Blow Lane); F-Troop; Frontline; Halfway Liners; NTO (Nutty Turn Out); The Treatment

Merthyr Tydfil: Merthyr Valley Line Firm

Newcastle United: Bender Crew; Gremlins; NME (Newcastle Mainline Express)

Newport AFC: NYF (Newport Youth Firm); The Trendies

Northampton Town: NAT (Northampton Affray Team)

Norwich City: Barclay Boot Boys; C Firm; C Squad; ETC (Executive Travel Club); NHS (Norwich Hit Squad); NR1; The Steins; The Trawlermen

Nottingham Forest: Naughty Forty; Red Dogs

Notts County: The Bullwell Crew; Executive Crew; Roadside Casuals

Oldham Athletic: Fine Young Casuals

Oxford United: The 850; Headington Casuals; The Oxford City Crew; The South Midlands Hit Squad; Warlords

Peterborough United: PTC (Peterborough Terrace Crew)

Plymouth Argyle: Devonport Boys; TCE (The Central Element); We Are The Lyndhurst

Port Vale: VLF (Vale Lunatic Fringe)

Portsmouth: 6.57 Crew

Preston North End: Leyland Boys

Queens Park Rangers: Fila Mob; Ladbroke Grove Mob

Reading: Berkshire Boot Boys; RYF (Reading Youth Firm)

Rotherham United: Rotherham Casuals; Section Five

Scunthorpe United: The Ironclad

Sheffield United: BBA (Bramall Barmy Army); BBC (Blades Business Crew)

Sheffield Wednesday: Inter-City Owls; OCS (Owls Crime Squad), later to become ITI (Is That It)

Shrewsbury Town: EBF (English Border Front)

Southampton: Inside Crew; Suburban Casuals; The Uglies

Southend United: CS Crew

Stockport County: The Company; Hit Squad; Stockport Hit Squad

Stoke City: Naughty Forty

Sunderland: Boss Lads; The Redskins; Seaburn Casuals; Vauxies

Swansea City: Jack Army; Jack Casuals; Stone Island Casuals; Swansea Jacks

Swindon Town: Gussethunters; SSC (South Side Crew) South Ciders; Southsiders; Town Enders

Torquay United: Torquay Youth

Tottenham Hotspur: N17s; The Paxton Boys; Tottenham Massive; The Yid Army or Yiddos

Tow Law: Tow Law Misfits

Tranmere Rovers: TSB (Tranmere Stanley Boys)

Walsall: Barmy Army; SPG (Special Patrol Group)

Watford: Category C; TWM (The Watford Men); Watford Youth

West Bromwich Albion: Section Five

West Ham United: ICF (Inter City Firm); Mile End Mob; Under Fives

Wigan Athletic: The Goon Squad

Woking: Woking Casuals
Wolverhampton Wanderers: Bridge Boys; Subway
Army
Wrexham: Frontline
York City: YNS (York Nomad Society)